Leading the localities

Manchester University Press

Leading the localities

Executive mayors in English local governance

Colin Copus

Manchester University Press
Manchester and New York
distributed exclusively in the USA by Palgrave

Published by Manchester University Press
Oxford Road, Manchester M13 9NR, UK
and Room 400, 175 Fifth Avenue, New York, NY 10010, USA
www.manchesteruniversitypress.co.uk

Distributed in the United States exclusively by
Palgrave Macmillan, 175 Fifth Avenue,
New York, NY 10010, USA

Distributed in Canada exclusively by
UBC Press, University of British Columbia, 2029 West Mall,
Vancouver, BC, Canada V6T 1Z2

British Library Cataloguing-in-Publication Data is available

Library of Congress Cataloging-in-Publication Data is available

ISBN 978 0 7190 7187 4 paperback

First published by Manchester University Press in hardback 2006

This paperback edition first published 2013

Printed by Lightning Source

Contents

List of tables and figures

Tables

Preface

The most controversial element of the local government modernisation project embarked upon by the Blair government has to have been the introduction into the English political landscape of the directly elected executive mayor. Transferring the power to choose the political head of the council from councillors – selecting the council leader – to the voters – electing the mayor in an at-large election – has the potential to fundamentally alter the political dynamics of the council, the community and the broader local governance network. Moreover, the opportunity offered to the electorate to change the political leadership of the council at a single stroke and the opening to political office that such at-large election provides for candidates from outside the main political parties were recognised and feared by local party political activists.

The Greater London Authority Act 1999 and the Local Government Act 2000 gave local government, and local citizens, an opportunity to experiment with direct election to local executive political office. These Acts of Parliament set the legal framework within which three different types of mayor would operate: the mayor of London; and, outside the new Greater London Authority, the directly elected mayor and cabinet, and the elected mayor and manager. The advent of elected mayors could, potentially, disrupt long-standing patterns of political behaviour, the dominance of political parties over local government and the relationship that exists between the local political leader and local citizens. Moreover, it makes very different demands on the way in which councillors conduct political affairs and council business.

Yet it is vital that the introduction of elected mayors is seen in the context of the long-term debate about the role of local government in the political representation of local communities and in the provision of important public services. Elected mayors have been parachuted into a landscape in which little else has changed other than the way in which the local political leader is selected. Lacking from this bold experiment was any fundamental reassessment of the role and nature of local government in England; mayors must govern with what they find when they arrive. They may be in a position to run the council, and to provide a high-profile public face of the authority to the local community, but, if that is all, then we are left with two key questions:

- What is the distinctive contribution elected mayors make, and could make, to the governance of the English localities?
- Have we given the new mayors sufficient powers and responsibilities to govern and lead the English localities?

It is these questions the book explores.

The book does not set out to evaluate the performance of the individual English elected mayors or to draw unnecessary and unhelpful comparisons between the skills and qualities of one mayor and those of another. Neither does it set out to tell the story of particular mayors, their journeys to office and what they as individuals have or have not done. Rather, what follows is an exploration of how this new office has so far contributed to notions of renewing and revitalising local government and democracy and refreshing local politics. The book searches for the conditions necessary to enable English elected mayors to make a distinctive contribution not only to the governance of their localities, but also to the wider political process of the country. Thus, the book uses the early experiences of the office of directly elected mayor to explore what this new form of local government can tell us about the future of English local democracy and local politics.

The research for this book was done in 2003/4 and written up to March 2005; it was conducted in all the mayoral authorities and included in-depth interviews with elected mayors, in-depth interviews with councillors and officers from mayoral and non-mayoral authorities, case study analysis and use of documentary evidence. In addition, a questionnaire survey was conducted among councillors sitting on mayoral authorities; a total of 531 questionnaires were circulated (though not to the councillors of Stoke-on-Trent because some of the questions were not appropriate for its mayor and manager system), and 253 were returned and usable for analysis – giving a response rate of 48 per cent.

All the mayors and councillors interviewed were assured that the interview data would be treated with absolute confidentiality and consequently the vast majority of elaborative quotes and comments used in this book have been anonymised. My thanks and gratitude go to the mayors who willingly and enthusiastically gave of their valuable time to be interviewed and who also provided documentary evidence and other material for the book. Thanks also go to officers and councillors of mayoral authorities for their cooperation and involvement in the research.

Throughout the book I have studiously avoided reporting anything that could result in the formation of any sort of league table for mayors. This is another reason for making much of the material unattributable.

Nor have I not identified which mayors fall into particular typologies and categories constructed on the basis of the research findings. This is because, as there are so few directly elected mayors in England, it would be unfair to suggest that some are better than others; to do so would provide political ammunition to opponents, and only the electorates concerned can make the judgement as to the quality of the mayor. Had England many more directly elected mayors, a book could not be picked over for what it said about the individuals' effectiveness (or otherwise). I respect the integrity and commitment of England's small and select group of elected mayors, and would not want to undermine them in any way. Also, I might need them for future research!

Many of the interviews were conducted by Alison Crow, a colleague at the Institute of Local Government Studies (INLOGOV) at the University of Birmingham, whose hard work during the research for the book was an invaluable part of this project. I would also like to thank Chris Game and Chris Skelcher, also colleagues at INLOGOV, who, throughout the research and during the writing of the book, provided encouragement and proved a constant source of ideas and insight. Finally, once again, thanks go to my wife, Julia, and two daughters, Emma and Harriet, who have supported me through another project and without whom I would never have finished.

Colin Copus

1

Introduction

The introduction of directly elected mayors into England generates a potential for a new and exciting approach to local governance. Directly elected mayors are a radical departure from past political structures and from ways of conducting local political decision-making; voters in English councils can now adopt a form of local presidential figure to replace the previously indirectly elected leader of the council. Thus, the book's focus is on the debate as it centres on the directly elected political leader rather than any indirectly elected alternative. It explores the English approach to the direct election of a local political leader and the way in which the first crop of mayors, elected in 2002, have gone about responding to and shaping this new office. It also explores the powers, roles, responsibilities and political dynamics of the English version of the elected mayor.

The book locates the English mayor firmly within the context of the continuing debate about the modernisation of local government and within a wider debate about the nature, conduct and relevance of local politics to the citizen and voter. It looks at how the new mayoral office can be part of a process of reconnecting local government to local communities and bringing new meaning and salience to local democracy, and at whether mayors can assist in transforming the nature of local politics. The book is deliberately written from the English experience; the comparative material included is there to help us understand the English approach to directly elected political leaders, how that approach may develop over time, and how local politics and government could be reconfigured.

While the book is based on the experience, so far, of English elected mayors, it is not the story of twelve individuals, nor is it an attempt to produce a league table of efficiency in office and the quality of political leadership provided. Rather, the book considers not only the experiences of particular mayors, but also the whole notion of directly elected political leadership and its place within English governance. The book draws out broad lessons from the mayoral experiment for local government and democracy, and offers a framework for understanding direct election to executive political office within the context of English local democracy.

In this chapter the recent and broad arguments that have resulted in the arrival of the directly elected mayor are briefly reviewed; the Blair government's modernisation agenda is placed within the context of arguments about the configuration of local political decision-making. The chapter also explores the different approaches taken to the government of London compared with local government in the rest of England. The chapter then briefly places directly elected mayors in an international perspective. It concludes by setting out a number of vital questions that are raised by the introduction of a directly elected form of local political leadership, questions that are addressed throughout the rest of the book.

**Local politics and local government:
a case for change and a not so modern agenda**

Local government in England has two distinct elements. First, there is a world of elected representatives, party politics, policy-making, public and private discourse and debate, the seeking of party advantage and the desire to secure a governing mandate from the local citizenry. The local council provides the main institutional setting for this process, with political parties and community or local action groups providing associated theatres for political interaction. Second, there is a complex set of institutional arrangements driven by managerial and technocratic concerns and aimed at the provision of important public services, services which, while needing to respond to local priorities and concerns, must meet national standards and considerations. Local government is the means by which the provision of local services is brought together with the world of politics, and party politics in particular.

The rediscovery of the representative, democratic and political role that local government could have is one of the most powerful changes that have occurred in local government in recent times and it has stimulated a debate about what local political leadership is and how it should be configured and conducted.[1] A key element of that debate is how citizens should select their local political leaders: either directly at an authority-wide election or by an indirect choice made for the voter, by local councillors of the majority party on the council.

Despite councillors being elected as politicians, with a clear political vision and more often than not a party label, they have not generally been expected – by governments or the public – to provide local political leadership to communities. Rather, they have been faced with the challenge of providing important and complex services, making decisions about the nature of that provision (within strict government guidelines) and being the vehicle through which the quality of those services and the officers running them are held to public account: services are, in the

British context, local government. Indeed, political leadership has been explored more fully in theory than in practice.[2]

That is not to say, however, that there have not been periods of intense political and party political activity within councils and between councils and central government, nor that political ideology and party advantage, locally and centrally, are not played out on the stage that is the local council, as was evident during the 1980s.[3] Such periods, however, are not examples of the usual conditions of local democracy and politics; nor did these times and events display what is now being sought by many from notions of local political leadership.

A vital element of the debate about local political leadership is whether a political body such as a council should be organised as a collective, uniform whole, responsible for all facets of political decision-making, or whether there should be a separation of the executive and representative functions and processes of local government, with responsibility for each located within a separate, if linked, political entity. Such a debate has not been the sole property of the Labour government's modernisation project. The Maud committee, which reported in 1967, suggested that the long-standing committee system within local government should be replaced by a management board of five to nine councillors, which would have control of the policy process and the formulation of the council's objectives. The Maud committee based its suggestions on the need for the provision of clear political leadership at local level, something which the introduction of directly elected mayors and executive council leaders was designed to facilitate some thirty years after Maud reported.[4]

Almost twenty years after Maud the Widdicombe committee recognised the advantages of the type of management committee of members that Maud had proposed and shared its enthusiasm for this approach to enhancing accountability and decision-making. Yet Widdicombe was concerned about concentrating power in too few hands and reducing the influence of councillors outside the executive. Further, when it came to direct election of the executive, Widdicombe's main concern was the potential risk of conflict that could arise between two separate governing bodies with competing mandates (i.e. the mayor and the council) and that deadlock could occur or, worse still, an intense political battle develop around which element of government had the strongest mandate. In addition, the personalisation of politics, seen as inherent in the mayoral system and accepted in 'countries with a presidential system', was thought to be 'generally disliked in Great Britain'. Finally, a concern was expressed that if the council and the mayor had different electoral cycles, the prospect could emerge of the mayor and council majority coming from a different party.[5] Widdicombe's analysis of the issues requiring reform was remarkably consistent with earlier reports and enquiries.

The Commission for Local Democracy (CLD) – an independent body launched in November 1993 – explored the state of local democracy at the time and ranged over issues such as: community identity and participation, the constitutional status of local government, the role of political parties, finance, and direct democracy at the local level. Much of the CLD's deliberations find an echo in the Blair local government modernisation project; for example, the problem of low turnout for local elections was seen to 'diminish the legitimacy of local councils and weaken the mandates of majority parties'.[6] Moreover, the central weaknesses of British local government were identified as:

> citizen ignorance of local politics and leadership; the gap between formal
> and informal accountability for decisions; excessive party involvement in
> local elections; and too much councillor time spent on management and
> not representation and scrutiny.[7]

The last point has been a consistent theme of research and explorations of the role of the councillor and a major criticism of the way in which councillors' time is allocated.[8] It is also an area of criticism made of councillor activity by both Conservative and Labour local government ministers. The CLD argued that local representative democracy would benefit from a healthy dose of participative and direct democratic practices, with referendums, local ballots and a range of consultative processes high on the Commission's agenda. The analysis set out by the CLD was largely accepted by the Blair government, yet some aspects of its findings sat less well with the current Westminster and Whitehall thinking, such as its criticisms of the citizen as customer and the priority of national standards over local concerns:

> The insistence on competitive tendering and the emphasis on the citizen as
> customer have changed the accountability functions of the council and its
> members. They are seen less as a reflecting mirror for local opinion, more
> as service managers. Performance is judged less on the basis of whether
> a service meets the professed needs of a particular community, more on
> whether it conforms to a national set standard.[9]

The CLD added prophetically: 'the growth of league tables for schools, hospitals and police forces, is one indicator of this trend'.[10] Such league tables are clearly now an indicator of how far central government views its own electoral fortunes as being bound to the quality and effectiveness of a range of public services, most of which are the responsibilities of providers other than the government itself.

The CLD pointed out that most local government in western Europe, at the time, was based on a form of separation of local powers and consisted of 'an elected assembly or council; an executive group or committee; and the permanent staff serving either of the political elements'. It suggested such a separation of powers in Britain would overcome 'public confusion, secrecy and inefficiency'.[11] The most radical aspect of the CLD's recommendations was that of the separate and direct election of a leader/mayor of the council, in an executive capacity, but less radically the CLD went on to suggest that while the directly elected leader or mayor would head the council administration, that office and its holder should be subordinate to the council, which would retain control of the budget and broad policy matters. Thus, the mayor would be required to negotiate with the council on a range of issues; the CLD had, thus, proposed a 'weak mayoral model'.[12]

Shortly after the CLD's suggestions, a parliamentary select committee, chaired by Lord Hunt, recommended that councils be free to experiment with their political management arrangements, a recommendation that he later followed with an unsuccessful Private Member's Bill.[13] Moreover, in the early 1990s the Conservative government had floated the idea of introducing directly elected mayors into Britain.[14]

Thus, the common themes of past examinations of local government have been: low levels of public awareness and engagement; the intensity and appropriateness of party politics; the legitimacy of local political action; the lack of visibility and transparency in political decision-making; the tensions between managing services and political representation; and the tensions between representative democracy and public participation. All have found a resonance in the modernisation of political decision-making that has resulted in the arrival of the directly elected mayor in the English political landscape. By exploring in more detail the arguments used by the Blair government for some form of local separation of powers, we can understand more fully the nature of the English version of directly elected mayors.

Local government: the need for a political executive?

More than thirty years after the Maud committee's deliberations, a political executive became a reality for English local government with the passing of the Local Government Act 2000. Before the passing of that Act, the modernisation agenda for local government, and the analysis on which that agenda was based, were set out in a number of key government publications: *Modernising Local Government: Local Democracy and Community Leadership*; *Modern Local Government: In Touch with the People*; and *Local Leadership: Local Choice*.[15] These themselves were preceded by the Labour Party's own publication in 1995 of its local government proposals, which, as well as unsurprisingly setting out the terms of the debate that would follow in government, also expressed a willingness to see experimentation with the CLD's suggestions for elected mayors.[16]

Certain key assumptions underpinned the modernisation agenda:
first, that there is a need to separate into distinct bodies the executive,
representational and scrutiny roles of the council; second, that the key
role of the council, and the councillor, is to provide political leadership to
the community; third, that councils are required to navigate a complex
and uncertain world of governance based on working in partnership with
other public and private bodies;[17] fourth, that political leadership and
decision-making should be transparent, open, visible and responsive
to citizens' concerns;[18] and fifth, that engagement between citizen and
council is vital and rests on councils employing a broad range of consultative and participatory mechanisms.

The committee system of political decision-making was roundly condemned as failing on all the above counts, as it was seen to be inefficient
and opaque and, indeed, was 'no basis for modern local government',
being a 'poor vehicle for developing and demonstrating community
leadership'. In addition, the committee system clouded political responsibility and, further, committee chairs, a vital part of the council's political
leadership, were often anonymous to the public. Committees had failed
to 'foster community leaders and leadership; and local people had no
direct say over their local leaders'.[19] Political leadership and the scrutiny of
those leaders were argued to be distinct and separate concepts and roles,
requiring politicians that specialised in one or the other. The separation
of roles, and ultimately the separation of local political powers, would
produce 'greater clarity about who is responsible for decisions and who
should be held to account for decisions'. Improved accountability and
scrutiny would be an automatic result of the separation of political roles
and responsibilities, as 'those councillors who have played no direct part
in the decisions taken will have a clear explicit responsibility to review
and question those decisions, whether or not they belong to the same
party as the executive'.[20]

Yet in 'most councils it is the political groups, meeting behind closed
doors, which make the big and significant decisions',[21] to which of course
can be added that in many councils even the small and insignificant
decisions are also made behind closed doors, in private party group
meetings.[22] Introducing a requirement on councillors to hold an executive
to account, even if it consists of party colleagues, is one thing; changing
long established and well understood patterns of political behaviour
among councillors is quite another. There is little evidence to suggest that
party group loyalty has been relegated to second place behind the need to
hold an executive to account.[23] Indeed, more generally, the government's
objectives for scrutiny are far from being achieved.[24] In addition, Stoker
has found that local stakeholders perceive political parties to dominate
the decision-making process more in non-mayoral than in mayoral
authorities.[25]

The government's analysis fails to provide anything like a robust and rigorous analysis of the political party group and group system. As a consequence, the place where real political decisions are taken and where political leadership is displayed – albeit privately – remains unmodernised, with no sign that it will be required to change, save, that is, for a belief on the part of the government that party 'whipping' is incompatible with overview and scrutiny, which has led suggestions that it be publicly declared in council when a whip is imposed.[26] Yet, despite the omission from the modernising analysis and project of any serious consideration of the role and power of political parties and party groups, the desire to do something about the public face and problems of local government resulted in the conclusion that the executive, representative and scrutiny roles of the council and councillor be separated. Indeed, the government declared it was 'very attracted' to the model of a strong, executive, directly elected mayor for the following reasons:

> Such a mayor would be a highly visible figure. He or she would have been elected by the people rather than the council or party and would therefore focus attention outwards in the direction of the people rather than inwards towards fellow councillors. The mayor would be a strong political and community leader with whom the electorate could identify. Mayors will have to become well known to their electorate which could help increase interest in and understanding of local government.[27]

In the 1998 white paper *Modern Local Government: In Touch with the People* the government elaborated its case for a local separation of powers and argued that such separation would enhance efficiency, transparency and accountability in local government:[28]

- *Efficiency.* A small executive, particularly where individuals have executive powers, can act more quickly, responsively and accurately to meet the needs and aspirations of the community.
- *Transparency.* It will be clear to the public who is responsible for decisions. The scrutiny process will help to clarify both the reasons for decisions and the facts and analysis on which policy and actions are based.
- *Accountability.* Increased transparency will enable people to measure the executive's actions against the policies on which it was elected. Councillors will no longer have to accept responsibility for decisions in which they took no part. That should sharpen local political debate and increase interest in elections to the council.

Modern Local Government presented the crystallisation of the government's thinking on what shape the mayoral council should take and that the role of the mayor would be as 'the political leader for the community, proposing policy for approval by the council and steering implementation by the cabinet through council officers.'[29]

The options available

Three options for the form of local government executive were set out in the 2000 Act, two of which involved a directly elected mayor. These options appear to have emerged from a series of discussions between senior politicians and friendly sources, rather than from any serious and fundamental review of various approaches to executive mayors that exist overseas, for example. The three options are available to all county, district and unitary authorities in England. The citizenry can petition for a referendum on either option for mayor, or the council can call the referendum; the leader and cabinet arrangement is not subject to a referendum.

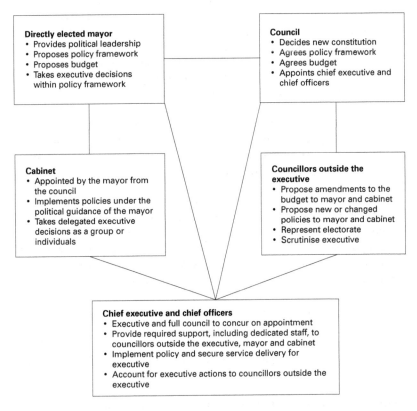

Directly elected mayor
- Provides political leadership
- Proposes policy framework
- Proposes budget
- Takes executive decisions within policy framework

Council
- Decides new constitution
- Agrees policy framework
- Agrees budget
- Appoints chief executive and chief officers

Cabinet
- Appointed by the mayor from the council
- Implements policies under the political guidance of the mayor
- Takes delegated executive decisions as a group or individuals

Councillors outside the executive
- Propose amendments to the budget to mayor and cabinet
- Propose new or changed policies to mayor and cabinet
- Represent electorate
- Scrutinise executive

Chief executive and chief officers
- Executive and full council to concur on appointment
- Provide required support, including dedicated staff, to councillors outside the executive, mayor and cabinet
- Implement policy and secure service delivery for executive
- Account for executive actions to councillors outside the executive

Figure 1.1 The mayor and cabinet executive arrangement. (Source: DETR, 1999. *Local Leadership: Local Choice*, London, DETR, para. 3.6.)

The first mayoral executive available under the 2000 Act is represented diagrammatically in Figure 1.1. This is the directly elected mayor and cabinet. The mayor is elected in an at-large election by all the local voters; he or she then appoints a cabinet from among the members of council, to a maximum of ten members in total.

The second executive option is that of an indirectly elected leader, appointed by the council, with a cabinet appointed either by the leader or by the council as a whole. It was pointed out that the indirectly elected

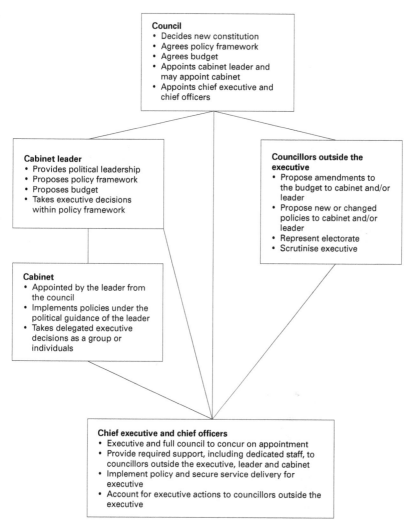

Figure 1.2 The indirectly elected leader and cabinet executive arrangement. (Source: DETR, 1999. *Local Leadership: Local Choice*, London, DETR, para. 3.6.)

leader's powers are broadly similar to those of an elected mayor, but are not so broad, because the leader has not been directly elected. Thus, there is little motivation for councils and citizens to experiment with an elected mayor, as he or she will have broadly similar powers to the council leader. Figure 1.2 presents the leader and cabinet executive arrangement.

The third executive option presented in the Act is a variation of a mayoral model: the mayor and council manager. Here there is an executive which consists of only two members: a directly elected mayor and a council manager, with the former giving a political lead to the latter. The

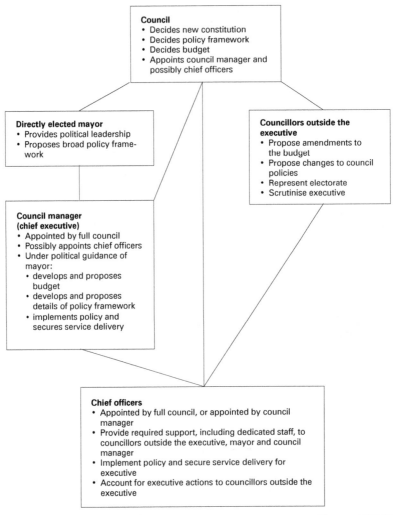

Council
• Decides new constitution
• Decides policy framework
• Decides budget
• Appoints council manager and
  possibly chief officers

Directly elected mayor
• Provides political leadership
• Proposes broad policy frame-
  work

**Councillors outside the
executive**
• Propose amendments to
  the budget
• Propose changes to council
  policies
• Represent electorate
• Scrutinise executive

**Council manager
(chief executive)**
• Appointed by full council
• Possibly appoints chief officers
• Under political guidance of
  mayor:
  • develops and proposes
    budget
  • develops and proposes
    details of policy framework
  • implements policy and
    secures service delivery

Chief officers
• Appointed by full council, or appointed by council
  manager
• Provide required support, including dedicated staff, to
  councillors outside the executive, mayor and council
  manager
• Implement policy and secure service delivery for
  executive
• Account for executive actions to councillors outside the
  executive

Figure 1.3 The mayor and manager executive arrangement. (Source: DETR, 1999. *Local Leadership: Local Choice*, London, DETR, para. 3.6.)

council manager represents a form of super chief executive, to whom strategic policy and day-to-day decision-making are delegated. The mayor is a political figurehead, giving guidance and leadership 'rather than direct decision-taking' and exerting influence over the council manager, who is appointed by the council. Figure 1.3 displays the mayor and manager option set out by the government. (This model at present has been adopted only in Stoke; all the other mayors fit the first option outlined above, and the second option is outside the focus of the book.)

In creating a carefully structured and limited approach to the three executive options open to local councils and citizens, the government had missed an opportunity to allow councils to borrow ideas about mayoral political leadership from overseas.[30]

The notion of consent

A vital element of the introduction of the mayoral political executive into English local government is the notion of consent. That is, before an elected mayor can be introduced as the political executive for any council area, a referendum must be held and a 'yes' vote secured to a question, the wording of which is specified in legislation:

> Are you in favour of the proposal for [name of local authority] to be run in a new way, which includes a mayor, who will be elected by the voters of the [city/borough], to be in charge of the council's services and to lead [name of local authority] and the community which it serves?[31]

Consent from the electorate adds legitimacy to the new office; not only is the holder sanctified by the public vote, but so is the office itself. Such consent, while not protecting the office of elected mayor from abolition by any future government, does provide it with an element of moral security. A referendum can be initiated either by a council itself or by a public petition, signed by a minimum of 5 per cent of the local electorate, but only if a complex set of regulations is adhered to.[32] Thus, the public now has a say over not only who governs them but also how they are governed. In addition, the Secretary of State (the local government minister or the Deputy Prime Minister) can direct a council to hold a referendum on the introduction of an elected mayor if, in his or her opinion, the council has not responded in such a way as to reflect the results of public con-sultation. Only one referendum is permissible in any council area in any five-year period, so as to prevent the risk of a community 'continuously over a number of years focusing primarily on how it should be governed', rather than on what those 'who are leading should be doing'.[33]

The 5 per cent threshold to trigger a referendum is a considerable hurdle for citizens organising a petition, particularly for those who are new to political activity. A petition circulating in Bradford at the time of writing requires some 19,000 signatures; a similar petition circulating in Northumberland County, which started as a response to the council's plans to reorganise education within the county, requires some 12,000 signatures. In addition, all signatures must be checked and verified by the council at which they are aimed. The five-year period between referendums is safeguard enough from frequent referendums.

Yet one councillor was happy to admit that his council had called a mayoral referendum safe in the knowledge that a 'no' vote would be returned. He commented in interview:

> We only went for a referendum because we knew that the people would understand it meant [named area] always picking the mayor because it's where the majority of the population live. The other six towns wouldn't get a look-in. If we thought there was a chance of a 'yes' vote we would never have gone for it.

Indeed, safeguards are needed not against community-inspired referendums but rather against councils and councillors manipulating the referendum process for their own purposes. As a backbench councillor on a mayoral authority commented in interview:

> We [councillors] didn't want this system and it's not working. People didn't understand what was happening or what mayors were about when they voted for it and we told them it wouldn't work; councillors don't have any power any more. When we win the mayoral election we are going to have a referendum and abolish it.

Yet referendums also represent a new way for those outside the existing political structure and processes to obtain political power, and despite the limitations on referendums and the complexity of the regulations governing the process, citizens in some areas have seen the new mayor come from outside the established local political elite.

Finally, the notion of consent to be governed by an elected mayor also operates in reverse and a referendum is required to remove the mayoral system as the local governing arrangement. While the mayoral system must be sanctioned in a referendum before its introduction and its demise is also sanctioned in this way, the only time the indirectly elected leader system requires a referendum is if it is to replace the mayoral arrangements.

The London case

For London, a directly elected mayor similarly had to be sanctioned by a referendum,[34] Yet the London mayor, under the Greater London

Authority Act 1999, has very different roles and sets of institutional and political arrangements from those for the mayors established by the 2000 Act.

London was always going to be different to the rest of the country when it came to modernising the system of government. The abolition of the Greater London Council (GLC) in 1986 and the transference of its responsibilities to the London boroughs, as well as to an array of other bodies created for the purpose, left the capital without a strategic layer of governance, something it had not lacked, in one form or another, since 1855, when the Metropolitan Board of Works was established.[35] While the Board of Works was not an elected body, the London County Council (LCC), which replaced it in 1889, did have the legitimacy of direct election. The struggle for political control of the London-wide body displayed characteristics and political dynamics that would be recognised today in council chambers throughout the country; from its outset, the LCC was a party politicised body.[36]

The GLC, which took over from the LCC in 1965, was based on an extended boundary compared with that of its predecessor, one which took in the more Conservative-oriented London suburbs, as the redrawing of the boundary recognised the difficulties of confining London within any sort of strictly drawn geographical demarcation (London now, as then, has the tendency to spill across any lines drawn on a map, to force new thinking about boundaries by government, policy-makers and local politicians). The GLC struggled with its role, particularly against the London boroughs, which jealously guarded their position and power. Indeed, while the GLC was the London-wide elected strategic authority, albeit a limited one, it was the boroughs that had the greater powers.[37]

It was the GLC that gave Ken Livingstone his first taste of London-wide governance, in 1981, when he became its leader and embarked on a new left-wing 'rainbow coalition' approach to politics across the capital and the construction of an alliance of the previously politically and socially excluded – an alliance that would later prove invaluable in Livingstone's bid to become the first directly elected mayor of London. Some five years after taking control of the GLC, Livingstone found his political platform and office snatched from him, not by the electorate but by the Conservative government, which, after publishing its consultation paper *Streamlining the Cities*, did just that, by abolishing the GLC and the six metropolitan counties.[38] Thus, London was left with no city-wide elected government and a complex mass of agencies – elected boroughs, unelected quangos and private organisations – competing, conflicting and cooperating in order to provide the capital with some semblance of governance.

It is perhaps no surprise that doing something about London was higher on the Blair government's modernisation agenda than the rest of local government. But there is a parallel in the reform of London government and the rest of the country, namely the separation of executive functions into a distinct political entity to be held to account by those outside the executive. In London, unlike in the rest of the country, mayoral accountability was to be assured by a separate organisation altogether, the London Assembly, the mayor and Assembly together comprising the Greater London Authority (GLA). The GLA was then to work in partnership with a range of external agencies to provide the capital with: good governance; a visible political leadership; a political decision-making arrangement that was transparent, inclusive and responsive; and clear lines of political accountability.

The government showcased its proposal for London government in the green paper *New Leadership for London* and the white paper *A Mayor and Assembly for London*.[39] While the themes of the wider modernisation agenda are reflected in these documents, and in the Greater London Authority Act 1999, which emerged from them, London was deemed by government to be a special case that required a different type of elected mayor from that which would become available to the rest of the country. Moreover, the reform of London governance was not an 'exercise in bringing back the Greater London Council or tinkering with existing local government structures'. Rather, it was about the creation of a 'new model of government, appropriate to a great capital city in the new millennium'.[40]

Thus, the new governance of London would look radically different from the rest of local government, and have a configuration of political relationships fundamentally different to those existing anywhere else. The GLA was not to be a traditional authority providing local services. Rather, it was to sit within a network of overlapping responsibilities, and its influence was to be shared with a number of other statutory and non-statutory bodies, with GLA members making up part of the membership of, and sometimes taking the chairs of, a range of organisations concerned with the governance of London. The GLA's relationships with the voluntary sector, central government and the London borough councils were to vary according to the task and partner in hand. But, before the mayoralty and Assembly could become a reality, a referendum was required.

Londoners gave consent to the new mayoralty on 7 May 1998, when a majority 'yes' vote was received in the referendum on a turnout of only 34 per cent. Yet, with 1,230,715 'yes' votes recorded (72%) and 478,413 'no' (28%) and with every London borough providing a majority 'yes' vote, the government had received its first public endorsement of executive mayoral government.

Alongside the elected mayor, the new Assembly consists of twenty-five members elected by the additional member system of proportional representation. There are fourteen members representing geographical constituency areas and an additional eleven members drawn from the results of a London-wide list; these eleven members are elected to seats allocated to ensure that the overall distribution of seats reflects the proportion of votes each party and independent list receives. So, a new type of representative assembly requires a new type of voting system; rather than providing a government, albeit a local one, the system was required to produce a representative chamber, and this it did. The first elections to the London Assembly, held in 2000, produced the following results: Conservative Party nine seats; Labour nine; Liberal Democrats four; and Green Party three.

The second set of Assembly elections, held in 2004, produced an even more intriguing and politically representative set of results: Conservative Party nine seats; Labour seven; Liberal Democrats five; Greens two; and the UK Independence Party two.

The GLA is a central part of a still complex and disintegrated approach to the government of the capital. It has a mayoral system that, while strong in relation to the London Assembly, is weak in relation to the outside world and especially of course central government. The London mayor is an elected figurehead for London who, outside of the GLA, wields influence, not power – a subtlety not lost on those in central government who designed the model. Yet, despite the limitations of the new office and the existence of an assembly which has no counterpart within the rest of English local government, the London mayor was the first directly elected English mayor to join the growing ranks of directly elected mayors overseas.

Elected mayors: an international movement

While in some countries directly elected mayors have been a long-established part of the local political system, there has been a recent trend towards the direct election of the local political leader in many western local democracies.[41] The shift from indirectly to directly elected leaders coincides with a shift from notions of local government to local governance, as well as with a move from hierarchical and closed government networks and a routinised policy structure to a more fragmented and decentralised set of local political networks, coupled with experiments in new forms of democracy.[42] The latter type of system requires a more personalised system of political leaders – one in which accountability and responsibility for political action or inaction can be readily focused on an individual.

Larsen provides another part of the driving force for the adoption of directly elected mayors in Europe when he notes that a directly elected mayor can make a superior claim to political legitimacy than his or her indirectly elected counterpart.[43] Other factors – such as economic regeneration and development, regionalism, shifts in central and local relationships, the emergence of new democracies, collapses in party political systems, the desire among regional or central governments for a single and powerful local politician with whom to do business, and the role of the supranational state – have also influenced the shift to directly elected local political leaders.[44] Alongside these macro-concerns are of course more micro-concerns, about local political accountability, citizen engagement, the need to promote effective local public policy and the reconfiguration of arrangements for service provision.[45] Moreover, changes in 'society, technology and intergovernmental relations' have often found local government wanting.[46] Thus, a myriad of factors have driven the international movement towards elected mayors, but the overriding factor has been the need for more effective, accountable and identifiable local political leadership.[47]

Yet related to the forces for change to a directly elected political leader is the question of whether a simple shift in the way local political leaders are selected is sufficient to enable them to respond effectively to the rapidly changing local and national political environment within which they find themselves. The powers that the local political leader may need are considered throughout the book, and it is sufficient to say here that the perceived and actual increases in political legitimacy and the greater political recognition of a directly elected mayor compared with those of an indirectly elected political leader do enhance their ability to deal with the challenges they face. However, such enhanced legitimacy cannot substitute for actual political power.

As well as a move toward elected mayors in established western democracies, it is noticeable that many emerging democracies among the former eastern bloc countries have also adopted the elected mayor for local government. In the 1990s directly elected mayors were introduced in Bulgaria, Hungary, Romania, Slovakia and Slovenia, and already existed in Albania, Russia and the Ukraine; in 2002 they were introduced in Poland.[48] Indeed, only the Baltic states and the Czech Republic (as of 2005) have a system of indirectly elected local political leaders. Much of the driving force for the change was the shift not only from totalitarianism to democracy but also from a centralised command economy to a market economy, and the impact of that shift on local economies and politics.[49]

Similarly, since the early 1990s mayors with a range of powers and a variety of relationships to the council have been directly elected across South America, in countries such as Argentina, Brazil, Columbia, Ecuador, El Salvador, Guatemala, Panama, Paraguay, Uruguay and Venezuela. Countries as politically, economically and culturally diverse as Uganda, Russia, Cyprus, Mozambique, Israel and the Indian states of West Bengal and Madhya Pradesh have adopted some version of a directly elected local political leader.

Despite the spread of directly elected mayors across the globe, the pattern of mayoral government is not unified; mayors exist at different tiers of local government, or share the local political landscape with indirectly elected counterparts; in other states the elected mayor is the only form of local political leadership; and in others only the council-appointed leader exists. Further, mayoral powers, responsibilities, relationships with political parties and influence with government also vary; Chapter 7 considers five mayoral systems in detail and sets out the lessons from them that can be drawn for the English version of mayoral local government.

The elected mayor exists, in one form or another, on every continent. Mayors come to office through a range of different voting systems, hold an array of powers and responsibilities, and have a relationship with their council that is partly driven by institutional arrangements, partly by cultural and political factors and partly by the personality of the mayor. Yet the search for effective local political leadership, the desire for a sound basis to central–local relationships and the need for an enhanced accountability in local politics have led many states towards the elected mayor to fulfil these needs. Whether the English version also meets these criteria and has incorporated the lessons from overseas is explored throughout the book.

Conclusions

By the late 1980s, the traditional committee system which had served local government since Victorian times and which was linked far more to the management of public services than to the demands of political representation had, in the government's view, become an anachronism. It was a product of a bygone age and was no longer suited to modern, or modernised, local government and to dealing with the complex network of governance arrangements, of which the elected council was just a part. Britain had avoided the separation of powers at the local level which was common across much of Europe but had been arguing, for over forty years or so, as committees of enquiry and royal commissions came and went, about the merits, or otherwise, of some form of executive–council separation.

The 2000 Act, while by no means ending the debate about the virtue of, or indeed the need for, a local separation of powers – or otherwise – has made that separation real. While the leader and cabinet executive arrangements simply formalised political practices already in existence across local government, the landscape of English local politics has been radically altered by the introduction of a directly elected mayor. A directly elected executive mayor has the potential to change both the way in which political decisions are made and the nature of the relationship between political leaders and citizens, and to reconfigure the balance of power in the local polity between political parties and political associations of a non-party nature.

The success or failure of the English experiment with elected mayors will be judged not so much by how many there are, although this is important. Rather, the office should be judged by its ability to provide effective, decisive and accountable local political leadership, and to enhance citizen engagement with local government, and by whether mayoral government can generate a local political culture that is demonstrably different from that in other areas.[50] When it comes to questions of political power, style, responsibilities, capacity and influence in the complex array of governance networks surrounding our localities, we should hold the English mayor not so much against the national counterpart of the indirectly elected leader but rather against mayors from overseas. It is here that we will see whether the mayoral experiment has introduced into England a new form of local governance and a reconfiguration of the political relationships between local government, political parties, local politicians and citizens, bringing them closer together,[51] or whether we simply have no more than a new route to the top job in local politics for the local politician.

To understand the position of the English elected mayor fully, it is necessary to identify factors that predominate in the development of this type of governance arrangement and in the formation of the dynamics of mayoral government. What the book aims to discover is whether the English mayor has added a new dimension to local political leadership – or has simply been accommodated within the existing dynamics and structures of local politics and government.

The English directly elected mayor operates within a very clearly defined set of institutional arrangements as part of the council. While the separation of powers between executive and council is by no way unique to the experiences of elected mayors across the globe – indeed, it is commonplace – the nature of these arrangements, the role of political parties within them and the way in which they serve to constrain and facilitate mayoral leadership all highlight the impotence of the current political decision-making structure within which the English elected mayor sits. In exploring how mayors inhabit these arrangements and navigate around them, we can discover the common themes and the distinctions between the ways in which our mayors have configured relationships with councillors and the political party groups to affect local politics and the dynamics of political decision-making.

The advent of directly elected mayors within English local government raises a wide but simple set of questions about the effect of direct election to executive political office on local democracy and representation, which the book addresses:

1 Does it strengthen or weaken the political relationship between the citizen and the governor?
2 Does it strengthen or weaken the nature of English local democracy and political representation at the local level?
3 Is the separation of powers at the local level a viable and achievable form of political organisation when set in the English context, in which much local political power, organisation and decision-making have been appropriated to the central government level?
4 Does the arrival of direct election to political office make local self-government a more or less desirable and obtainable concept?
5 What are the lessons for the broader politics of England from the way in which local government develops as a political institution with a written constitution?
6 What are the lessons from the mayoral experiment for the constitutional position of local government in England?

These questions are addressed throughout the book.

Structure of the book

Chapter 2 explores the arrival of the elected mayor within English local government through referendums and subsequent elections. That chapter also explores the elected mayors' roles, responsibilities and powers. It asks whether the English elected mayor is an office able to revitalise local government and alter the dynamics of local politics, or whether it is simply a very English compromise between the competing desires to pursue change but to do so cognisant of the objection from the local political elite and local government establishment to any disturbance in the established patterns of political interaction.

Chapter 3 explores notions of local political leadership and asks what is meant by this concept in England and how it applies to elected mayors, council leaders and councillors.

Chapter 4 goes on to investigate how elected mayors face the competing pressures of both running a large public service bureaucracy that is a council and leading the local community.

Chapter 5 looks in detail at the political power of the English elected mayor, how mayors have carved out a role for themselves locally and how they have operated within a framework set out in both legalisation and a written local constitution. The chapter also theorises on direct election to executive political office.

Chapter 6 explores, through three case studies, how mayors have engaged with local political issues that have stimulated intense public interest and political activity. It looks at what the office of elected mayor can bring to resolving the tension between governing an area and reconciling communities of place within it.

In Chapter 7 the approach to mayoral local government in five countries is explored in detail and lessons for the English version are considered from this overseas experience.

Chapter 8 explores the role of the councillor serving alongside an elected mayor, and looks at the reactions and experiences of councillors to working with an elected mayor.

In the last chapter the powers, responsibilities and activities of English mayors are considered against the expectation that the office will be an integral part of a new form of local governance and that elected mayors will be a new type of highly visible and accountable local politician and political leader. The chapter provides a framework for the development of the office of elected mayor in England and sets out some options for how that development might occur.

Notes

1 Leach, S. and D. Wilson, 2000. *Local Political Leadership*, Bristol, Policy Press.
2 Hill, D.M., 1974. *Democratic Theory and Local Government*, London, George Allen and Unwin; Bulpitt, J., 1983. *Territory and Power in the United Kingdom*, Manchester University Press.
3 Blunkett, D., and K. Jackson, 1987. *Democracy in Crisis: The Town Halls Respond*, London, Hogarth Press; Wainwright, H., 1987. *Labour: A Tale of Two Parties*, London, Hogarth Press.
4 Committee on the Management of Local Government, 1967 (henceforth Maud committee). *Report of the Committee, Vol. I*, London, HMSO.
5 Committee of Inquiry into the Conduct of Local Authority Business (henceforth Widdicombe committee), 1986. *Report of the Committee into the Conduct of Local Authority Business*, London, HMSO, para. 5.26.
6 CLD, 1995. *Final Report. Taking Charge: The Rebirth of Local Democracy*, London, Municipal Journal Books.
7 *Ibid.*, para. 4.4.
8 Maud committee, *Report*; Committee of Inquiry into the System of Remuneration of Members of Local Authorities (Robinson committee), 1977. *Remuneration of Councillors, Vol. I: Report; Vol. II: The Surveys of Councillors and Local Authorities*, London, HMSO; Widdicombe committee, *Report*; Young, K. and N. Rao, 1994. *Coming to Terms with Change: The Local Government Councillor in 1993*, York, Joseph Rowntree Foundation.
9 CLD, *Final Report*, para 3.15.
10 *Ibid.*
11 *Ibid.*, para. 4.2.
12 *Ibid.*, para 4.9.

13 House of Lords Select Committee on Relations Between Central and Local Government, 1996. *Report, Vol. I; Report, Vol. II: Oral Evidence and Associated Memoranda*, London, HMSO.

14 DoE, 1991. *Local Government Review. The Structure of Local Government in England: A Consultation Paper*, London, DoE; Working Party on the Internal Management of Local Authorities in England, 1993. *Community Leadership and Representation: Unlocking the Potential*, London, HMSO.

15 All published by the Department of Environment, Transport and the Regions, the first two in 1998 and the last 1999.

16 Labour Party, 1995. *Renewing Democracy, Rebuilding Communities*, London, Labour Party, p. 14.

17 DETR, 1998. *Modernising Local Government: Local Democracy and Community Leadership*, London, DETR.

18 DETR, 1998. *Modern Local Government: In Touch with the People*, London, DETR; DETR, 1999. *Local Leadership: Local Choice*, London, DETR.

19 DETR, *Modernising Local Government*, paras 5.1 and 5.7.

20 *Ibid.*, paras 5.9, 5.11.

21 *Ibid.*, para. 5.4.

22 Copus, C., 1999. 'The Councillor and Party Group Loyalty', *Policy and Politics*, Vol. 27, No. 3, July, pp. 309–324; Copus, C., 1999. 'The Party Group: A Barrier to Democratic Renewal', *Local Government Studies* (special edition), Vol. 25, No. 4, Winter, pp. 77–98; Copus, C., 2004. *Party Politics and Local Government*, Manchester University Press.

23 Leach, S. and C. Copus, 2004. 'Scrutiny and the Political Party Group in UK Local Government: New Models of Behaviour', *Public Administration*, Vol. 82, No. 2, pp. 331–354.

24 Leach, S., 2001. *Making Overview and Scrutiny Work*, London, Local Government Association; Snape, S., S. Leach and C. Copus, 2002. *The Development of Overview and Scrutiny in Local Government*, London, ODPM.

25 Stoker, G., 2004. *How Are Mayors Measuring Up? Preliminary Findings – ELG Team*, London, ODPM, p. 23.

26 DETR, 2000. *New Council Constitutions: Modular Constitutions for English Local Authorities*, London, DETR, para. 3.45.

27 DETR, *Modernising Local Government*, para. 5.14.

28 DETR, *Modern Local Government*, para. 3.14.

29 *Ibid.*, para. 3.19.

30 Larsen, H., 2002. 'Directly Elected Mayors: Democratic Renewal or Constitutional Confusion?', in J. Caufield and H.O. Larsen (eds), *Local Government at the Millennium*, Opladen, Leske and Budrich, pp. 111–133.

31 The Local Authorities (Conduct of Referendums) (England) Regulations, 2001.

32 DETR, 2000. *Petitioning for a Mayor: Information Pack*, London, DETR.

33 DETR, *Local Leadership*, para. 2.15.

34 Travers, T., 2004, *The Politics of London: Governing an Ungovernable City*, Basingstoke, Palgrave Macmillan.

35 Owen, D., 1982. *The Government of Victorian London 1855–1889: The Metropolitan Board of Works, the Vestries and the City Corporation*, Harvard University Press.

36 Young, K., *Local Politics and the Rise of Party: The London Municipal Society and the Conservative Intervention in Local Elections, 1894–1963*, Leicester University Press, 1975; Young, K. and P. Garside, 1982. *Metropolitan London: Politics and Urban Change 1837–1981*, London, Edward Arnold.

37 Travers, *The Politics of London*, pp. 28–35.

38 DoE, 1983. *Streamlining the Cities*, London, HMSO.

39 DETR, 1998. *New Leadership for London: The Government's Proposals for a Greater London Authority*, London, DETR; DETR, 1998. *A Mayor and Assembly for London*, London, DETR.

40 DETR, *A Mayor and Assembly for London*, para. 109.

41 Larsen, 'Directly Elected Mayors'; Back, H., 2005, 'Institutional Settings of Leadership and Community Involvement', in M. Haus, H. Heinelt and M. Stewart (eds), *Urban Governance and Democracy: Leadership and Community Involvement*, London, Routledge, pp. 65–101.

42 John, P., 2001. *Local Governance in Western Europe*, London, Sage.

43 Larsen, 'Directly Elected Mayors', p. 113.

44 Loughlin, J., 2000. *Subnational Democracy in the European Union: Challenges and Opportunities*, Oxford University Press; John, *Local Governance in Western Europe*; Haus, M., H. Heinelt and M. Stewart (eds), 2005. *Urban Governance and Democracy: Leadership and Community Involvement*, London, Routledge.

45 Savitch, H. and P. Kantor, 2002. *Cities in the International Market Place*, Princeton University Press; Stewart, J., 2003. *Modernising British Local Government: An Assessment of Labour's Reform Programme*, Basingstoke, Palgrave Macmillan; Stoker, G. and D. Wilson, 2004. *British Local Government into the 21st Century*, Basingstoke, Palgrave Macmillan.

46 Streib, G., 1995. 'Strategic Capacity in Council–Manager Municipalities: Exploring Limits and Horizons', in H.G. Frederickson (ed.), *Ideal and Practice in Council–Manager Government*, Washington, DC, International City Management Association.

47 Frederickson, H.G., G. Johnson and C. Wood, 2004. *The Adapted City: Institutional Dynamics and Structural Change*, New York, Sharpe.

48 Kirchner, E. (ed.), 1999. *Decentralisation and Transition in the Visegrad*, London, Macmillan; Soos, G., G. Toka and G. Wright (eds), 2002. *The State of Local Democracy in Central Europe*, Budapest, Open Society Institute; Swianiewicz, P., 2005. 'Cities in Transition', in M. Haus, H. Heinelt and M. Stewart (eds), *Urban Governance and Democracy: Leadership and Community Involvement*, London, Routledge, pp. 102–128.

49 Hegedus, J., 1999. 'Hungarian Local Government', in E. Kirchner (ed.), *Decentralisation and Transition in the Visegrad*, London, Macmillan, pp. 132–159.

50 John, P. and A. Cole, 2000. 'When Do Institutions, Policy Sectors and Cities Matter? Comparing Networks of Local Policy-Makers in Britain and France', *Comparative Political Studies*, Vol. 33, No. 2, pp. 248–268.

51 Taylor, M., 2000. 'Communities in the Lead: Organisational Capacity and Social Capital', *Urban Studies*, Vol. 37, Nos 5–6, pp. 1019–1035.

2

Mayors: a new form of local politics or a very English compromise?

Introduction

The use of the term 'mayor' to denote the political leader of a council is not a new departure for English local government. Recently, however, and before the Local Government Act 2000, the mayor, in those councils which had one, was the symbolic first citizen of the locality. The traditional mayor presides at meetings of the full council, rising above the fray of party politics, and acts in an ambassadorial role for the council and its communities. The political head of the council and its administration is the 'leader', who is very much part of the political fray, being drawn from the majority party (where there is one).

The shift in political power away from the mayor to the council leader was a gradual one: England has known powerful, politically skilful mayors in the past, both directly and indirectly elected. First, at various points during the development of the medieval English borough, various local communities were able, by grant of the monarch (and often in return for some payment) to directly elect a number of local officials with executive responsibilities, such as reeves, sheriffs, bailiffs and, indeed, even a mayor.[1] While the electorate was not what we would recognise today or resemble anything like a mass democracy, and such elections must be seen for what they were – a gift from the monarch which could be rescinded – direct election to local executive office is not something which is totally alien to the English experience.

Second, the development of local government throughout the Victorian period often saw local mayors wield considerable power and influence, both within the council and across England's major cities: Manchester, Birmingham, Leeds and other major urban centres saw their municipalisation and politics dominated by powerful local politicians who held the office of mayor. Individuals such as Joseph Chamberlain in Birmingham and John Barran in Leeds used the office of mayor to pursue their own political philosophies and translate them into practical local agendas.[2] While Victorian mayors such as Chamberlain had of course

been supported by party machines, the gradual process of the nationalisation of local politics and the regularisation of local party politics by
national parties saw a change in roles and powers.[3] Over time, mayors
came to retain only symbolic power and duties, while political power was
transferred to council leaders, who in turn faded into the background
and often, though not always, lacked the public prominence of a chain-
wearing mayor.

To add to the opaque nature of the political responsibility that rested
in the hands of council leaders, the appointment to such an office, before
the 2000 Act, was neither a legal requirement nor even recognised in
legislation. Moreover, some councils existed without a member taking
on the title of leader and confusingly in some councils, but not many,
the mayor was still the political head. It was in these rare circumstances
that the mayor (or council chair) took on more of a leadership role, a
role, however, that again was not recognised in legislation. The legislative
framework before 2000 almost ignored the existence of politics and party
politics; political party groups were recognised in the Local Government
and Housing Act 1989 only in the appointment of political advisers/
assistants to party groups and seat allocation to committees.[4]

Neither the political head of the council – the leader – nor the party
political network on which his or her position rested was acknowledged
in legislation. A widely recognised myth about the absence of party
politics in local government had been sanctified and perpetuated in legislation until the 2000 Act. To those political leaders abroad who held the
title 'mayor', whether directly elected or not, the position of the British
'council leader' was a mystery. As one former metropolitan borough
council leader recounted in interview in relation to his meetings with
overseas mayors: 'I could never adequately explain what a council leader
was and they all just referred to me as mayor anyway'.

A greater degree of clarity and a much more distinct and open explanation of the role, position, power and responsibilities of the political
head of a council were required if political accountability was to be
enhanced. Moreover, greater visibility and a higher public profile for
the local political leader would enable the voter to become more quickly
aware about where political responsibility lay. Direct election is one
simple way of achieving these aims. The next section explores how the
voter has responded to the prospect of being able to directly elect the
local political leader by reviewing the referendums held so far. The third
section examines what the first set of elections to the office, held in 2002,
can tell us about the nature of the mayoral experiment and local politics.
The fourth section sets out the powers of the elected mayor in England
and compares them with those of the council leader. The concluding section draws out the lessons from England's experiences of electing mayors
and what we can learn about the power we have granted them.

The elected mayor: a difficult journey

The Local Government Act 2000 required all councils to consult the public on the three options for executive arrangements: indirectly elected leader and cabinet, directly elected mayor and cabinet, and directly elected mayor and council manager (see Chapter 1). If that consultation indicated a preference among the public for a directly elected mayor, then a referendum should be held and this, coupled with the public's right to petition for a referendum on mayoral government, allowed Westminster and Whitehall to feel secure that the framework had been provided to encourage the public to take the initiative when it came to the way in which they were governed locally. Moreover, regulations were laid down to ensure that the conduct of any referendum would be fair.[5]

Direct election would enable the mayor to act on behalf of the whole area, promoting and protecting its interests far beyond the council boundaries. Indeed, the mayor would be the embodiment of the area he or she served: speaking for it on local, regional and national platforms; acting as the focal point for major projects; and linking territorial politics, where appropriate, into a national, European and even global network. Moreover, the mayoral office would be the first port of call for those seeking to apportion praise or blame for the success or failure of some local initiative. All this could be achieved because of the mayor's direct mandate. Yet, despite the hopes that elected mayors would spark a blaze of public interest in local political leadership and ignite wider public involvement in local democracy, the response from the public to the possibility of being governed by this new political office has been less than enthusiastic.

Thirty mayoral referendums had been held at the time of writing (excluding the London one) and Table 2.1 sets out the results.[6]

The mayoral experiment has clearly not succeeded in stimulating widespread public interest or excitement; nor has it motivated greater public engagement in local politics. At the time of writing only six mayoral referendums had resulted from public petition; the opportunity to decide on the structure of local political leadership and to take control of the shape and nature of how the area should be governed has met largely with national indifference. All but one of the non-petition-generated referendums have been a council initiative and not all the councils supported the mayoral option – some saw a referendum as a way of removing the issue from the public agenda, at least for five years. The referendum held in the London Borough of Southwark was imposed by the Secretary of State (the minister for local government), as public consultation appeared to favour a mayor yet the council opted for an indirectly elected council leader. Rather than the inaccuracies of public consultation, the resulting 'no' vote in the referendum indicates more

Table 2.1 Results in the first thirty English mayoral referendums

Council	Date	Result	Number (%) of votes for	Number (%) of votes against	Turn-out	Type of election
Berwick-upon-Tweed	7 June 2001	No	3,617 (26%)	10,212 (74%)	64%	Poll at general election
Cheltenham	28 June 2001	No	8,083 (33%)	16,602 (67%)	31%	All postal
Gloucester	28 June 2001	No	7,731 (31%)	16,317 (69%)	31%	All postal
Watford	12 July 2001	Yes	7,636 (52%)	7,140 (48%)	25%	All postal
Doncaster	20 September 2001	Yes	35,453 (65%)	19,398 (35%)	25%	All postal
Kirklees	4 October 2001	No	10,169 (27%)	27,977 (73%)	13%	Normal
Sunderland	11 October 2001	No	9,593 (43%)	12,209 (57%)	10%	Normal
Hartlepool	18 October 2001	Yes	10,667 (51%)	10,294 (49%)	31%	All postal
London Borough of Lewisham	18 October 2001	Yes	16,822 (51%)	15,914 (49%)	18%	All postal
North Tyneside	18 October 2001	Yes	30,262 (58%)	22,296 (42%)	36%	All postal
Middlesbrough	18 October 2001	Yes	29,067 (84%)	5,422 (16%)	34%	All postal
Sedgefield	18 October 2001	No	10,628 (47%)	11,869 (53%)	33%	All postal
Brighton and Hove	18 October 2001	No	22,724 (38%)	37,214 (62%)	32%	All postal
Redditch	8 November 2001	No	7,250 (44%)	9,198 (56%)	28%	All postal
Durham	20 November 2001	No	8,327 (41%)	11,974 (59%)	29%	All postal
Harrow	7 December 2001	No	17,502 (42%)	23,554 (58%)	26%	All postal
Plymouth	24 January 2002	No	29,553 (41%)	42,811 (59%)	40%	All postal
Harlow	24 January 2002	No	5,296 (25%)	15,490 (75%)	36%	All postal
London Borough of Newham	31 January 2002	Yes	27,163 (68%)	12,687 (32%)	26%	All postal
Shepway	31 January 2002	No	11,357 (44%)	14,438 (56%)	36%	All postal

London Borough of Southwark	31 January 2002	No	6,054 (31%)	13,217 (69%)	11%	Normal
West Devon	31 January 2002	No	3,555 (23%)	12,190 (77%)	42%	All postal
Bedford	21 February 2002	Yes	11,316 (67%)	5,537 (33%)	16%	Normal
London Borough of Hackney	2 May 2002	Yes	24,697 (59%)	10,547 (41%)	32%	All postal
Mansfield	2 May 2002	Yes	8,973 (55%)	7,350 (45%)	21%	Normal
Newcastle under Lyme	2 May 2002	No	12,912 (44%)	16,468 (56%)	32%	Normal
Oxford	2 May 2002	No	14,692 (44%)	18,686 (56%)	34%	Normal
Stoke-on-Trent	2 May 2002	Yes	28,601 (58%)	20,578 (42%)	28%	Normal
Corby	3 October 2002	No	5,351 (46%)	6,239 (54%)	31%	All postal
London Borough of Ealing	12 December 2002	No	9,454 (45%)	11,655 (55%)	10%	Combination postal and ballot

Source: The New Local Government Network website, April 2003: www.nlgn.org.uk.

the ability of local politicians and parties to campaign for, and achieve, a result they want from an electoral process.[7]

The way in which parties have fought referendum campaigns has fallen into four broad types: first, all three main parties have combined to seek a particular result; second, the dominant local party has controlled the campaign, with other parties sidelined; third, parties have agreed to disagree internally and 'pro' and 'anti' groups within parties have campaigned separately; fourth, a strong independent, normally 'pro' mayor group has emerged to challenge the domination of the referendum campaign by political parties, of which the 'Mayor 4 Stoke', Bedford and Mansfield campaigns were notable examples. Whichever type of campaign is fought, one thing is clear: the role played by political parties and the vote they campaign for is crucial to the outcome of the referendum.

In the majority of campaigns so far, the three main political parties, or at least two of them, have backed a 'no' result. Exceptions have occurred, a notable one of which was the Newham referendum campaign, in which a few Labour councillors campaigned against the overwhelming majority of their colleagues, on the council and in the local Labour Party, for a 'yes' vote; securing the support of West Ham United was a master stroke in the Newham 'yes' campaign and lifted it out of the usual dry political campaign into something linked to the wider community.

The arguments used in the referendum campaigns have had similar themes, with 'yes' campaigns reflecting the arguments set out by the government in favour of elected mayors and the 'no' campaigns focusing on the concentration of power into a single office, remote from the public and 'vulnerable to corruption.'[8] Yet, as we shall see later, the powers of the elected mayor are not very different from those of the council leader and the anti-mayoral camp has displayed no unease about the concentration of power into hands of an indirectly elected leader, chosen by only a few councillors from the council's majority party. Nonetheless, 'no' campaigners have expressed considerable concern about similar power being placed in the hands of an individual selected by the electorate. It appears that it is the constituency selecting the powerful leader that really counts and not the power that leader goes on to wield. Little robust intellectual argument has been put forward by the 'no' campaigners in any of the referendums.

The referendum campaigns and results so far have demonstrated that despite the power of local political parties, a strong, well resourced and organised independent campaign can succeed against the local political elite. Such independent campaigns have built on existing political and social organisations and have acted as an umbrella group for those within the local civil society concerned to influence the dynamics of local politics or holding a grievance over some council policy decision. The results also indicate that tacit government support for certain local changes is insufficient to generate public enthusiasm and acceptance; a more robust, efficient and clear explanation of the reason for change is required for local voters to respond positively to mayoral government. Moreover, much more groundwork was required in the Labour Party nationally to secure some support for the model beyond that expressed in a few 'New Labour' councils.

So, at the time of writing England now had twelve directly elected mayors dotted around the country, with four, including the mayor of London, located in London. These mayors had joined their directly elected counterparts across the globe in providing a very distinctive approach to the governance of the localities. It is an approach which in many cases overseas reflects the political culture, traditions and, importantly, an approach to national government and politics under presidential systems. The directly elected mayor in England has no such national counterpart, nor reflects in any particular way the political culture, traditions or structure of government in England. So, we need to examine whether this new political office as it is currently constructed is a radical departure from the political norm, or a merely a repackaging of familiar local political powers and political decision-making arrangements.

Electing the mayor: a new experience for the English voter

In May 2002 electors in Doncaster, Hartlepool, Middlesbrough, North Tyneside, Watford and the London Boroughs of Lewisham and Newham elected the first mayors to office outside of the already existing office of mayor of London; these were followed in October 2002 by the voters in Bedford, Mansfield, Stoke-on-Trent and the London Borough of Hackney. For the first time, these voters were able to choose for themselves the individual they wished to hold the political leadership of the council and to head the council's executive, rather than having that choice made for them by their local councillors.

Mayors are elected at large and, while they are a member of the council, they do not represent a ward as do the councillors who serve alongside them. Councillors campaign for election in their wards based on local activity and a borough-wide manifesto, or set of policy pronouncements. Yet that manifesto will receive only an aggregated electoral legitimacy from the votes cast for party candidates standing in the wards; the manifesto is not subject to any strict authority-wide test. Indeed, voters at ward level will be influenced by a range of factors, not all of which will be relevant to the locality concerned. Moreover, the blurring of electoral accountability inherent in the difficulty of disaggregating the components of voting helps to maintain the view that national concerns dominate local elections.[9]

Whatever the motivations behind the casting of a vote and whether or not the electors' political preferences transcend local concerns, we are left with a question: exactly whom or what does the councillor represent? Is it the political party, the council party group, the council of which he or she is a member, or the ward or division from which the councillor was elected? Confusion over the question of whom or what the councillor represents amounts to 'representative failure', and a weakening of the link between councillors and their ward or division. The truth is, however, that as councillors are expected to represent the interests of at least three distinct concerns, they must balance these, arbitrate between them and act accordingly. Yet the directly elected mayor is supposed to be free from the very local connection to a ward and also in receipt of a governing mandate granted directly by the electorate, rather than aggregated and assumed from a party receiving a majority of council seats. Moreover, the production of mayoral manifestos by candidates in the first elections displayed the recognition that an authority-wide mandate to govern was being sought from the voter. We shall see later whether disconnection from the interests of a ward guarantees that mayors govern in the interests of the whole district, even if, at the same time, they are expected to respond to very local issues.

The electoral system used for mayoral elections emphasises the governing role of the mayor. The CLD, reporting in 1995, suggested the use of the alternative vote for mayoral elections. Here candidates are ranked in order of preference by the voter and if no candidate receives 50 per cent of the vote on the first count the candidate receiving the least votes is eliminated and his or her second preferences are redistributed until a candidate receives over half the votes cast.[10]

The government, however, preferred the supplementary vote system. Here voters use an 'X' to indicate only their first and second choices of candidate; if no candidate receives 50 per cent of the vote on the first count, all but the top two candidates are eliminated and the second choice of the voters is redistributed to those two remaining candidates. The government believed that the supplementary vote was 'simple and easy to use and can result in a clear winner'.[11] The object of the supplementary vote system for mayoral elections was to ensure that the mayor had a clear popular mandate and to ensure, as Deputy Prime Minister John Prescott stated in Parliament, that as 'many people as possible agree to support a mayor'.[12] Yet, as Van der Kolk *et al.* have very clearly shown, that system cannot guarantee the election of a candidate with the type of support the government wished to see and the alternative vote, for example, could produce a different result to that achieved by the supplementary vote.[13]

Whatever the arguments about the advantages of one electoral system over another, the voter expresses a preference on a ballot paper. The overriding issue is that all voters across the locality are faced with the same choice of candidates for mayoral office and are able to grant support to a particular mayoral manifesto, in a way that is not possible in non-mayoral councils: direct, authority-wide election brings with it a mandate all of its own. With an authority-wide mandate the moral and political leverage is granted to a mayor to speak for and on behalf of an entire area, to a range of diverse local, regional, national and international bodies, and to act in an ambassadorial role for that community. While a council leader is not precluded from developing such a role, indirect election by a small number of councillors simply does not carry the moral and political weight attached by direct election.

Because of the mayor's direct mandate, the potential contact between mayors and citizens, and particularly the organised citizen group, is vast. Such direct contact between political leadership and the community has the potential to disturb the existing local political dynamic. Direct election thereby has the potential to affect the role and primacy of the political party and the party group within local politics, and to shift the definitions of what constitutes local politics within a local representative democracy.[14] But, before the mayor can set about altering the local political status quo and changing the nature of the political elite, or indeed defending the same, he or she must first get elected to office. It is in the very act of election to mayoral office that we can start to see the impact of the mayoral experiment on the interplay of local politics and the dominance of the local politics by political parties.

The first mayoral results: 2002

At the first mayoral elections, held in 2002, an interesting question was whether or not the elections would follow the London example and reflect the stunning success of the then independent London mayoral candidate, Ken Livingstone. The results of the May and October mayoral contests in 2002 do indicate, to a degree, the fragility of the hold that political parties have over local politics, at least when voters have the ability to change control of the council at a single stroke.

Table 2.2 sets out the results of the mayoral elections held in 2002. Independent candidates or candidates of no political party were successful in five of the eleven mayoral contests held in 2002. With London mayor Ken Livingstone included in the figures, at least before his re-election as the official Labour candidate in 2004, then six of the twelve mayors across England were independent of party politics. Of the five independent mayors outside London, two were initially faced with a party majority on the council, and the other three with a council with no overall control, although of course political parties were still

Table 2.2 English mayoral election results, May and October 2002

Council	Winning candidate	Political affiliation	Elected on first or second count	Electorate	Turnout (%)
May 2002 election					
Doncaster	Martin Winter	Labour	Second	216,097	27
Hartlepool	Stuart Drummond	Independent	Second	67,903	29
London Borough of Lewisham	Steve Bullock	Labour	Second	179,835	25
Middlesbrough	Ray Mallon	Independent	First	101,570	41
London Borough of Newham	Robin Wales	Labour	First	157,505	26
North Tyneside	Chris Morgan	Conservative	Second	143,804	42
Watford	Dorothy Thornhill	Liberal Democrat	Second	61,359	36
October 2002 election					
Bedford	Frank Branston	Independent	Second	109,318	25
London Borough of Hackney	Jules Pipe	Labour	Second	130,657	26
Mansfield	Tony Egginton	Independent	Second	72,242	18
Stoke-on-Trent	Mike Wolfe	Mayor 4 Stoke	Second	182,967	24

Source: The New Local Government Network website: http://nlgn.org.uk.

predominant. The council election results for 2003 and 2004 and the change in party fortunes are considered in Chapter 9 and assessed for whether any swing can be detected for or against an incumbent mayor and his or her party or political association. In this section, the concern is with the first mayoral elections.

At the mayoral elections of 2002, four Labour mayors were installed alongside Labour-controlled councils; one Liberal Democrat mayor operated with a council which had no one party in overall control (but which subsequently achieved a Liberal Democrat majority). A Conservative mayor was elected alongside a Labour council majority on North Tyneside but he subsequently resigned, and on 12 June 2003 North Tyneside held the first mayoral by-election since the 2000 Act introduced the new office. The Conservative candidate was elected after second preference votes were counted; the council, at the time of writing, had twenty-seven Conservative, twenty-six Labour and seven Liberal Democrat councillors.

The results show that voters used the elections either to signal discontent with the local political elite or to support its regime and policies. They also indicate that mayoral elections can usher into local politics a new uncertainty for political parties. The realisation that a 'party' may not win every mayoral contest destabilises not only the conduct of elections but also local politics more generally. Parties are now faced with reconfiguring the relationships they have with their own voters and supporters, the wider electorate, other parties and the local political leader.

Potentially, the advent of elected mayors demands a different response from political parties to the business of campaigning, selecting candidates and conducting local politics. Indeed, parties will have to be far more energetic and sophisticated when it comes to fighting elections. Different campaign tactics, approaches and skills will be needed when filling the office of mayor from those used for the election of councillors, and for that matter a different type of candidate will be required. The office of directly elected mayor demands that parties view the local political world from the outside, in a wholly new way, and not as the sole property of political parties. Elected mayors overseas have long recognised that they must rely on much wider support than a party, both inside and outside the council chamber, which is something to which English mayors may have to become accustomed. Indeed, as the first mayor of North Tyneside found out, being in office need not be the same as being in power.

Another telling lesson from the first mayoral elections is that a change of governance arrangements does not necessarily excite the English voter enough to want to participate in choosing the political leader of the locality. As Table 2.2 displays and as Game reminds us, the contests so far have failed to turn any enhanced awareness of political candidates and leaders into a 'greater readiness to vote, let alone participate in other ways'.[15] Turnout figures as low as 18 per cent in Mansfield and barely reaching a quarter to a third of the electorate in a number of other contests clearly show that the elected mayoral system of governance failed to stimulate voters into making the most of being able to select the local political leader. Perhaps, however, this is less of a statement about deep-seated political apathy – especially when we look at the case studies in Chapter 6 – and more about the lack of power of local government and local mayors to make things happen.

The elected mayor: a powerful political leader?

The government wanted the mayoral experiment to produce a new kind of political leader; but what factors would tempt a new type of local politician to emerge? Is it the power available to the holder of the office or the ability to forge and pursue a clear political agenda for the locality that will inspire a new kind of local politician? Or will direct election make no difference to the type of politician elected to office, but rather simply provide another route for those who would seek political power in whatever guise it manifested itself? In this section the powers of the directly elected mayor are considered in terms of whether they represent a new departure for English local politics and whether they lay the groundwork for a new type and style of local political leader to emerge.

Power and responsibility

The Local Government Act 2000 and the regulations and guidance which flowed from it set out the powers and responsibilities of England's elected mayors.[16] That these also cover the powers of a council leader indicate the similarities that exist within these executive structures and that, for Whitehall and Westminster purposes, they can be seen jointly as local government. Indeed, from the very outset it was made clear that the elected mayor: is to be treated as a councillor for the purposes of any legislation; is subject to the same rules of qualification for, and disqualification from, being elected; is covered by the same ethical framework and code of conduct as all councillors; and is to be included as part of his or her party group in the calculation of the proportional allocation of committee seats.[17]

The council executive, whether in the form of mayor or leader, has certain common features related to its role in the political leadership of the council and wider community. The executive is expected to lead the community planning process and the preparation of plans and policies adopted by the council; executives are also expected to lead the development of Local Strategic Partnerships (LSPs). Yet what we see in these broad notions of the leadership role is: first, no distinction between a mayor's cabinet and a leader's cabinet; and second, a role focused on leadership in terms of management of a set of council organisational processes and service responsibilities. There is little here that really speaks of political leadership and the development of a political vision for and with the community.[18]

The mayor and leader cannot exceed ten members (including themselves) when putting together a cabinet (the mayor and council manager model has an executive of two: the mayor and council manager), all of whom must be elected members of the council. A wider choice is available to the London mayor, whose choice of cabinet appointments is not limited to members of the GLA and who has a different cabinet arrangement to 2000 Act mayors.

The 2000 Act mayor can select his or her cabinet without reference to the council; in turn, the council can grant the council leader the power to select his or her cabinet or can appoint one itself. In reality, the latter means that the cabinet is selected and appointed by the council majority group, with whom the leader will negotiate to select cabinet members, or have cabinet members imposed upon him or her by the group, or, if able, the leader may ignore the majority group and appoint whom he or she wishes – it depends on the political dynamics of the council and its ruling group. The mayor cannot have a cabinet membership imposed on him or her to suit the demands of the majority group, unless he or she wants to be so driven.

The main constraint on the mayor in forming a cabinet is that of appointing from among the council membership. In addition, the standing orders of the national political parties can of course be written to restrict the mayor's ability to select a cabinet to include members from outside the mayor's party group. Yet the standing orders of the three main political parties give mayors considerable implicit, if not explicit, freedom in appointing their cabinets – far more than might be expected.[19]

When it comes to the delegation of functions to individual cabinet members, the cabinet collectively or some other arrangement, the elected mayor sets out the nature of that delegation. Again, not much is different from the council leader, particularly if the leader is able to select the cabinet; where the leader does not have such a free hand in cabinet selection, then the council sets the scheme of delegation for decision-making.[20]

It is only around the issue of the executive's relationship with the council that we see (at least in the guidance and regulations) any real distinguishing feature of mayoral authority. Thus:

> The elected mayor and cabinet will be responsible for most of the functions of the local authority. In addition, although the full council will be

responsible for approval and adoption of the policy framework and the budget, the elected mayor and cabinet have overall responsibility for the development of the draft budget and draft plans and strategies for submission to the full council for approval.

It will be for the elected mayor to choose how to involve other members of the local authority, including the overview and scrutiny committee, and the wider community in preparing the draft of the budget and the plans and strategies which make up the policy framework.[21]

The responsibilities of the mayor and cabinet set out in these sections do provide a broad framework for action. Yet that action is set with the same requirements as exist for the council leader for consultation with officers (particularly with the monitoring officer), on financial and legal aspects, for recording decisions, and on the production of a forward plan for major decisions. What is clear is that the powers of the mayor, and for that matter council leader, are legally constrained, which, in turn, constrains (but does not negate) any one mayor's ability to develop a distinctive political regime to suit the locality.

The power of appointment

With the directly elected mayor comes a series of institutional checks and balances which serve to determine whether it is either the mayor or the council which is dominant. One of the indicators of that dominance is the arrangements for the appointment of the head of the local civil service – in England the council chief executive – and whether it is the mayor or council which appoints that managerial head and other senior officers. Practice varies across the globe and within the same country regarding whether it is the elected mayor or the full body of councillors who have the power of such appointment. In US cities with a strong mayoral system it is the mayor; in places with a weak mayoral system it is the council. At the municipal level in Turkey the mayor appoints all chief officials; in the areas of Germany where directly elected mayors are in office the council appoints the officers; in larger Slovakian municipalities the head of the local civil service is appointed by the council on the recommendation of the mayor; an Italian mayor can appoint and dismiss the heads of all offices and services. Overseas practice is thus very diverse, but the power of appointment is an indicator of where the balance of power rests: mayor or council.

In England, whatever the form of executive arrangement, mayor or council leader, it is the council that appoints and dismisses the chief executive, which represents a power balance tipped towards the council. In the mayor and manager model, the manager is appointed by the council and the manager is then responsible for appointing council staff. The precise mechanisms for appointing chief officers and the levels of delegation will vary with each council's constitution. With a council controlled by the same party as the mayor, internal party negotiation over candidates for appointed office would ensure some degree of mayoral influence in the process; in authorities controlled by parties other than the mayor's, or where the mayor is an independent, mayoral exclusion from the process could be engineered. What we see here, as with everything else in local politics, is that so long as the legal framework is adhered to, the political dynamics of the authority will control decision-making.

The London mayor has a much broader power of appointment available than the 2000 Act mayors, a power which reflects the intention that the GLA would not be a service provider in the traditional, local authority sense. Rather, the activities for which it is responsible are provided by a range of bodies headed by boards that are wholly or partly appointed by the mayor.[22] Travers has summarised the appointment powers of the mayor of London and shows that the membership of, and the chairs of, Transport for London and the London Development Agency are subject to mayoral patronage, as too are the appointment of twelve of the twenty-three members of the Metropolitan Police Authority, which then goes on to appoint its own chair; the mayor appoints seventeen members of the London Fire and Emergency Planning Authority and its chair, with a further eight nominations made by the London boroughs.[23]

The elected mayors created under the 2000 Act have no such broad powers of appointment to outside functional bodies as does the mayor of London. Moreover, neither type of mayor has access to appointment of investigatory commissions or bodies in the same way as the mayor of New York or the Italian elected mayor.[24] Thus, the English elected mayor is denied a valuable and potentially powerful resource and patronage tool. The lack of such a resource reflects government thinking on the role that overview and scrutiny should play in policy initiation and development. Elected mayors (and for that matter council leaders) and their executives can commission reports or investigations for the purposes of overview and scrutiny, but they are not solely a mayoral resource. Moreover, the membership of a scrutiny committee is not subject to mayoral patronage, as this would undermine its ability to hold the mayor to account and to act as a powerful check and balance on executive activity.[25] Yet this is distinct from the mayoral commission, appointed by and responsible to the mayor as a policy and political resource.

Deputies, advisers and support staff

Mayoral influence and power can, in part, be measured by the direct access the mayor has to resources, advisers and support staff, and whether these form the basis of a mayor's office or are shared with the council. Moreover, the independence of mayoral support and advice from the civil service of the local authority also serves to strengthen the mayor's hand as a political leader. Finally, whether such support staff and deputies can act as mayoral enforcers for policy and political decisions, or whether they are merely advisers with no power over civil servants, will affect the mayor's ability to govern.

The mayor of London is able, under the provisions of section 67 of the Greater London Authority Act 1999, to appoint not more than two political advisers and up to a maximum of ten other members of staff as mayoral support. Such staff are employees of the GLA but with employment linked to the mayor's term of office and which cannot extend beyond it. Thus, they are support not to the mayor as such but to the particular individual holding that office. Importantly for the mayor, such appointments are personal to him or her and do not have to be subject to the usual recruitment process.

The first incumbent of the London mayoralty, Ken Livingstone, negotiated with the London Assembly to secure appointment of his staff and was granted (again by the Assembly) additional funding for further support and research staff; Livingstone's office grew as a consequence to around thirty people.[26] Livingstone has shown that it is possible to stretch the confines of the legislation when it comes to advice and support and thus extend, with Assembly agreement, the resources available for the mayor to pursue policy initiative and provide London with broad political leadership. The London mayor must appoint a deputy mayor, and that individual must be selected from among the elected members of the London Assembly but cannot hold the position of chair of the Assembly at the same time.

The situation for England's other elected mayors when it comes to support and advisers is somewhat different to the experience of the London mayor and reflects two long-standing traditions of local government: its service-providing role; and a united officer core serving the whole council equally. The notion of an officer core serving all members equally is one long propagated by chief executives and leaders of majority parties. The reality, as any backbencher and minority group member will attest, is somewhat different. Yet it is a notion the government also continues to propagate in stating that 'officers will continue to work and serve the local authority as a whole'. It also recognises, however, that officers will be spending most of their time supporting the executive – mayor or leader – in its work.[27]

The advice and support officers provide to the mayor are not solely policy oriented but are also congruent with their role as service providers in general and as specific service managers, rather than as a resource for the mayor as the political leader of the community. There is no distinction between the role of the officer in serving the elected mayor or the indirectly elected council leader. Yet the arrival of a political executive has placed a great strain on the notion of a unified officer core serving the whole council, and evidence is beginning to emerge that this approach is fracturing. We may find, over time, that officers specialise in supporting an executive, in overview and scrutiny, or in service management.[28]

There is a gap between what regulations and guidance say and what individual mayors and leaders are able to accrue in terms of officer support. While the mayor, and leaders, will have almost day-to-day contact with the chief executive and other senior officers, mayors also require powerful and independent political advice and support, separate from the traditional officer structure, with its focus on public services. English mayors have had different degrees of success in obtaining any support and advice from their authorities. As two of the English mayors interviewed agreed, the level of preparation for their arrival by the authority was minimal, to say the least. One mayor went as far as to comment:

> I arrived at the town hall the morning after the election. There was no one to meet me; no office space had been made available; no office equipment was available; and no secretary. It was like no one was expecting me, but I know they knew I was coming – the election was the give-away.
>
> I had to fight for office space and everything else you see here. It was as though the council was saying 'All right, so you've got a mayor, but we'll make sure he can't do anything'. It's better now, as you can see.

While a mayor's assistant and secretary and a mayor's office are commonplace in mayoral authorities, the role of these varies from purely administrative and secretarial support on the one hand to political advice and support on the other. In leader and cabinet authorities a leader's office and a cabinet office are also commonplace, alongside secretarial, administrative and political support available to the leader. There is nothing unique in the levels of support given to elected mayors that stands apart from that available to leaders, nor anything that recognises this new office as a different approach to the governance and political leadership of the community. The resources mayors in England accrue from the council are a result of their own political skills.

England's elected mayors are required by law to appoint a member of the council as a deputy mayor; the mayor can also dismiss that individual. There is no legal requirement for the appointment of a deputy council leader, only for provisions to deputise in the leader's absence. Yet the post of deputy leader proliferates across the country (and did before the 2000 Act); among other things, the post of deputy leader provides political patronage to either the leader or his or her party group, and can be used by the group to keep the leader in check, or to provide him or her with a powerful political ally.

The role of a deputy mayor varies enormously between mayoral systems across the globe; in some the deputy is a powerful politician, enforcing mayoral policy; in others the deputy acts as the head of a particular service department. The English approach to the deputy mayor is that the deputy is just that: someone who deputises in the mayor's absence. But, again, the rules are often different from the reality and some English deputy mayors are clearly powerful political players in their own right. The role of deputy mayor and for that matter deputy leader can provide holders with a position from which to involve themselves in a range of council activities and to roam across executive portfolios. Or the deputy can be given a specific role by the mayor, or leader, to pursue a particular policy initiative. The English deputy mayor makes the most of his or her office based on political skill and what the mayor wants the role to be.

Conflict resolution

Another clue in deciding how the checks and balances play themselves out between mayor and council can be seen in the arrangements for resolving conflict between the mayor and council. Here again, the practice varies enormously between systems and nations. In some of the larger US cities the mayor has a form of broad veto over council decisions.[29] The English solution to the resolution of conflict between mayor and council, or council leader and council, is one which reflects the belief that the mayor's direct mandate should count for something. Also at the heart of the resolution process is an expectation that a solution will be negotiated between mature, consensus-oriented politicians not seeking party political gain.

Any conflict resolution must be based on recognition of the differing roles of executive and council, and, in the English context, recognition that the separated powers have been granted different responsibilities for aspects of council business and functions, within a framework produced by Parliament. Moreover, the workings of a system for conflict resolution depend on who disagrees with whom. Local authorities cannot leave conflict resolution to chance or negotiations alone: they are required to adopt a mechanism that will resolve disagreement between the executive and the council.

The process is almost the same for elected mayor and leader where disagreement exists about a full council decision which is contrary to the executive's budget, plan or strategy and there must be a five-day period of grace before such a decision takes effect. Once an objection is registered by the mayor or leader the council must meet to reconsider its proposal but the council can insist on its decision standing. Such mandatory provisions are a delaying mechanism for the mayor or leader to employ to carve a space for further negotiation, should it be required.

It is in the majority required in full council that the different status of mayor and leader is reflected: with a council leader the council can insist on its decision standing with an overall majority, or a qualified majority previously agreed by the council and set out in the constitution. A two-thirds majority is required to override the mayor rather than a simple majority and this pays homage to the mayor's direct mandate. This provision applies only to the budget and policy framework, in either mayor or leader authorities, and is not employable where the executive is acting upon matters solely of its preserve. Here, it is the overview and scrutiny committees which can challenge, question and delay executive decisions, but not override or veto them.

So, on the face of it, the mayor and for that matter council leader can delay a council decision (or the council an executive decision) and, if the council fails to provide an appropriate majority in support of its original decision, the executive prevails. The process is not, however, a mayoral veto and nor is there, strictly, a council veto over mayoral decisions – or the council leader. The separation of powers in the English local context, while acknowledging the potential for political conflict, overcomes that potential by granting specific powers to act, in specific areas, to either the executive or the council and the balance here is tipped towards the executive.

When either the executive or the council is acting in its own specified field, then the power of delay, rather than veto, exists for its counterpart. The originator of the decision can decide to alter that decision or for it to stand, once the process of negotiation has been completed. There is little difference in this process for either elected mayor or council leader; the real difference comes in the political dynamics of the council concerned. One mayoral authority has found itself immersed in interminable wrangling over the precise meaning and interpretation of a two-thirds majority and how it should be obtained, and what the conflict resolution majority should be at any meetings after the two-thirds has been achieved or not achieved, when and how it was achieved, by whom and how many times. It was here the mayor found that being in office did not necessarily mean that he was in power, which is something that could affect any elected mayor.

Term of office

To many opposed to elected mayors, the four-year term of office indicates the overwhelming power of the mayor.[30] It is true that councillors cannot remove the mayor during his or her term of office but, as they were not responsible for the mayor's election, why should they be able to? The problems some mayors have experienced with councils that their party, or independent grouping, does not control indicate that some councillors would seek to use any removal powers simply because they did not like the result of the mayoral election! But mayors can be removed from office between elections in exactly the same way as councillors and for the same reasons: breaking the law or the ethical framework and code of conduct. The removal of the mayor from office cannot, in England, be actioned as a form of political expedient or to rerun the mayoral election in another form.

The real weakness in the legislation is not that councillors cannot remove the mayor, but that the public does not have the right to force a recall election. Recall is something that strikes at the heart of the British approach to representative democracy, the role of the representative within it and political accountability. The last, in England, is a *post hoc* experience, a judgement cast on past action and a political record; the citizen can remove a politician only at a scheduled election; any other opportunity for the electorate to remove a politician would mean that representative would be dangerously responsive to the views of the governed.

The term of office of the mayor is the same as that of the councillor and it is not unknown for ruling groups, before the 2000 Act, to have elected council leaders for a two- and even four-year term themselves. Indeed, leaders with two-year terms have not been unknown since the passing of the Act. It appears it is not the term of office that is the real bone of contention for those opposed to elected mayors but rather who it is who does the electing. However, a four-year term of office for the mayor gives at least some consistency to political governance and here the tenure of the local political leader cannot be overturned on the whim of the ruling group – or just because someone in that group wants the job.

The election of a council leader is often about the internal machination of the ruling group, and good leaders have been removed from office and bad leaders re-elected because it suited the group's internal political balance and the ambitions of group members. A four-year term of office for the mayor reflects the need for a sufficient period for mayoral policies to have an impact, so the electorate can judge their effects at the next election, while not being too long to distance the mayor from the community governed. Yet short terms of office are a sensible check and balance, and an easy means of enhancing accountability and political responsiveness; there is a powerful argument for reducing mayoral (and councillor) terms of office to three years, for just that reason.

Conclusions

While the elected mayor is at the heart of the project to modernise local government, it is fair to conclude that the innovation has failed to capture widespread public enthusiasm and interest. Even where interest has been generated and referendums held, around two-thirds of such votes have returned a 'no' result – some quite resoundingly. The public appear uninterested in and unconvinced about this form of local political leadership, a position which sits uneasily with the government's own findings about public interest in, and support for, elected mayors.[31] Moreover, no more than a casual glance at the turnout figures for both referendums and mayoral elections indicates that they have failed to ignite public interest in the local political contest and even to stimulate much input to decisions about how the area will be governed.

Direct election may give the mayor a clear electoral mandate to govern, unlike the assumed mandate of the council leader and his or her majority party or administration, but the legal and administrative framework and the political and institutional arrangements the mayor inhabits do not provide any new or enhanced powers for the mayor significantly different from those existing for the council leader. While the mayor's ability to place in the cabinet any member of the council he or she wishes seems a small reward for securing the office in the first place, it does worry many councillors. A member of a mayoral authority summed up in interview the views of many of her colleagues thus:

> They [the mayor] can put in the cabinet whoever they like, you know; we have no say over it. These are powerful posts; cabinet members can make decisions on all sorts of things; it's an executive and can make decisions. It can't just be up to one person who's in and who's out.

Another councillor, who stressed the need for anonymity for his comment, simply said 'You have to be a member of an ethnic minority group to get in the mayor's cabinet'. Both comments, however, miss the point of course: that the council leader can have exactly the same power, if the council decides to grant it.

The mayor is able to construct for himself or herself a high public profile, but this is not something beyond the wit of the competent council leader. Public profile, coupled with direct election, does provide for some political leverage over other bodies and organisations involved in the governance of local communities and, to some extent, with the business community. Yet the successful mayor must look outwards, towards the area governed, and to be responsive, as far as political ideology will allow, to the demands and opinions of various communities of interest and place. England now has a structure of political leadership that requires a political dynamic that extends beyond the narrow confines of the party and the council if the incumbent is to be successful in office.

The elected mayor in England has resources, some of them structural, which can be used to develop the influence attached to the office – the power of appointment to cabinet (though not of the head of the paid officer service), and the appointment of a deputy and support staff – but, again, this is regulated by central government. The conflict resolution mechanisms put in place can tip the balance towards a mayor in conflict with his or her council, but in practice use of this has shown that it is not simply a mayoral trump card when faced with a recalcitrant council.

The arguments that the proponents of the mayoral model put forward stress its ability to transform the exercise of power at the local level, to improve the dynamism of policy-making and to increase local government's ability to command resources from the centre, but this ability has been hamstrung within a model which does not provide the power for it to achieve much that is unique to the office.[32] Stoker and Wolman see elected mayors as a way of breaking the circle of political inertia that can exist within local politics and of fostering the development of political leadership.[33] Stoker has gone as far as to say that elected mayors:

> deliver a leadership capacity better suited to the new tasks and challenges that face local politics and governance ... leadership in these circumstances is not about seizing control of the state machine: it is about building coalitions, developing networks and steering in a complex environment.[34]

But English mayors are hard pressed to meet such high expectations, set as they are within a legislative framework that provides them with little institutional and political capacity to act as political leaders. Nor does the legislative framework provide elected mayors with significant distinctions when compared with their council leader counterparts, other than that of direct election. The dominance of politics in Britain by the centre, and the continuing Westminster and Whitehall fear of powerful alternative centres of political action and loyalty in the localities, have acted to undermine the development of a new form of local governance. Indeed, mayoral authorities, as the rest of local government, lack real powers with which to act in accordance with local preferences.[35]

Elected mayors in England have neither the power nor the political resources to adequately face the complex array of governing pressures they experience. Yet some in government were convinced of the radical nature of the mayoral experiment and of the power that was to go with these new politicians. As Game and Goymen noted, a former English local government minister said at a local government conference in New Zealand: 'some of our ideas may not seem too radical to you. You are use to directly elected mayor and city managers'. Game and Goymen point out that the New Zealand mayor has 'few formal powers'; what may seem like a radical reconfiguration of power to some can work out as little or no change in practice.[36]

It would be wrong, however, to conclude from these observations that the elected mayor experiment in England is already a failure. As will be shown in following chapters, individual elected mayors are carving out a distinct approach to the governance of their areas and using their offices in interesting new ways to provide dynamic local political leadership; others are struggling with the limitations of their office and a hostile local political environment.

The legislative, constitutional and political constraints placed on the English elected mayor mean we are left with a new political office that represents a typical English compromise: a compromise between the recognition, by some, of a need for change, and the desire of local political elites and the local government establishment not to change too much, for fear of destabilising long-established political dynamics and relationships. In addition, we have a new type of political leader who sits within the constitutional settlement of a supreme Parliament and a unitary state. Thus, there can be no conflict between centre and localities that the centre cannot be guaranteed to win; territorial government is always low politics and subservient to the centre.[37] Any other approach to sub-national government would demand a radical modernisation of the entire British political system.

It remains to be seen whether the English elected mayors can offer a new form of local governance to their communities and whether they can become political leaders rather than elected heads of service-providing corporations. It is to how mayors have taken up to their role and their position as a local political leader that the next chapter turns.

Notes

1 Tait, J., 1936. *The Medieval English Borough: Studies on Its Origins and Constitutional History*, Manchester University Press; Redlich, J. and F.W. Hirst, 1958. *The History of Local Government in England*, London, Macmillan; Jewell, H., 1972. *English Local Administration in the Middle Ages*, Newton Abbot, David and Charles.

2 Jones, G.W., 1969. *Borough Politics: A Study of Wolverhampton Borough Council 1888–1964*, London, Macmillan; Hennock, E.P., 1973. *Fit and Proper Persons: Ideal and Reality in Nineteenth-Century Urban Government*, London, Edward Arnold; Saint, A., 1989. *Politics and the People of London: The London County Council 1889–1965*, London, Hambledon Press.

3 Schofield, M., 1977. 'The Nationalisation of Local Politics', *New Society*, 28 April, pp. 165–166; Gyford, J., 1985. 'The Politicisation of Local Government', in M. Loughlin, M. Gelfand and K. Young (eds), *Half a Century of Municipal Decline*, London, Allen and Unwin, pp. 77–97.

4 Local Government and Housing Act 1989. See also the Local Government (Committees and Political Groups) Regulations 1990 (SI 1990 No. 1553).

5 The Local Authorities (Conduct of Referendums) (England) Regulations, 2001.

6 Two further referendums have been held since. In the only referendum to have been held in Wales, the people of Ceredigion Borough Council voted 'no' to an elected mayor in a petition-inspired referendum held in 2004.

On the other hand, Torbay returned a 'yes' vote in July 2005 (by 18,074 to 14,682, on a 32 per cent turnout) and a mayor was duly elected the following October.

7 Copus, C., 2000. 'Consulting the Public on New Political Management Arrangements: A Review and Observations', *Local Governance*, Vol. 26, No. 3, Autumn, pp. 177–186.

8 Rallings, C., M. Thrasher and D. Cowling, 2002. 'Mayoral Referendums and Elections', *Local Government Studies*, Vol. 28, No. 4, Winter, pp. 67–90.

9 Green, G., 1972. 'National, City and Ward Components of Local Voting', *Policy and Politics*, Vol. 1, No. 1, September, pp. 45–54, at p. 45; Newton, K., 1976. *Second City Politics: Democratic Processes and Decision-Making in Birmingham*, Oxford, Clarendon Press, p. 7, p. 17, and p. 223; Jones, G.W. and J. Stewart, 1983. *The Case for Local Government*, London, Allen and Unwin, pp. 16–18; Committee of Inquiry into the Conduct of Local Authority Business, 1986. *Research, Vol. I: The Political Organisation of Local Authorities*, p. 25, and p. 197, and *Research, Vol. III: The Local Government Elector*, p. 31, London, HMSO; Rallings, C. and M. Thrasher, 1997. *Local Elections in Britain*, London, Routledge.

10 CLD, 1995. *Final Report. Taking Charge: The Rebirth Of Local Democracy*, London, Municipal Journal Books.

11 DETR, 1999. *Local Leadership: Local Choice*, London, DETR, para. 3.52.

12 *Hansard*, 25 March 1998, Vol. 209, Col. 511.

13 Van der Kolk, H., C. Rallings and M. Thrasher, 2004. 'Electing Mayors: A Comparison of Different Electoral Procedures', *Local Government Studies*, Vol. 30, No. 4, pp. 598–608.

14 Wheeland, C., 1994. 'A Profile of a Facilitative Mayor: Mayor Betty Jo Rhea of Rock Hill, South Carolina', in J. Svara (ed.), *Facilitative Leadership in Local Government*, San Francisco, CA, Jossey-Bass, pp. 136–159; Mouritzen, P.E. and J. Svara, 2002. *Leadership at the Apex: Politicians and Administrators in Western Local Government*, University of Pittsburgh Press.

15 Game, C., 2002. 'Elected Mayors: More Distraction than Attraction?', paper presented to the Eleventh One-Day Conference of the Political Studies Association Urban Politics Specialist Group, November, p. 10.

16 The Local Authorities (Functions and Responsibilities) (England) Regulations, 2000; ODPM, 2000 (updated 2001). *New Council Constitutions: Guidance to English Local Authorities*, London, ODPM.

17 ODPM, *New Council Constitutions*, paras 4.9, 4.25.

18 Leach, S. and D. Wilson, 2000. *Local Political Leadership*, Bristol, Policy Press.

19 ALDC (Association of Liberal Democrat Councillors), 2000 (updated 2001). *Model Standing Orders for Liberal Democrat Council Groups*, Hebden Bridge, ALDC; Conservative Party, 1998 (revised 2001). *Conservative Council Groups: Draft Model Rules*, London, Conservative Party; Labour Party, 2001 (updated 2002). *Labour Group Model Standing Orders*, London, Labour Party.

20 ODPM, *New Council Constitutions*, paras 4.54, 4.71–75.

21 *Ibid.*, paras 4.58 and 4.59.

22 DETR, 1997. *New Leadership for London: The Government's Proposals for a Greater London Authority*, London, DETR; DETR, 1998. *A Mayor and Assembly for London*, London, DETR.

23 Travers, T., 2004. *The Politics of London: Governing an Ungovernable City*, Basingstoke, Palgrave Macmillan, pp. 126–130, table 5.1, p. 128.

24 Giuliani, R., 2002. *Leadership*, New York, Little, Brown; Kirtzman, A., 2000. *Rudy Giuliani, Emperor of the City*, New York, W. Morrow; Fabbrini, S., 2000. 'The Presidentialisation of Italian Local Government? The Nature and the Effects of Semiparliamentarism', paper presented to a workshop on Presidentialisation of Parliamentary Democracies, ECPR, Copenhagen, Denmark, 14–19 April.

25 Snape, S., S. Leach and C. Copus, 2002. *The Development of Overview and Scrutiny in Local Government*, London, ODPM; Leach, S. and C. Copus, 2004. 'Scrutiny and the Political Party Group in UK Local Government: New Models of Behaviour', *Public Administration*, Vol. 82, No. 2, pp. 331–354.

26 Travers, *The Politics of London*, p. 87.

27 ODPM, *New Council Constitutions*, para. 4.49.

28 Fox, P. and S. Leach, 1999. *Officers and Members in the New Democratic Structures*, London, Local Government Information Unit.

29 Frederickson, H.G., G. Johnson and C. Wood, 2004. *The Adapted City: Institutional Dynamics and Structural Change*, New York, Sharpe.

30 In practice the first term of office has been of variable length, to bring electoral cycles into line, but this is only a transitional arrangement.

31 DETR, 2001. *Public Attitudes to Directly Elected Mayors*, London, DETR.

32 John, P., 2001. *Local Governance in Western Europe*, London, Sage.

33 Stoker, G. and H. Wolman, 1992. 'Drawing Lessons from US Experience: An Elected Mayor for British Local Government', *Public Administration*, Vol. 70, No. 2, pp. 241–267.

34 Cited by Tomaney, J., 2001. 'The New Governance of London: A Case of Post-democracy?', *City*, Vol. 5, No. 2, pp. 225–248.

35 Page, E. and M. Goldsmith, 1987. *Central and Local Government Relations*, London, Sage.

36 Game, C. and K. Goymen, 2001, 'Directly Elected Wizards or Dragons: Some Reflections on Turkish Mayors' Contribution to Political Participation, Legitimacy and Accountability', paper presented to the Political Studies Association Annual Conference, Manchester, April.

37 Bulpitt, J., 1983. *Territory and Power in the United Kingdom*, Manchester University Press.

3

Local political leadership and mayoral government

Introduction

The introduction of directly elected mayors into the English local political landscape has brought an additional dimension to political representation and new electoral opportunities for the voters to cast a judgement on their local political leaders. Moreover, the office of elected mayor throws into sharp relief distinctions between representative democracy and representative government: the former comprises political processes which allow citizens to have an 'indirect' participation in decision-making by electing representatives; the latter comprises the institutions and arrangements for the making of political decisions or for the display of political leadership. While the term 'representative' has been described as 'demanding the need to be responsible in governing', it also brings with it an expectation on behalf of the citizenry, if not a requirement of political leaders, to be responsive to the views of citizens.[1]

While the office of elected mayor provides additional opportunities for voters to decide on who will become political leaders, elected mayors do not equate with participatory democracy or necessarily any greater political participation in decision-making by citizens. The local political system remains a representative one. However, the prominence granted to a local politician by an at-large election, and the expectation, for it is no more than that, that such election brings with it an incumbent responsive to citizen input, create a potential for a new form of local politics – that is, a form of politics no longer dominated solely by political parties.[2] This new form of local politics enables a range of non-party political organisations (called here 'political associations' – see below) to enter and exit the political system as issues and circumstances demand, thus providing an outlet for political activity focused on salient local concerns, rather than on party interest.

Elected mayors potentially interfere with the usual mechanism for the transference of political views from the citizen to the political leader: the party. Parties have a well and long established dominance over the conduct of local politics, a dominance partly secured by the nature of the electoral system, which serves to make it harder for smaller parties or non-party candidates to secure election.[3] Party dominance has also been secured by an imbalance in resources and organisational capacity between parties and political associations.

The term 'political association' is used here to describe a broad range of organisations that are formed within a strictly local context and that have their origins in either the political world or the local civil society, but which straddle both. They are bodies that are not primarily designed as broad platform organisations and they may or may not have been formed with an original aim of securing political office; if they do not indulge in electioneering themselves they may lend support by way of endorsement, or other resources, to a particular mayoral (or other) candidate. Alternatively, a political association may be formed with the specific objective of securing the election of a particular candidate; the term would therefore also cover a local organisation that for electoral convenience uses the term 'party', such as the Better Bedford Party, which supports the elected mayor of Bedford. Moreover, a residents' association that did or did not seek for its members election to a council or mayoral office would also be a political association, alongside tenants' associations and other groups of this type.

Political associations therefore sit alongside political parties insofar as they share the aim of securing political control, or at least political influence, but they may not, unlike parties, see themselves as having the long-term goal of a political existence or any national focus or interest. They may rise to political and public prominence and even office if the public are roused, by a sufficiently salient issue or set of political circumstances, into some interest and involvement in local politics. When the issue that was the catalyst for the formation of a political association has receded, the association may transform itself into a broader-based local political movement and seek a more permanent presence on the local political scene. Alternatively, it may voluntarily dissolve and remove itself from the political theatre.[4]

Political associations in the local context may come and go, as do the issues that stimulate their arrival; whether a temporary or permanent part of the political landscape set within a particular council, an association is ideal for the business of providing a potential coalition partner for a candidate seeking mayoral office, or for a mayor seeking to broaden support outside of his or her party, or for one working without a party base. The political association provides fertile ground for those mayors predisposed to a different style of local political leadership from what has hitherto been the case in English local government and politics. The political association serves to remove from the conduct and processes of local politics the worst excesses of party political behaviour.[5]

That the office of directly elected mayor has produced the potential for the dominance of local politics by parties to be undermined is not itself an indication that a new form of local politics will necessarily emerge from the mayoral experiment. Yet direct election to executive political authority also produces the conditions for a much clearer, more visible and more accountable local political leadership.

The notion of local political leadership was identified in Chapter 2 as one of the more radical aspects of the modernisation agenda – perhaps unintentionally so; this chapter explores the role of the elected mayor as a political leader. The next section considers what is meant by local political leadership in the context of English local politics. It explores whether the office of elected mayor, as currently configured, can engender such leadership and whether the nature and conduct of local politics have been changed as a result of the arrival of elected mayors. The chapter goes on to explore how the separation of powers within mayoral authorities operates and considers the checks and balances within the political decision-making system. The final section examines the pressures faced by English elected mayors to respond to the political demands generated by a range of local interests, especially political parties.

New political leadership: the big idea for English local politics

A key element of the current reform agenda for local government is the provision of political leadership to the local community. The absence of such leadership was clearly articulated by the Prime Minister when he called for local government to have 'recognised leaders' and for visibility of those 'politically responsible' for decisions.[6] Put more starkly, the problem was that in local government 'there is little clear political leadership' and that:

> People often do not know who is really taking the decisions. They do not know who to praise, who to blame or who to contact with their problems. People identify most readily with an individual, yet there is rarely any identifiable figure leading the local community.[7]

While the absence of political leadership has been identified, what political leadership is and how it displays itself locally have been less well articulated by the government, save for the creation of new political structures from which that leadership may be provided. Moreover, the political role of local government has long been submerged beneath its functioning as a provider of public services, the standards and financing of which are closely monitored by central government. As the functions of local government and the complex relationships between local and central government over the provision of public services have developed – through notions of the 'hollowing out' of the state[8] to notions of a congested state emerging from network governance, 'post-hollowing out'[9] – local government's political and governing role has remained largely submerged under service provision concerns. If it does not reposition itself as the authoritative political leadership of a locality, local government is faced with a steady and continued erosion of its position.[10] If the English elected mayor is to provide visible, transparent and accountable local political leadership, how that concept relates to local politics needs to be articulated.

Much of our current understanding of political leadership comes from research in the US, particularly among elected mayors. In the 1970s Kotter and Lawrence explored mayoral political leadership and found that it displayed itself in distinct behavioural patterns, whereby individual mayors would focus on aspects of leadership, either policy setting or policy implementation, or focus on the management of the service-delivering bureaucracy.[11] Kotter and Lawrence went on to identify the importance to assessing the effectiveness of mayoral governance in terms of control of the political/policy agenda, demonstrable task achievement and network building and maintenance. They also identified five types of mayor: ceremonial, caretaker, personality/individualist, executive and programme entrepreneur.[12]

Such typologies provide an insight to how US mayors operate within a distinct political system. While some mayors will of course display the characteristics of more than one type, a dominant tendency in mayoral approach and focus will be discernible; such typologies therefore help us to understand the balance in mayoral government between the pressures generated for a particular approach to government by the political and institutional system itself and by the mayor's personal choice of a style and focus in his or her governing activity.

An assessment of the way in which mayoral political leadership displays itself in any political context will initially focus on the mayor's ability to bring resources, of one sort or another, to bear on political problems in such a way as to effect action, or of course to prevent action or a decision with which the mayor disagrees.[13] Whether the mayoral system is considered either 'strong' or 'weak', with strong mayors having a high degree of individual control and weak mayors sharing power through some institutional arrangement, mayors can be judged by what they make happen through the employment of institutional and political power, or through the use of political influence, alliances and discourse.[14]

Mayoral power and the ability to provide political leadership rest on acting in a range of governance networks which extend beyond the locality. Here, the English mayor is constrained in the process of political leadership by the 'structural characteristics' of the mayoral system.[15] Yet Svara has shown that even when faced with strong counterbalancing forces within the governance arrangements, mayors can provide political leadership and act as a demonstrable force for change, or resistance to it; mayors can rise above system constraints.[16]

Hambleton and Sweeting suggest three factors should be taken into account when making comparisons of local political leadership provided in the UK: the policy environment, institutional arrangements and relationships with followers.[17] These factors have a bearing on the scope, effectiveness and legitimacy of the leadership provided, in this case by the elected mayor. They recognise that these factors do not diminish the importance of the personal qualities that individual mayors display in providing leadership, but that those qualities are constrained and shaped by external and system factors. In concluding that the power of party political groups in controlling the 'behaviour of local leaders seems to be declining' and that the English elected mayor can be expected to 'exercise more independent leadership than the typical U.K. council leader', they do underestimate the power and resilience of the party group system in local government and its ability to constrain mayoral leadership. In addition, the linkages between local and national parties in England serve to bind party mayors to their local party.[18]

Leach and Wilson have produced a comprehensive and powerful analysis of local political leadership in the UK and provided a valuable framework through which to analyse the effectiveness, or otherwise, of the political leadership displayed by the English elected mayor.[19] They highlight the importance of leadership as a behaviour pattern, rather than the mere holding of a position;[20] they are interested in leadership as an inspirational process, inducing others to follow the lead given rather than responding mechanistically to system-driven instruction – the leader's ability to inspire and persuade can overcome system constraints on mayoral power. Mayoral leadership is about style and skill, and it is these factors that can help the mayor transcend system constraints.

Leach and Wilson see the key tasks of the local political leader as: maintaining the cohesiveness of the authority, developing strategic and policy direction, representing the authority to the external world, and ensuring the accomplishment of political tasks. Yet they also recognise that the political context in which leaders find themselves greatly influences their ability to 'lead' and to achieve the key leadership tasks. Indeed, they remind us that urban regime theory distinguishes between the idea of holding political power (or office) and governing.[21]

Yet to achieve any form of political success beyond the pursuance of statutory duties and functions, the political leader must look beyond the context of his or her party to a broader contextual setting. He or she must forge coalitions of interest around what regime theorists normally see as growth machines, following an economic development objective. While local government bodies in England must work with a broad range of partners in formal and semi-formal arrangements and may even be seen to be leading the way, as with LSPs, simply being the council is not sufficient to be leading the community.[22] But are elected mayors better placed than the council leader to forge governing coalitions beyond the confines of statutory responsibilities and powers and beyond the council as an institution, and how are local political parties and party groups responding to a mayor who attempts to broaden his or her support base beyond the party?

Randle, in a study for the New Local Government Network, and in other unpublished research, has developed a typology of English mayors which helps us to understand how mayors are responding to the need to move beyond the normal patterns of party political behaviour if mayoral leadership potential is to be fulfilled.[23] She has categorised mayors as follows. First, there is the *visionary*, elected on a platform of radical change and distanced from the previous council leadership; the visionary will probably be elected from a non-party political background. Second, there is the *strong leader*, who exercises strong internal leadership of the council and places this over developing a high community profile and developing broader relationships with the outside world; this type of mayor has a strong focus on services and drives a clear service-oriented agenda. Third, the *mediator* operates a consensual and inclusive form of leadership, while having a strategic approach which is carefully designed not to raise expectations of mayoral achievement too high; the mediator can and does play a number of different roles as the need arises, but nevertheless the focus is on results. Finally, the *populist* is unlikely to have been involved in local government before election and is typically elected on an anti-council platform; the populist mayor will view himself or herself as a 'people person', rather than be identified as a council spokesperson. The populist is concerned for public engagement and has a firm belief that local government can be remote and unresponsive.

Stoker has also constructed a typology of English mayors, but he presents them as one of three types: a *change agent*, arriving on the scene to change a 'failed system' and leading the council out of a period of 'turmoil' and away from past failed political regimes; a *community representative – advocate*, pursing a policy of developing links with citizens and giving priority to speaking for the area as a whole; and a *builder on past strengths*, where a former leader has become mayor and pursued continuity rather than change. Stoker's typologies, as he points out, are not context free; rather, context has a powerful influence on the development of mayoral government.[24]

The most powerful context in which English mayors find themselves is the domination of local politics by political parties. The rules and regulations of local parties and party groups set a framework which both influences and reflects the culture of the party concerned. While interpretations of concepts such as democracy, representation, politics and government vary across the parties, similarities also exist in the way parties make sense of the local political world.[25] Placing these mayoral typologies in a political and party political context enables us to refine what we have so far considered about mayoral leadership.

Refining English mayoral leadership

If we are to improve our understanding of the potential impact of elected mayors in England, it is vital to refine what we know already about local political leadership. There are of course shared characteristics which all political leaders, however they are elected to office, will display, and there are common constraints and power resources affecting them. Moreover, political leaders' own political philosophies will result in them stimulating, dampening or preventing political action. But has the English mayor added a new dimension to local political leadership – or has it simply been accommodated by existing political dynamics and structures? And what are the factors which will enable us to make a judgement on the impact of mayoral politics on the politics of English localities?

By exploring the English version of the local *separation of powers* we can start to address the effect of the directly elected mayor as a system of local government. In looking at the how mayors inhabit and navigate around their institutional arrangements we can discover the common themes in, and distinctions between, the way in which English mayors have developed relationships with councillors and party groups to alter the dynamics of local politics. In addition, we can tell not only whether mayors can govern locally, but in what context and what effect on mayoral activity the existing series of checks and balance can have. Linked to this is the need to consider how the separation of powers enables the mayor to control or at least influence the policy agenda, both in the confines of the council and its responsibilities and in wider local governance networks.

The *political focus* of any English mayor depends on a complex mix of personal, political, structural and locality-based influences, as well as quite simply the mayor's interest, predilection and time to reach beyond the confines of the council and out into local communities. There are two dimensions to the mayor's broad governing focus: whether the mayor is from a political party or a political association (the latter, for convenience, includes those standing on an independent ticket); and how personally tied, rather than institutionally tied, the mayor is to his or her political party. Does he or she see the party as a legitimate counterbalance to community assertiveness and involvement and as an institution which shares a broad governing perspective with the mayor? Or does the mayor seek to stretch – perhaps to the limit – his or her relationship with the party in a search for a broad, alliance-based governing approach?

The mayor without party affiliation will, it is widely assumed, look beyond the council to seek either a series of single-issue alliances or a broad governing alliance; or he or she may operate on the basis of a grand coalition of interests, one which exists outside the council. The mayor without party affiliation will need to play a dual alliance-building role: building governing or single-issue alliances within the council and building governing or single-issue alliances outside the council with the aim of pursuing policy decisions through the council. Thus, there is an internal political focus to these activities, distinct from community leadership. A mayor facing a council without having a majority of councillors automatically supporting him or her makes this sort of alliance-building distinct from other community governance activities, as it is designed to secure leverage over councillors.

How much mayors balance the dual pressure between running a service-based bureaucracy as a form of elected 'over-manager' and how far they delegate this (legally or informally) to councillors and managers will dictate how much time they are able to give to broader community political concerns: the manager/politician dichotomy is as real for the mayor as it is for councillors. The notion of a *mayoral dichotomy* between public service provision and political governance is fully explored in the next chapter.

These factors – the *separation of powers*, the *mayoral political focus* and the *mayoral dichotomy* – bring together a range of issues which help uncover the richness of the English experiment with elected mayors, but which also explain the frustrations inherent in any attempts at radical reform of the structure of local political decision-making. They also relate to how structural and contextual settings have influenced the English mayoral experiment.

The separation of powers: checks and balances

The local separation of powers is a new concept for English local government and alongside the development of notions of local political leadership it is part of the radical edge to the government's reform agenda. Moreover, the separation of powers is what causes the local government establishment and local political elites the most concern, as it threatens to sweep away existing power balances, patterns of behaviour and long-established processes for making political decisions. In addition, such a separation of powers removes the collective veil behind which councillors can hide when it comes to the allocation of responsibility for political action or inaction. Yet a form of separation of powers is a common feature of local government overseas, whether the political head of the executive is directly or indirectly elected. What varies is the nature of the interaction between the executive and the main body of councillors, and the balance of power between them. Most elected mayors sit happily in a system with a separation of powers, checks and balances between executive and council, and with a secure knowledge of in whose favour that balance is tipped.[26]

The separation of powers within English mayoral councils has the elected mayor as the head of the executive *and* political head of the council; the legislative element of that separation (although ironically with no legislative power) is the full council, which forms a number of overview and scrutiny committees to initiate and review policy and to provide a robust mechanism for holding the mayor to account. Further, the standards committee of the council could be seen as a form of judiciary, ensuring the ethical framework of local government introduced by Part III of the 2000 Act, and the code of conduct, are complied with.

There is of course in English local government a forum for political discourse and decision-making of which the separation of powers takes no account: the political party group. Yet the party group exists alongside the formal theatres of political action and any analysis of the executive arrangements in English local government that does not account for the relationship between the party group, its members and the formal council settings provides only a partial picture of the workings of the political system.[27] English mayors, as we shall see, are beginning to develop a range of relationships and dynamics with the local party groups, as well as to navigate the more formal aspects of the separation of powers.

Acting with a separation of powers

The evidence collected from the English mayors suggests that they have mostly warmed to the idea of a clear distinction between the political leadership of the council centred in the executive and a body of councillors acting as a check and balance. Indeed, if the mayors are correct, it is their fellow councillors and not they who often struggle with the concept and have yet to develop a robust means by which to hold mayors to account. As one party mayor commented in interview, 'I would love someone to scrutinise me, to offer some challenge, or debate, but scrutiny just isn't doing it yet'. Another mayor, from a different political party, offered this suggestion in relation to overview and scrutiny: 'They have to come off the fence and tackle issues they are unhappy about rather than moaning in group meetings about this or that'. Added to this was a comment that:

> I feel overview and scrutiny is well resourced; I've asked them to look into problems for me and come up with suggestions and they think I'm trying to tell them what to do; on the other hand, they complain loudly when I do things, or don't respond to some of their points as they want.

There also appears, however, to be a focus developing on overview and scrutiny as the area in which the mayor can be safely challenged and some mayors reported a rigorous scrutiny process in their councils. It is the approach councillors take to mayoral challenge that mayors use to identify whether scrutiny is a useful area in which to test mayoral initiatives or, if the approach to scrutiny becomes an obstructive mechanism, it is a mechanism seemingly misused by opposition councillors. Complaints were raised by mayors that overview and scrutiny were being 'misused' for party political purposes, alongside an excessive use of 'call-in' procedures. Call-in by overview and scrutiny has the effect of delaying a mayoral decision while a committee explores the issue or questions the mayor and executive. Ultimately, however, if the mayor's decision is compliant with the policy framework, the mayor, or for that matter the council leader, can override any overview and scrutiny objections. Call-in procedures are defined within each council's written constitution and will vary from council to council. One mayor commented that:

> it appears they [opposition councillors] have a policy of calling in anything I do, mostly on pretty spurious grounds and just to delay things; we waste a lot of time with these types of call-in that are done for political reasons only. I don't think they [councillors] have grasped the idea that the mayor can do things and doesn't have to ask their permission. If they disagree politically they call it in, which isn't what the system's for; I've got to be able to get on with things otherwise it just makes a mockery of the [mayoral] election.

What is evident is that those mayors who ran on an election platform in opposition to the council, or more accurately in opposition to the ruling group, have found that the separation of powers has been used as a barrier to mayoral initiative. It is mostly, but not exclusively, the independent mayors who have experienced a form of institutional blockage to mayoral policy. The tussle over who governs an area – mayor or majority party – is potentially complex and difficult when an independent mayor faces party councillors set within a separation of powers, a written constitution and a high degree of party politicisation. That tussle can become more acute when a mayor from one party is faced by a council controlled by another. Here the potential for conflict is intensified by the existence of party political considerations and dynamics that may extend beyond the council into national political concerns.

While the legislation and the nature of any separation of local powers make it clear that the mayor is the political head of the council, if the mayor's own party is in a minority the party political dynamics of a council do not make the matter of political leadership and control clear cut. One mayor in such circumstances reported political life to be a constant struggle to assert the role and responsibilities of the mayoral office against a majority party deprived by the electorate of the mayoralty. This mayor faced opposition from the majority group over certain key aspects of his mayoral manifesto. He claimed, however, the right to pursue his manifesto by dint of his direct election; the council majority party claimed a similar right to pursue their policies and to oppose the mayor by dint of being elected to a majority of seats.

In such circumstances political deadlock could occur if political maturity is absent. The issue becomes one of a mayoral right to govern. The mayor on this council saw his policies as being unnecessarily 'picked over' by his political opponents, who he thought were seeking to find ways in which to obstruct him from achieving his political objectives. The mayor, who had drawn his cabinet from the council minority group, was insistent that his direct election meant that these political circumstances did not meet the traditional definition of a hung council. He claimed leadership and political responsibility from direct election, thus conceptually relegating the council majority to a subservient political status – one that they should recognise and work appropriately from as a consequence. This notion, unsurprisingly, was one that the council majority party did not accept.

A senior majority group councillor rejected emphatically accusations of obstructionism or misuse of the council's constitution to prevent the mayor from taking action. She saw the majority group's role as probing and exploring mayoral policy proposals and the broader executive agenda, and seeking out weakness of substance and process that required improvement. She also saw the group's role as holding mayoral policy up to public, critical, scrutiny and challenge, and although this might frustrate the mayor it was clearly the responsibility of the council to undertake such action.

What is clear in this council, at least, is that a previously dominant political party had been deprived of the mechanisms of power but still remained in a position to act as though it were in power. Moreover, the nature of the relationship between the party groups before the election of a mayor accounted for the state of inter-party relationships. Changing institutional arrangements is only a small part of changing party political dynamics, as political power is hard fought for by parties and they do not give it up easily. Time is needed for the parties to adjust to new political realities and dynamics and to new institutions, and these factors are at the heart of the way in which the mayor and cabinet executive develop.

There are also examples of the system checks and balances being used to block individual mayoral policies, rather than to challenge wholesale a mayor's right to govern. Even councillors from the same party as the mayor have proved not unwilling to challenge the mayor publicly when other means have failed to bring about a change in mayoral policy. One mayor provided an example of the majority group, of the same political affiliation as the mayor, using the council checks and balances to alter a particular mayoral policy which had split the group. The mayor requested that the policy be not identified as, at the time of writing, the issue had yet to be resolved. The issue itself is not what is important here though; rather, it is that the mayor's group, or at least large sections of it, were prepared to employ formal council mechanisms to effect a rescinding of the decision, which indicates that some councillors are willing to employ challenge on an issue-by-issue basis. Importantly, the councillors concerned displayed a willingness to move outside the confines of the party group to change mayoral policy and into the formal settings of overview and scrutiny and full council. The mayor, while frustrated about the issue and particular decision, was not, however, frustrated by the overall operation of the system. Moreover, while the mayor's group was willing to gather support in overview and scrutiny from councillors in other parties, the mayor expressed no reluctance to negotiate with other parties to secure the votes needed to override council objections.

The process here, to some, will appear to be de-politicising council policy-making; it is not. Rather, it is an indication that the worst excesses of party politicking can be negated when the executive and councillors recognise their executive and scrutiny role as transcending party label. Such an approach is real politics: the politics of discourse, negotiation, compromise, the search for agreement, alliances and coalitions, which adherence to rigid party boundaries removes from the political system.

The political dynamics of mayoral authorities

Evidence collected from mayoral authorities suggests that a number of factors affect the nature of the relationship between the elected mayor and the councillors forming the rest of his or her council:

- *Political party.* Is the mayor from the same party as the majority group or does the mayor face a majority formed by another party? Does the mayor face a council on which no party has an overall majority? Or is the mayor independent of party and face a majority formed by a political party, or a group or grouping of independents or councillors from a political association?
- *The political culture of the council.* Is it cooperative or antagonistic, intensely or mildly party political, broadly traditional in outlook or willing to experiment and open to public involvement and discourse, inward looking, introspective and defensive or outward looking, strategic and confident in its ability to govern? Is it willing to change in response to new political circumstances and governance arrangements?

- *The relationship between the mayor and councillors.* This relationship depends on the interpretations each has of the other's role and the political recognition that the mayor has an authority-wide mandate to govern, while councillors have an institutionalised role as a mechanism for mayoral accountability and local representation.

Mayors have attested to the importance of these factors to their own ability to develop individual and collective relationships with councillors. It is commonplace in much literature, and rather formulaic, to emphasise the importance of the personality of the mayor (or other political leader) in forming a political dynamic and set of relationships that enable the mayor to pursue his or her policy goals. The personality of the political leader does have a role to play in the formation and development of a conflictual or cooperative political culture and relationships with council members. Yet it is only one aspect of that process: how mayors treat councillors rests on ideological, political, party political and institutional factors, as well as the mayor's (and councillors') own predisposition towards conflictual or cooperative politics.

The English mayors display different traits when it comes to relationships with council members. For the party mayor, while the existence of a large in-built bloc of support among councillors may on first sight appear comforting, the reality can be very different. For the independent mayor, or the mayor faced with a majority of councillors from another party, the processes of developing good working relationships can appear, in the words of one mayor, 'daunting; like a mountain to climb', but the mayor's task in this case was made easier because he 'enjoyed a good fight'.

In addition, whether councillors supported the introduction of an elected mayor to the authority, and whether they were pleased or not with the outcome of the election – that is, whether their party had won or lost – played a part in the development of the relationship between mayors and council. The independent mayors had experienced the fallout from councillors' attitudes towards elected mayors and the results of the mayoral elections rather more abruptly than the party mayors who sat with a council consisting of a majority of their colleagues. An independent mayor summarised the reactions of party councillors to his victory thus:

> Shock, anger; they tried to make my experience as difficult as possible from the outset; most were very cold; most of them thought I was a bit of a joke and were waiting for me to fail. They tried to test me to see how I would respond. Some false stories were circulated in the press saying I was doing this or that when I wasn't; they were just stirring really. But, over time, they have come round.

Other independent mayors painted a similar picture of the reaction from party councillors to the election of a non-party mayor. What becomes clear is that these mayors are faced with a council on which they may have no political allies and so must set about finding support – because of the public rigidity of party groups this has been difficult for them, except behind the scenes. Independent mayors have tended thus far to find allies wherever they can, and particularly have worked to develop support among officers of the council. While one independent mayor reported that council officers were as shocked by an independent victory as the councillors, all have found officers a ready source of advice and support. In one council where a chief executive was not in place at the time of the mayor's election, the process of forging working relationships with officers was made easier because the mayor could put a stamp on the appointment, although the council, not the mayor, controlled the process.

The willingness of mayors to reach out to councillors also generates a climate of cooperation, although that reaching out can be a hard process, with some mayors reporting that councillors were simply unwilling to cooperate in mayoral activities or governance. Some even questioned why councillors had troubled with becoming elected in the first place.

The process of developing a form of working dynamic with council members has progressed, as would be expected, at a different pace in each of the mayoral authorities, although it is clear that the mayors faced with a council controlled by his or her party have had a head start. This staggered development of a working dynamic is partly a result of the newness of the system. It is not only how the mayors have coped that counts, but also how councillors cope in an entirely new set of circumstances and processes, to which they are unaccustomed. There are no clear patterns of initial relationships between mayors and councillors: some have had a troublesome and conflictual start; others a more supportive and cooperative reaction from councillors. (Councillors' reactions to mayoral government are explored in Chapter 8.)

The research for the book indicated the powerful effect of a mayor's skill in cabinet-making when it came to forming a working relationship between mayor and council. Mayors reported different approaches to cabinet-making, some of which were driven by necessity, others by political culture and some element of political expediency. The composition of mayoral cabinets, at the time of writing, is set out in Table 3.1

While party mayors demonstrate a preference for party colleagues when it comes to cabinet membership, some of this is against a backdrop of the overwhelming control of the council by the majority party. In the 2002 London borough elections for example, Labour in Lewisham won forty-five seats out of fifty-four; in Hackney the party won forty-five seats of fifty-seven; and in Newham Labour took fifty-nine of sixty seats. In these circumstances a preference for party colleagues to the exclusion of a cabinet seat for others is understandable. At the time of writing,

Table 3.1 Mayoral cabinet composition (pre-May 2004 local elections and 2005 mayoral elections)

Council	Size of cabinet (including mayor)	Party composition of cabinet
Bedford	10	Labour, 3; Conservative, 3; independent, 2; Better Bedford Party, including the mayor, 2
Doncaster	10	All Labour
Hackney	9	All Labour
Hartlepool	7	Labour, 4; Conservative, 1; independent, including the mayor, 2
Lewisham	10	All Labour
Mansfield	7	Independent, including the mayor, 4; Liberal Democrat, 1; Independent Forum, 1; vacancy, 1
Middlesbrough	10	Labour, 7; Conservative, 1; independent, including the mayor, 2
Newham	10	All Labour
North Tyneside	9	All Conservative
Watford	5	All Liberal Democrat

Note: Stoke-on-Trent is excluded from the table as it operates the mayor and council manager option, in which no cabinet members are selected from among councillors.

all mayors elected as a party candidate have cabinets formed exclusively from their own party.

It is the independent mayors who find themselves faced with a more difficult task and with putting together a cabinet of a mixed political composition, both from necessity and from inclination. Independent mayors also report 'requesting' applications from councillors for a seat in the cabinet and conducting a form of interview and selection process for cabinet members. Partly this is a result of needing to select from a range of very different candidates with different levels of support for mayoral policy, but also simply because a new independent mayor may just not know who the councillors are and what personal qualities they have. Moreover, they will not use party label as a means of including or excluding councillors from cabinet membership. Independent mayors speak of looking for 'talent', 'quality' or 'merit' rather than party allegiance when it comes to a cabinet place. The mayors also report cabinets of mixed compositions as 'working well', 'surprisingly coherent' and 'a good mix of ability and political acumen'. The independent mayors learnt very quickly that the small size of the cabinet provided an opportunity to develop a cohesive team with a defined purpose and unity to it, and they have capitalised on this to build cabinets of mixed compositions. Equally as important, as one mayor admitted, was the ability of a mixed cabinet to 'have a foot in every camp, which really helps smooth out problems and helps to get things done'.

Mayoral cabinet-making is an area where mayors can redress a party balance (cabinets are not required to be proportional) and they can draw on a wider range of talent from across the council, rather than be corralled into selecting from just one party; and it is a process which can be used by the mayor as a check and balance on the rest of the council. The formation of a cabinet, the allocation of portfolios, the area those portfolios cover, the cabinet meetings themselves and the unity of purpose the cabinet displays provide, for a mayor of any party or none, a lever to control the policy process and to pursue mayoral initiatives. Skilful cabinet-making serves to make mayoral control far more secure than the institutional arrangement of the council would indicate.

Mayors obtain some but not all of the power and influence they wield from the structure of the council and their relationship to it. Political actors and the institutions they inhabit have a mutually influencing relationship.[28] Mayors can and do increase that power and influence by creating a political dynamic supportive of their governance initiatives and policy direction and by creating a cabinet that enables them to focus confidently outwards, on the community, while the cabinet focuses inwards, on the council. So the political focus of the mayor is partly choice and partly created by the mayor and cabinet's own political intelligence. Mayors have indicated that they are prepared to share the outward focus they develop with the cabinet collectively and individually, as this strengthens the mayor's position in the broader world of governance.

Mayoral political focus: party or people?

All elected representatives face competing pressures for them to concentrate political activity on pursing and articulating the concerns of a range of political interests; the competition is to ensure that the representative places one particular set of interests above all others. While it will not be possible for the representative to exclude all other concerns, the representative's primary focus of attention will be at the centre of his or her political activity and, in the case of a clash of opinions, the interests of one particular political concern will transcend all those competing for attention. That focus of representative attention has been described, variously, as: 'a geographical unit, a party, a pressure group or an administrative organisation';[29] a 'broad section of the community, a particular organised group, another local authority or individual citizens';[30] or the borough on which a councillors sits, or the ward from which he or she was elected.[31] The reality for the vast majority of councillors in England is that the political party of which he or she is a member is the primary, and for some the only, focus of attention and loyalty.[32]

While the party political mayor will be subject to pressure from the party and party group of councillors to place party political interest at the centre of mayoral attention, the independent mayor will not face such pressure. The independent mayor may, however, face pressure from an independent group or a political association (whether represented on the council or not) to pursue its concerns; if working with a multi-party cabinet, the mayor may face pressure to place the concerns of the parties in the cabinet at centre stage. Such pressure of course is not the same as that experienced and responded to by the party mayor, as it lacks any underpinning from shared party membership and the political, emotional and psychological factors which help bind party colleagues together – at least in public.

A clear indication of the mayor's approach to political leadership is displayed in how he or she deals with the competing pressures to place a party, or some other articulated set of interests, at the centre of his or her activity as a local political leader. It is a tension that is not unique to the English mayor of course, but how the English mayors cope with these pressures has the potential to alter the long-standing political dynamics of at least some small sections of English local government. Of the current elected mayors in England (see Table 2.2 on page 32 and the Postscript for an update with the 2005 elections), six come from a party political background (seven including the mayor of London) and the other five are independents or backed by a political association (one of whom has been a member of a political party in the past). Of the six party mayors, all had been councillors or were councillors at the time of being elected mayor; four had been leaders of the council for which they were elected to mayoral office; and one had held the office of the traditional civic mayor. The political party pedigree of these six mayors is not in doubt; they are long-standing, dedicated and loyal members of the party and active within it beyond the council area. While this is a very small sample, it is an important one to explore for indications of the strength of the relationship between mayor and party.

Political focus: the party mayor

The evidence collected from party mayors indicates that there are two dimensions affecting the relationships between the mayor and his or her party group of councillors and the wider local party: first, the personal predilections about party unity and loyalty and the personal style of governance and politics the mayor brings to the office; and second, systemic factors emanating either from the separation of powers within the council or from the institutional arrangements of the political party concerned. What is apparent is that while political affiliation obviously affects the policy direction the mayor takes, it is less of a discriminator than would be expected when it comes to mayoral–party relationships. It is here that the personal style and predisposition towards the conduct of politics comes into play.

It is in the model standing orders for party political groups produced by the Labour Party nationally in which we find the most carefully drawn set of procedures to bring the mayor and party group together as a cohesive unit, although these do, at the same time, recognise the separate mandate of the mayor and his or her right to govern based on that mandate. [33] The group and mayor are expected to work closely together to pursue Labour policy at the local level and to cooperate in public on mayoral initiatives. However, the notion of councillors challenging and holding the mayor to account through public overview and scrutiny represents a fracturing of past Labour Party expectations of complete public unity between its councillors. Moreover, Labour members now have a role, permissible in party rules, to pursue ward-based concerns, so long as they avoid criticising the policy or decisions of a Labour-controlled council.

The intention of the rules is to avoid public disagreement between mayor and council group and, where that is not possible, and in recognition of the different mandate of mayor and council, to ensure such disagreement is dealt with either within a group meeting or through the separation of powers within the council. While the current standing orders may to some appear unduly restrictive on mayoral and councillor action and initiative, they are a giant leap forward from the nature of past party standing orders and do provide councillors and mayors with freedom and room for political manoeuvre.

The Liberal Democrats and Conservatives have no such rule-induced arrangements to drive the relationship between the mayor and party group. Indeed, the Conservative Party had, at the time of writing, not resolved the consultation process around the nationally produced set of group rules that was launched in 1998 and revised in 2001. Yet the model standing orders produced by the Association of Liberal Democrat Councillors and the consultative draft for group rules produced by the Conservative Party do seek to ensure that disagreement between elected mayor and councillors is reduced to a minimum and, as far as is politically possible, confined to private forums rather than aired in public.[34]

Providing a set of rules and procedures which at one and the same time are designed to draw together group and mayor and to provide political freedom of movement to both is only one part of the story. Mayors and their party groups must be willing to act in an interdependent and, indeed, an independent fashion so as to develop notions of political leadership at the local level. The party mayors, and their groups, reported different approaches to the degrees of independence between these two political elements of the separation of powers and different degrees of willingness to indulge in open public debate around mayoral initiatives. They also reported variations in the way in which the mayor either became deliberately embedded in the group or sought to distance himself or herself from it, at least operationally. An extra dimension to the relationship between the party mayor and the party group of councillors is whether or not the party holds a majority of seats; where no overall majority exists, the mayoral–group relationship becomes a mayor–group–council one. Thus, additional pressure is placed on the mayor to be seen to be loyal to the party and on the group to support the mayor. The evidence suggests that not all party mayors are responding to these pressures in the same way and they fall into two categories: the *party-detached* mayor and the *party-loyalist.*

The party-detached mayor deliberately places some distance between himself or herself and the party group of councillors. As one mayor described it in interview:

> It is important to the public not to be seen to be 'on the council's side' and a mayor should not end up defending, excusing or supporting the council, particularly over poor performance.... I need to get outside of the party so the decisions I make are as well and widely informed as possible.

Interestingly, this suggests that the mayor, in placing some degree of distance between the office of mayor, the council and the party, almost inverts the scrutiny process by adopting a form of scrutiny role over the council.

A mayor from a different political party suggested that the mayor should be 'the council's harshest critic and not spend time defending it to the public', to which the following was added:

> It is wrong to only speak to your own party; you have to engage with as many people as possible in as many places as possible and, yes, that includes talking to other political parties. That's what it takes to be a community champion and my party must learn that as well as everyone else.

Party-detached mayors have deployed the technique of appointing a deputy mayor, with a cabinet seat and sometimes a portfolio, but also with a distinctly political role of negotiating with and managing the party group, thus freeing the mayor from the need to micro-manage the political tensions and needs of that group. Party-detached mayors admitted to appointing a deputy specifically to play the role of party group manager. In these cases the mayor and deputy mayor were identified by councillors on those councils as presenting a very close-knit team and that when the deputy spoke to the group it was either to support the mayor or it was as though the mayor were speaking. It also had the benefit of removing the mayor not only from the need to micro-manage the group, but from becoming embroiled in some interminable internal group political or personal dispute. Deputies here are political, rather than policy enforcers – but enforcers they are all the same.

All the party-detached mayors reported attending group meetings as a matter of course, but practice varied in whether the mayors remained for all or part of the group meeting and varied in the dynamics they had created with their group. Mayors here presented the issues for discussion they wished debated or considered, listened to parts of the group discussion on other matters raised by the group and either left the meeting at an agreed point after mayor's business or stayed for the whole meeting. What was common to these mayors was that it had been made clear to the group that the mayor would also be discussing the same issues with a wide range of other political associations and organisations before a decision was made. The group represented one of many varied elements of a discursive process that extended beyond the usual party political boundaries.

All the party-detached mayors attested, however, to strong party political identification, loyalty to the party locally and nationally, and taking part in a wide range of party political and electioneering activity – they were not detached in that sense, but only in how they approached the business of mayoral government.

The party-loyalist mayors, on the other hand, displayed no predilection for distancing themselves from the party group and saw themselves as an integrated part of the group. There was a tendency among this type of mayor to want to micro-manage all aspects of group activity and to ensure the group supported, as fully as possible, mayoral policy and initiatives. These mayors were still strong leaders – in fact were particularly strong – as they left nothing to chance and wished to prevent, rather than encourage, the group publicly debating party concerns, preferring to keep such issue to the privacy of a group meeting.

The party-loyalist was as willing as the party-detached mayor to discuss social and political problems and solutions with a wide range of political associations, stakeholder groups and citizens, but for the party-loyalist, the party and party group dominated the discursive process and took primacy over all other contributors when it came to making a final decision. The party-loyalist wanted to take the party and group with him or her on the same political journey and arrive at the same political conclusion; these mayors tolerated internal disunity and were willing to exploit it but they preferred external unity, unless of course disagreement was exposed within the proper checks and balances of the council – mainly overview and scrutiny. As one party-loyalist mayor said:

The party is important; I wouldn't be here if it wasn't for the party. I know it is dangerous for us to appear disunited in public. Even though I have a different mandate to the group, the public will forget that and just see us as arguing amongst ourselves if we don't secure an agreed line – which of course, as mayor, should be mine!

Even for the party-loyalist mayor, securing agreement may not be easy and, while not bound by decisions of the group, the mayor's political preference here was to avoid public disagreement and to secure a unity of purpose between the mayor and the group. The party-loyalist mayor was also likely to be the council loyalist mayor and tie his or her public profile to the council, being prepared if necessary to defend it from critics and to seek reasons for poor performance as well as improvement.

Political focus: the independent or political association mayor

Independent mayors and mayors backed by a local political association do not face party political pressure in the same way as party mayors. They are not members of a party and may even have secured election on an anti-party or an anti-council platform, as in Hartlepool, Middlesbrough, Mansfield and Bedford. Yet mayors in these circumstances reported experiencing all the political tensions and pressures experienced by their party counterparts, although they manifested themselves in different ways and there is clearly no underlying expectation on behalf of councillors that the mayor and council will speak politically as one.

The independent mayors reported repelling pressure from parties to take on aspects of a party platform and to operate on other than an issue-by-issue basis. They achieved this by playing to their mayoral strengths, by relying on the fact of direct election for a separate mandate and developing political alliances outside the council; by these means they sought to counterbalance the pressures from the parties on the council. One mayor in particular operated around the parties and produced an appearance of almost ignoring them, as was stated quite simply in interview when referring to party councillors: 'I am the mayor, not them'. Another mayor added in similar fashion, 'they did what they could to stop me when I arrived, so I do what I can to work around them now'. He did admit that the situation had since improved and a form of unwritten accommodation had been reached in how the mayor and council would work with each other.

Independent mayors reported experiencing a very particular political tension. One mayor saw his council moving from party control to independent control after his election as providing only part of a solution to seeking a good working relationship between mayor and council. He reported that the previous administration had reacted 'hatefully' to his election and that the leader of the council had refused to vacate his office to provide the mayor with the office space he needed. The majority party had operated to block mayoral policy and to 'discredit him and the independent cause'. When independents secured control of the council the political environment changed but, as the mayor commented, 'the independents truly act as independents, rather than as a group; they all take up an individual position on an issue and just because they are independent I cannot guarantee they will support me'.

Another independent mayor, backed by a political association with a small number of council seats, admitted the association's councillors acted in a way that resembled a proper group – although they did not impose a whip. They did, however, look to the mayor for support, guidance and advice and to provide them with support in their council and wider political activities, particularly at election time. The need for a mutually supportive relationship was clear but, as the mayor admitted, 'there just isn't enough of them [councillors sharing his label] to make a difference and council meetings are still dominated by political parties'. He added, rather ruefully, 'it appears the electors want an independent mayor, but want parties running the council – we just have to get on with it as best we can – that's the mature approach to politics'.

Yet local politics is not just what political parties do; nor is it about how parties choose to define it. Rather, local politics, through the office of an elected mayor, is open to many comers and different interpretations of meaning and approach. The independent mayors do have a political focus, but it is one not constrained by notions of party loyalty, nor by the need to present a united and cohesive public face on the part of the mayor and fellow independent or political association councillors. Indeed, party mayors had emulated some of the practices of their independent counterparts and were finding ways of working that rested less and less on old notions of rigid party boundaries and public unity within the party.

The political focus of the independent mayor, even when faced with an independent-controlled council, is turned outward from the council almost by definition and inclination. An independent mayor faced with a council controlled by one political party and with few independent councillors admitted to:

> getting on very well now with all the parties ... which is just what I said to them from day one ... but I try to keep out of the party politics to be honest ... also, I'm very much decide on the issue as to how I will approach it: sometimes I go along with the public and they with me, other times not. There is always more than one side to a story and you will always find some people backing you and happy and others not.

Independent mayoral politics is inherently more complex than party politics in that it demands a constant search for support for aspects of mayoral policy, rather than guaranteed support from a bloc of councillors to a comprehensive policy platform. Independent mayors are required to build political support for their approach and policies and cannot take such support for granted.

What all the independent mayors reported, however, was that, whatever the state of the parties and the reaction from them, things were working: policy frameworks were set; mayoral initiatives were pursued and duly scrutinised; decisions were made; difficult budget negotiations were conducted and concluded between mayor and parties; and political compromise was sought and achieved. This is not to give an overly rosy picture; the independent mayors did report that some councillors in the political parties had yet to come to terms with mayoral governance and that blocking and obstruction, rather than robust and genuine scrutiny, were often experienced. As one mayor stated: 'Some councillors still don't like the idea of an elected mayor; it offends them and they will do what they can to oppose me, and I suspect any mayor. Although one of their lot would probably have an easier ride as mayor'. Another commented: 'Labour are doing nothing, just sitting back and waiting to win the mayoralty'.

Independent mayors, while experiencing political difficulties over specific issues, and some obstructiveness from one or all political parties on the council, did not equate this with preventing the effective operation of mayoral governance. Neither did they report problems caused by political dynamics and relationships in developing a range of external networks and integrating themselves into broader governance networks beyond the council. This is partly because political parties are so focused on the running of the council that they fail to recognise such broader governance activities. In addition, what the mayor does outside the council is safe territory, as it does not reflect on councillors or a party's stewardship of the council and its services.

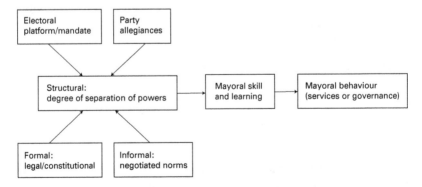

Figure 3.1 Factors affecting the development of mayoral governance.

The way in which English mayors develop is related to the nature and degree of the separation of powers at the local level and to their ideological world view. Moreover, that ideological world view will also reflect the mayor's membership of a political party or his or her independent status; party mayors, however, despite party political differences, will share interpretations and meanings assigned to concepts such as democracy, representation, citizen participation and the role of the political party in local affairs. Yet mayors as individuals will have different levels of skill and personal qualities when it comes to learning from their experiences and the pressure of the post. That ability to learn will help them navigate the formal structure within which they find themselves and adapt to the political culture of the council with which they find themselves working. The whole process is set out diagrammatically in Figure 3.1. The process set out in the model forms the basis of the discussion in the next chapter.

Conclusions

Councillors in England have, over time, seen their role as a political representative submerged beneath the responsibility they have for monitoring and maintaining the provision of important public services. Indeed, the majority of their time is spent in meetings focused on those services.[35] Political leadership, on the other hand, is something that has not been an expectation, or a requirement, of our local elected representatives. That is not to say that many council leaders have not developed a high local or national political profile. Some have, and have acted in a leadership capacity of a very specific political nature. Names from the 1980s such as Derek Hatton in Liverpool, Ken Livingstone at the GLC, Ted Knight and Linda Bellos in Lambeth, David Blunkett in Sheffield, Eric Pickles in Bradford, Shirley Porter in Westminster and Paul Beresford at Wandsworth all gained notoriety locally and nationally as leaders of a party political kind.

Such high-profile local political leaders are a rarity in the English context. Most of what passes for political leadership in local government is in reality organisational leadership with a party political tinge – a form of overview and direction to the managerial and service provision process. While the current big idea for local politics is political leadership, the concept has been rather poorly defined by the government in its modernising agenda. The findings from empirical research into local political leadership brings us to the conclusion that, while there are criteria for judging its existence and effectiveness, it is largely understood in terms of what local political leaders do rather than what they should or could be doing.

Coupled to this is the need to contextualise local political leadership within the separation of powers at the local level introduced by the 2000 Act. That separation, and the checks and balances within it, set the boundaries within which the elected mayor operates. It is the political style and political focus of the mayor that will determine whether the separation of powers acts as a constraint on mayoral initiative or whether the mayor is able to rise above those constraints to provide clear, visible and accountable leadership to the locality.

The concept of political leadership is one which helps to reconnect local elected representatives with their political roots and their role as a representative within a democratic system. Councillors are to be leaders of the communities based within the wards or divisions they represent; council leaders and elected mayors are to provide broader political leadership and to take a governing perspective across the whole of the authority area and, indeed, to extend beyond it. Thus, the two geographical dimensions of English local government – the ward/division and the authority – have elected representatives to 'lead' within their own areas.

Common factors have emerged from the experiences of England's elected mayors in the development of the role of a political leader:

- the need to accommodate the power of the political party group of councillors;
- where the political composition of the council dictates, developing political leadership based on creating alliances or coalitions of support around specific political problems or mayoral initiatives;
- where the political composition of the council dictates, managing the tensions and dynamics of a large party group of councillors;
- creating a cohesive cabinet with a focus on mayoral initiative and policy;
- developing networks of general mayoral support across the community;
- integrating into wider networks of governance beyond the boundaries of the authority;
- developing and maintaining a high public political profile;
- facing the need to lead and govern the community while also leading the service-oriented organisation that is the council.

Mayors in England do face the dual pressure to provide high-profile local political leadership and to act in a governing capacity across the locality, set against the need to lead a bureaucracy charged with providing a range of important public services. The dual pressure between governing and leading an area and controlling a bureaucracy is not a false dichotomy, as the mayor must balance the tensions and pressures of these two roles and the competing directions in which they may be pulling mayoral focus and initiatives. It is the mayoral dichotomy of running council services and governing a locality that the next chapter explores.

Notes

1 Judge, D., 1999. *Representation: Theory and Practice in Britain*, London, Routledge.
2 Young, K., 1975. *Local Politics and the Rise of Party: The London Municipal Society and the Conservative Intervention in Local Elections, 1894–1963*, Leicester University Press; Copus, C., 2004. *Party Politics and Local Government*, Manchester University Press.
3 Stanyer, J., 1970. 'Social and Rational Models of Man: Alternative Approaches to the Study of Local Elections', *Advancement of Science*, Vol. 26, pp. 399–407; Rallings, C. and M. Thrasher, 1997. *Local Elections in Britain*, London, Routledge; Parry, G., G. Moyser and N. Day, 1992. *Political Participation and Democracy in Britain*, Cambridge University Press; Copus, C., 1998. 'The Councillor: Representing a Locality and the Party Group', *Local Governance*, Vol. 24, No. 3, Autumn, pp. 215–224.
4 Cochrane, A., 1986. 'Community Politics and Democracy', in D. Held and C. Pollit (eds), *New Forms of Democracy*, London, Sage, pp. 51–77; Held, D., 1993. *Models of Democracy*, Cambridge, Polity Press.
5 Ostrogorski, M., 1902. *Democracy and the Organisation of Political Parties, Vols I and II*, New York, Macmillan.
6 Blair, T., 1998. *Leading the Way: A New Vision for Local Government*, London, Institute of Public Policy Research.
7 DETR, 1998. *Modern Local Government: In Touch with the People*, London, DETR, para. 3.7.
8 Rhodes, R., 1997. *Understanding Governance: Policy Networks, Governance, Reflexivity and Accountability*, Open University Press; Stewart, J., 2003. *Modernising British Local Government: An Assessment of Labour's Reform Programme*, Basingstoke, Palgrave Macmillan.
9 Sullivan, H. and C. Skelcher, 2002. *Working Across Boundaries: Partnerships in the Public Sector*, Basingstoke, Palgrave Macmillan.
10 Young, K. and N. Rao, 1997. *Local Government Since 1945*, Oxford, Basil Blackwell.
11 Kotter, J.P. and P. Lawrence, 1974. *Mayors in Action: Five Approaches to Urban Governance*, London, John Wiley.
12 *Ibid.*, pp. 105–121.
13 Stone, C., 1995. 'Political Leadership in Urban Politics', in D. Judge, G. Stoker and H. Wolman (eds), *Theories of Urban Politics*, London, Sage, pp. 96–116.
14 Svara, J., 1990. *Official Leadership in the City: Patterns of Conflict and Co-operation*, Oxford University Press; Svara, J., 1994. *Facilitative Leadership in Local Government: Lessons from Successful Mayors and Chairpersons*, San Francisco, CA, Jossey-Bass; Mouritzen, P.E. and J. Svara, 2002. *Leadership at the Apex: Politicians and Administrators in Western Local Governments*, University of Pittsburgh Press; Frederickson, H.G., G. Johnson and C. Wood,

2004. *The Adapted City: Institutional Dynamics and Structural Change*, New York, Sharpe.

15 Morgan, D. and S. Watson, 1996. 'Mayors of American Cities: An Analysis of Powers and Responsibilities', *American Review of Public Administration*, Vol. 26, No. 1, March, pp. 113–125.

16 Svara, *Official Leadership in the City*.

17 Hambleton, R. and D. Sweeting, 2004. 'U.S. Style Leadership for English Local Government', *Public Administration Review*, Vol. 64, No. 4, July/August, pp. 474–488.

18 Copus, *Party Politics and Local Government*, chapters 5 and 9.

19 Leach, S. and D. Wilson, 2000. *Local Political Leadership*, Bristol, Policy Press.

20 *Ibid.*, p. 11.

21 To this end Leach and Wilson (*ibid.*) cite Dunleavy, P., K. Dowding and H. Margetts, 1995. 'Regime Politics in London Local Government', paper presented to the ESRC Local Governance Programme Conference, Exeter; and Harding, A., 2000. 'Regime Formation in Manchester and Edinburgh', in G. Stoker (ed.), *The New Politics of British Local Governance*, Basingstoke, Macmillan, pp. 54–71.

22 Sullivan and Skelcher, *Working Across Boundaries*.

23 Randle, A., 2004. *Mayors Mid-Term: Lessons from the First Eighteen Months of Directly Elected Mayors*, London, New Local Government Network.

24 Stoker, G., 2004. *How Are Mayors Measuring Up? Preliminary Findings – ELG Team*, London, ODPM, table 2, pp. 16–17.

25 Copus, C., 1999. 'The Attitudes of Councillors Since Widdicombe: A Focus on Democratic Engagement', *Public Policy and Administration*, Vol. 14, No. 4, pp. 87–100; Copus, C., 2000. 'Community, Party and the Crisis of Representation', in N. Rao (ed.), *Representation and Community in Western Democracies*, London, Macmillan, 2000, pp. 93–113.

26 Batley, R. and A. Campbell (eds), 1992. *The Political Executive: Politicians and Management in European Local Government*, London, Frank Cass.

27 Leach, S. and C. Copus, 2004. 'Scrutiny and the Political Party Group in UK Local Government: New Models of Behaviour', *Public Administration*, Vol. 82, No. 2, pp. 331–354; Copus, *Party Politics and Local Government*.

28 Lowndes, V. and S. Leach, 2004. 'Understanding Local Political Leadership: Constitutions, Contexts and Capabilities', *Local Government Studies*, Special Edition, Vol. 30, No. 4, pp. 557–575.

29 Eulau, H., J. Whalke, W. Buchanan and L. Ferguson, 1959. 'The Role of the Representative: Some Empirical Observations on the Theory of Edmund Burke', *American Political Science Review*, Vol. 53, No. 3, September, pp. 742–756.

30 Jones, G.W., 1975. 'Varieties of Local Politics', *Local Government Studies*, Vol. 1, No. 2, pp. 17–32.

31 Glassberg, A., 1981. *Representation and Urban Community*, London, Macmillan.

32 Copus, *Party Politics and Local Government*.

33 Labour Party, 2001, updated 2002. *Labour Group Model Standing Orders*, London, Labour Party.

34 Conservative Party, 1998, revised 2001. *Conservative Council Groups: Draft Model Rules*, London, Conservative Party; ALDC 2000, updated 2001. *Model Standing Orders for Liberal Democrat Council Groups*, Hebden Bridge, ALDC.

35 Committee on the Management of Local Government, 1967. *Research, Vol. II: The Local Government Councillor*, London, HMSO; Committee of Inquiry into the Conduct of Local Authority Business, 1986. *Research, Vol. II: The Local Government Councillor*, London, HMSO; Young, K. and N. Rao, 1994. *Coming to Terms with Change: The Local Government Councillor in 1993*, York, Joseph Rowntree Foundation.

4

Running the council or leading the community? A mayoral dichotomy

Introduction

As we saw in the last chapter, three factors affect the development of the roles and responsibilities of the English directly elected mayor: first, the separation of powers at the local level; second, mayoral political focus; and third, the mayoral dichotomy between political leadership of a locality and the running of a service-based bureaucracy. The mayoral dichotomy arises because governance and organisational concerns represent two distinct demands on mayoral attention. They are not, though, mutually incompatible: political governance can be enhanced through organisational leadership and capacity, but only if the mayor is leading and not managing the public service bureaucracy.

While an elected mayor can choose to focus on political governance or organisational leadership, the mayor will, by circumstances and pressures exerted from central government, other agencies and the public, be pulled into focusing more on one than the other. The successful mayor of course must keep these two sides in balance. Even though the elected mayor was then a new political office, those elected in 2002 did not start work in a context-free environment. Rather they took office at a time when predetermined policy constraints and the complexities of service delivery would limit their initial influence and ability to effect radical change in either governance or control of the public bureaucracy. Mayoral councils, as all others, must develop strategies to promote service improvement over a varied time scale. Some issues demand fairly straightforward, short-term solutions, which simply require the political will and tenacity to see them through. Others require a medium- or long-term strategic plan to deal with complex, cross-cutting concerns about quality and cost; some of these concerns will extend beyond the responsibility of the council itself.

Yet the long-term strategic planning required for the delivery and improvement of public services, and the political skill to achieve that vision, has a technocratic edge to it, and when running and providing public services the input of any elected representative is optional rather than necessary. Services can be run without political input and control, but, because our local government is synonymous with service delivery, politicians elected locally will become bound up with services. Local government is, rightly or wrongly, about public services and the political and managerial processes are therefore inextricably linked – to such a degree that some present the notion that community governance and leadership can come about only if local government has a major role in providing services.[1]

This chapter explores the way in which English directly elected mayors have so far dealt with the competing, but linked, pressures of providing political leadership and governance to communities while also ensuring the provision of important public services. The next section explores how the tensions between political governance and service provision have manifested themselves for the English elected mayors and how the mayors have come to terms with balancing those tensions. The following section looks at mayoral focus on service concerns and examines the pressures on mayors that may lead them to become embroiled in the organisational and management concerns of the council, at the cost of a new style of local political leadership. The chapter concludes by drawing out the lessons for mayors when it comes to balancing organisational and political leadership.

Reconciling competing pressures

In the 2002 mayoral elections, a mix of candidates standing on an anti-council or anti-local political elite platform and those more closely linked to the council (pro-local political elite) were elected and took from their election a signal of public either disquiet or satisfaction with the state of the local council. While all mayors recognised the role that the council played in service provision, they also displayed recognition that the council was only one part of a complex web of institutional arrangements and relationships that were responsible for providing services and thereby affecting the local quality of life. Mayors were acutely aware of the need to look beyond what the council could do, to working with other agencies; even those who had little or no local government experience recognised the need to draw on the resources of a range of bodies to tackle local problems.

In Middlesbrough Ray Mallon – former Cleveland Police Superintendent – stood on an anti-crime platform and after election focused heavily on the relationship between the council and the police, as well as other agencies involved in crime reduction. He has worked across institutional boundaries to tackle crime and disorder issues, but has not had to rely only on the police for his initiatives. The mayor has also been able to deploy community wardens (known in the area as 'Robocop's army') and anti-social behaviour wardens to improve the local quality of life and reduce crime and the fear of it. Yet the English mayor, including the mayor of London, does not have direct powers over the local police as do his or her big-city US counterparts, or even the level of control over local police that some Latin American elected mayors enjoy.[2] Independent Stuart Drummond in Hartlepool also worked with the police, fire brigade and probation service on crime and disorder issues in 'Operation Clean Sweep', in which a range of organisations were brought together, on the mayor's initiative, to focus on visible environmental improvements in specific areas of Hartlepool.

The mayor of Doncaster has launched an initiative to clear the streets of litter and abandoned cars, and has focused on the regional development agency as a key partner in service-delivery matters. The mayor of Mansfield has focused on economic regeneration and the creation of employment opportunities; he set out his four-year plan in this regard on a DVD which presents a mayoral vision for Mansfield – a vision which crosses a range of institutions dedicated to providing services. The mayor of Newham tied his political support to the successful London Olympic bid, which was linked with improving leisure facilities within the borough, which is set to be a major host for the Games in 2012. The mayoral initiative focused on encouraging the participation of children in experiencing first-hand the range of sporting events to be held. Some 63,000 sporting activities were undertaken by children in the borough over the course of a year, and swimming in municipal pools was made free for children over the summer of 2004 as part of linking the Olympic bid to tangible service improvements for local people.

None of these examples, however, is specific to a directly elected mayor – council leaders could conduct such negotiations and many indeed are focusing on how to work alongside a range of service providers. What is clear from mayoral initiatives, however, is that public services are at the centre of what they are doing; furthermore, the range of services with which they are engaging extends beyond the responsibility of the council. Again, there is nothing unique here to the directly elected mayor, save that an individual with a direct authority-wide mandate can speak to a range of organisations with a greater degree of legitimacy than a council leader, yet the mayor does not have the power to control or direct other agencies. The service agenda for the mayor is about long-term development and strategies to bring together a range of agencies to promote and improve the broad quality of life of local citizens: a political objective. Yet again, we see that there is nothing here that is special to an elected mayor, except that action which rests on the mayoral office does stem from a broader governing mandate and recognition among stakeholders of the value of working with the mayor. What differs for the mayor is the feeling that he or she, as one mayor put it, 'can get things done, without interminable and dense committee meetings pouring over the details'. He went on to add 'I can set a ball rolling and see where it goes'.

So the picture emerging of the English mayor is one just as focused on public services, on quality-of-life issues and on the quality of council provision as that of any other local councillor or council leader. What is it, then, that distinguishes the processes of politics, government and representation from the management of public services? Can a mayor govern without control of services? The answer to the latter question lies in the power of the office of mayor as a political agency, rather than in the institutional arrangement for providing services. In other words, can mayors govern as independent political agents with political power to make things happen, or do they govern through what they provide and how they negotiate with other providers?

Mayors do identify themselves as 'in charge' of a large, multifaceted organisation and as being responsible for a range of services, and recognise that, in the public mind, both the council and the mayor are closely linked with the quality and effectiveness of those services. Yet they also recognise that they have a much broader political and governing role, which extends beyond concerns for services, whether provided by the council or some other agency. One mayor summed up the position thus:

> If we define ourselves by the way our councils deliver services there will be little opportunity to exploit our new role. I am not just the mayor of the council: I am the mayor of the whole borough and the added value of the new system will come as much outside the town hall as it does inside.... Neither must I neglect my role as a politician. Elected mayors will be seen as the leaders of their local parties to an extent that leaders of party groups rarely were.

As suggested by the last point, the pressure to run the council and to be identified with the quality of council services remains. As one mayor commented:

> It always comes back to what the council does; if we don't deliver on the street and if we don't improve education, housing, or services to the elderly, then we can fail because that is what the public will judge us [mayors] on. We [mayors] have to find new ways of working though; we have to use the political leverage; we have to try new things and to be at the very front of our communities. I'm not just the boss of the council; I represent the whole of [the borough].

Another mayor added:

> Yes, it's about a broad remit to get on with things and to talk to as many people and organisations as possible, but I have to be careful. I can't say

to someone outside the council – you must improve X and this is how to do it and they reply 'Oh yes and you got a "bad" [overall service grading] in the CPA' [Comprehensive Performance Assessment – see below]. You must have your own house in order to encourage improvement elsewhere. It's also about consultation and communication; I'm proud of the way in which we involve people in council services and policy and I say to others, like the NHS and police, that they should be doing that as well – leading by example and from the front.

What we see here is not service concerns smothering the governing role of the mayor. Rather, council services are being used as a political tool to bring about change elsewhere. There is still a danger, however, that mayors are drawn too closely into the running of the administrative and management machine and thus into specific managerial concerns, rather than focusing on political leadership and the processes of governance. As one mayor summed it up, 'They [the officers] seem to come to me for everything; I just want them to get on with running their departments and let me get on with what I was elected to do: think and act like a politician'. However, not all mayors agree. As one commented: 'I'm not a politician; that's what the councillors are for'.

The tension between political responsibility for public services and a broader governing responsibility is clearly seen in the way in which mayors have formed their cabinet and allocated portfolios to cabinet members. While individual mayors have constructed cabinets unique to their own requirements, certain trends have emerged. Three types of configuration of cabinet and portfolios emerge: first, those cabinets with portfolios clearly tied to service areas; second, those where the predominant tendency is

Table 4.1 Mayors' cabinet portfolios (pre-May 2004 local elections and 2005 mayoral elections)

Council	Size of cabinet (including the mayor)	Portfolios		
		Mainly service based	Mainly cross-cutting and governance	Mixed approach
Bedford	10			♦
Doncaster	10			♦
Hackney	9		♦	
Hartlepool	7		♦	
Lewisham	10		♦	
Mansfield	7	♦		
Middlesbrough	10	♦		
Newham	10		♦	
North Tyneside	9	♦		
Watford	5	♦		

for cross-cutting portfolios linked to broader issues of governance; and third, a mix of service-based and political governance portfolios. Table 4.1 shows the mayoral approach to portfolio allocation.

Whether the mayor takes a portfolio is very much a personal choice, but one driven by political priorities. Three mayors had taken on a portfolio: the mayor of Lewisham, for regeneration; the mayor of Hartlepool, for 'liveability'; and the mayor of Bedford, for economic development, regeneration and land and property (one portfolio). These mayors gave particular priority to the area covered by the portfolio they had decided to hold within the mayoral office. Others have preferred to remain, in the words of one mayor, 'unencumbered by worrying about a department'. In only three authorities did the deputy mayor have a specific portfolio. In two authorities a series of mayoral advisers operated outside the cabinet (and outside overview and scrutiny), both as a mayoral policy resource and as a way of linking the mayor and cabinet more firmly into the rest of a very large political group on the council.

The mayoral cabinet portfolios only in part reflect mayoral preference for a governing perspective or a service focus. The portfolios also reflect the needs of the council officers for a clear line of reporting responsibility and accountability, and the organisational need for a point of reference when it comes to decision-making. A further pressure exists when it comes to mayors creating cabinets. As one mayor summed it up: 'I was surprised by how much the CPA results dictated what I should do with my cabinet'. The results of the Comprehensive Performance Assessment (CPA), the grade given to each authority by the Audit Commission within the CPA, and whether an authority is part of a government-monitored recovery programme can and do act as a tremendous pull on the way in which the mayor wishes to govern and the focus he or she can place on improving service performance or developing a governing mandate through political leadership of the community.

While the CPA involves an assessment of council services, it also assesses the effectiveness of the governance arrangements and it is here that the individual mayor comes into his or her own. An Audit Commission report into Middlesbrough's new mayoral government concluded that the mayoral system there was successful primarily due to the calibre of the mayor and the subsequent support he received from councillors, officers, partners and, most importantly, local people.[3] In Hackney the Audit Commission recognised the high level of commitment from the mayor and councillors to improving the council's performance and that they had 'begun to develop into an effective body that can formulate longer term policy and plans and focus on their implementation'.[4]

The assessment the mayor and mayoral arrangements receive from such external inspections may not of course be reflected in the overall assessment of the council. Such government-inspired external audits, from CPA to OFSTED inspections, have a profound effect on the mayoral focus and can serve to draw mayors away from notions of governing and towards managing a large public bureaucracy. The CPA assesses not only a council's current performance but also its capacity to improve that performance. The assessment is based on six service blocks, depending on the type of council. Services are graded excellent, good, fair, weak, or poor, and different services from the same council can sit in different categories. The council is also given an overall grading. It is the corporate assessment which judges the ability of the council to improve its performance.[5]

Yet such assessments of the complex processes of local government are arbitrary and fail to reflect the realities of community life, service demands and, most importantly, the political realities of life on any one council. They do, however, have the power to deflect local authorities, mayors and councillors from identifying and responding to community priorities and, vitally, limit the willingness of elected representatives to experiment in developing new forms of political leadership.

The CPA results for the mayoral authorities are set out in Table 4.2.

Mayors reported that the CPAs and the final results of those assessments fix their attention and that of councillors and officers on the notion of continual service improvement, and that when faced with a low grading the CPA acts as a magnet drawing focus away from the idea of governance and political leadership. Moreover, they reported that the council became fixed on the issues drawn out by inspectors, rather

Table 4.2 The results of Comprehensive Performance Assessments in mayoral authorities, 2002–4

Council	2002	2003	2004
Doncaster	Fair	Fair	Good
Hackney	Poor	Poor	Weak
Hartlepool	Excellent	Excellent	Excellent
Lewisham	Good	Good	Good
Middlesborough	Good	Good	Good
Newham	Fair	Good	Good
North Tyneside	Poor	Poor	Fair
Stoke-on-Trent	Fair	Fair	Good
Bedford	–	–	Good
Mansfield	–	–	Weak
Watford	–	–	Weak

Note: A number of authorities, such as Hackney and North Tyneside, have greatly improved their positions, as recorded in Audit Commission re-inspection reports, which are not reflected in the figures above.

than on more pressing local concerns. Mayors and councils can thereby be prevented from using their role as a service-based organisation as a tool for governance and become trapped by the need to focus on managerial specifics. The mayors were, however, conscious of this and to some degree had all developed tactics to avoid this trap. As one stated: 'You can't get away from the CPA. But you don't have to be obsessed by it; that's up to the officers!'

The CPA, coupled with the executive's responsibility for leading the search for best value, places a profound stress on the direction that mayoral governance can take.[6] It can distort the priorities of the mayor and the processes of political leadership; all external assessment, however good its intention, removes autonomy from local government – whether mayoral or not. While mayors clearly recognise the pressure they are exposed to by external audits of one sort or another, they also recognise that if the office of elected mayor is to change the nature of local governance and the relationship between councils and citizens, not only must mayors drive the political and public service agenda, taking governing decisions that reflect political and public priorities, but they must also be seen to be doing so. In developing a new perspective on political leadership and balancing that with public service provision, mayors are not working alone, but alongside the councillors serving on mayoral authorities.

Councillors: a perspective on governing and service provision

Councillors sitting on each of the mayoral authorities (excluding the London Assembly) were asked to respond to a questionnaire survey. Stoke-on-Trent was excluded from the survey because many of the questions were not appropriate for that mayor and council manager system. A total of 531 questionnaires were circulated and 253 returned and usable for the analysis, giving a response rate of 48 per cent.

Councillors were asked a number of questions about their experiences of working alongside an elected mayor. The main results of the findings are set out in Chapter 8, but a number of the questions sought to explore how councillors saw the elected mayor's role in relation to service provision and quality, as well as the wider concerns for political leadership of the local community, and how the mayor should balance these two facets, and these results are reported here. It was made clear that the statements in this section of the questionnaire were about the political office of the directly elected mayor and not about the current holder of that office.

Councillors were presented with a number of statements and were asked to express levels of agreement (agree, agree strongly, disagree, disagree strongly) with how important it was for the elected mayor:

- to govern the local authority area;
- to ensure the council provides high-quality services;
- to represent the interests of the people of the area;
- to negotiate with organisations outside the council;
- to provide clear, high-profile and visible political leadership to the area.

They were also asked to indicate their level of agreement to the following two statements:

- The mayor does not spend enough time running council services.
- The mayor spends too much time thinking about issues outside the council's remit.

Tables 4.3 and 4.4 present the responses received from councillors, by party. The figures do not necessarily total to 100 per cent because of rounding and removing the neutral response option from the tables. The aggregated 'agree' and 'disagree' responses are shown because the results were heavily skewed in that direction.

Table 4.3 indicates a high level of agreement among councillors that it is important for an elected mayor to play a part in the governance of the locality. Conservative and Labour councillors, and to a slightly lesser degree independents, shared the view that the mayor has an important governing role to play; Liberal Democrats were markedly less convinced that this was so.

What is clear from Table 4.3 is that the councillors believed that elected mayors should be heavily focused on the quality of the public services provided by the council. There is little room for ambiguity or doubt in the responses councillors gave to this issue and it reflects the long-standing relationship between councillors and their role in the provision of services. The responses also indicate that councillors were willing to share this role with a mayor and, indeed, that it was deemed somewhat more important for a mayor to focus on services than on governing an area.

Interviews with councillors conducted for this book underpinned the questionnaire results and indicated that councillors inextricably linked their role in service provision to notions of government and representation; for councillors, politics is about public services, and councils govern through services. Thus, they expect mayors to follow this long-standing approach to local politics and to focus on service concerns. There was little difference between the parties when it came to this aspect of mayoral activity.

One Labour councillor commented in interview: 'We provide services that are important to people's day-to-day life; some are vital, like

Table 4.3 Percentage of councillors agreeing and disagreeing with statements regarding important roles of the mayor, by party affiliation

Statements and party	Agree	Disagree
An important role of the mayor is to govern the local authority area		
Conservative	78	7
Labour	71	12
Liberal Democrat	45	24
Independent	60	19
An important role of the mayor is to ensure the council provides high-quality services		
Conservative	100	0
Labour	90	10
Liberal Democrat	93	7
Independent	82	18
An important role of the mayor is to represent the interests of the people of the area		
Conservative	86	0
Labour	90	6
Liberal Democrat	84	3
Independent	82	12
An important role of the mayor is to negotiate with organisations outside the council		
Conservative	72	7
Labour	78	8
Liberal Democrat	90	7
Independent	88	6
An important role of the mayor is to provide clear, high-profile and visible political leadership to the area		
Conservative	50	29
Labour	77	11
Liberal Democrat	72	22
Independent	65	29

education, social services and housing. The mayor must work to improve all those services.'

A Liberal Democrat councillor added:

> I'm not really sure what political leadership means, or if it's the right thing for us to be doing. But I know when one of my constituents can't get a place in a care home, or the local school has a disastrous inspection; that's the sort of thing the mayor should look at.

The responses displayed in Tables 4.3, however, also show recognition among councillors that mayors have a wide political role in representing the views of the entire council's electorate and range of communities. Moreover, the mayor was recognised as the public face of the council, particularly in negotiating and working alongside stakeholders and other agencies. Yet again, there is little to distinguish between councillors from different political parties in this regard, save that Labour councillors had marginally stronger views on the importance of the mayor in representing the interests of the whole community, and Liberal Democrats outstripped their Conservative, Labour and independent counterparts when it came to the mayor negotiating with other organisations. But these results reflect degrees rather than differences of opinion.

It is on the question of the importance of the mayor's role in providing high-profile political leadership to the locality that we start to see some divergence in opinion between the parties, as shown in Table 4.3. Here a divergence emerged between the views of Conservative councillors, who were less convinced that the mayor should have such a role, and those of the Labour and Liberal Democrat councillors. Independents, while not as sceptical as Conservatives on the matter, did not wholly share the feelings of most Labour and Liberal Democrat councillors.

A Conservative councillor summed up the views of some of his fellow councillors thus: 'Governments provide political leadership; councils are responsible for local services'. Not all Conservatives were of this view, however, as one councillor commented:

> If we are going to have a mayor there is no point in him getting bogged down in all the things the council does. They have to rise above that and provide strong leadership, much like a company director; you wouldn't expect the director to spend all day on the production line making boxes, would you?

Table 4.4 indicates that councillors had differing views about the amount of time the mayor gave to the running of services, but a majority (with Labour indicating the greatest satisfaction with the time allocation) felt that the time mayors invested in running services was about right. Again, though, in the mind of the councillor council services are a clear focus for mayoral attention.

The results displayed in Table 4.4 also show that the councillors across the political spectrum had different views about the allocation of mayoral time to matters other than the services the council provides. While a majority of Conservative and Labour councillors felt it was the case that the mayor did not spend too much time away from council services, Liberal Democrat and independent councillors were more evenly divided on the matter.

The responses tell us that councillors recognise that the elected mayor has an important role in governing the locality, except that Liberal

Table 4.4 Percentage of councillors agreeing and disagreeing with statements regarding mayoral priorities

Statement and party	Agree	Disagree
The mayor does not spend enough time running council services		
Conservative	46	43
Labour	18	67
Liberal Democrat	34	48
Independent	35	53
The mayor spends too much time thinking about issues outside the council's remit		
Conservative	31	50
Labour	17	56
Liberal Democrat	21	24
Independent	35	47

Democrats are less convinced about the importance of this to a mayor than other councillors. Moreover, there is also recognition of the important external focus to the mayor's activities as a broad political actor. Conservative councillors, however, do appear to balk somewhat at the notion of the mayor as a political leader. As with other national surveys, political affiliation does appear to be a discriminator of councillor opinion, at least on some aspects of the importance of the various facets of mayoral activity.[7]

The responses also tell us a lot about the way in which councillors respond to certain key terms and how they interpret those terms. On the one hand, in relation to mayoral government, phrases like 'represent the interests of the people of the area' and 'negotiate with organisations outside the council' elicited high levels of support from councillors across the political spectrum. One the other hand, phrases like 'govern an area' and 'high-profile and visible political leadership' saw distinctions between the parties become more acute. These distinctions rest on interpretations of those phrases and on what councillors from a certain political perspective felt the role of an elected mayor should be. Interestingly, very high levels of agreement existed across the parties and independents to the idea that the mayor should be focused on council services. Thus, local politics – even in mayoral systems – is about running services.

In interview, councillors displayed unease at the tension that exists between a politically representative role for both themselves and the mayor and the processes of providing and overseeing council services. Councillors recognised themselves and mayors as politicians but many did not clearly articulate what that means. Being a councillor for many was about a close involvement in running the council and the services it provides. As one long-standing Labour councillor said:

> Councils do things; we provide for services for people. All these quangos have taken away our role and taken away democratic control of services. All these partnerships and the LSP shouldn't be there – it's the council that should be doing these things. We had real power thirty years ago, ran things and it's all been taken away. I've seen the borough become little more than a parish council over the years.

Yet many councillors also recognised that the political leadership provided by the mayor, far from eroding the position of the council, strengthened local democracy and enhanced local representation. Echoing the words of a mayor quoted above, a Labour councillor from another authority articulated a view about political leadership that was shared by some Conservatives and Liberal Democrats:

> I feel we got into too much detail about this or that area and still do to some extent; that detail keeps us away from developing a broader, more political perspective on being a councillor. We have a mayor, which I supported, and he is there to lead not only the council but to provide leadership across the entire community. Our job is to make sure he does his job. It's much more exciting because I can stay involved in all those things I was involved in before being elected to the council, but up until we had a mayor I was expected to forget about, because they weren't about what the council does.

The tension between service provision and governing/political leadership is as clear for councillors as it is for elected mayors. But for mayors who become too immersed in service minutiae the consequences are stark: they will be unable to develop a broader focus on the needs of the community and the area, and they will fail to provide that political leadership in which elected mayors overseas specialise. Indeed, the mayor and manager model which exists in New Zealand (Stoke-on-Trent has a similar model) is designed so that the mayor provides that focus for community leadership and acts as a figure-head for the council and community, while the council manager and council focus on the running of council services. Indeed, the New Zealand elected mayor has been described as both 'powerful and powerless'. While sub-national government in New Zealand is more closely connected to a wider range of services than the English council, from police to involvement in gas supply, it is the council and not the mayor that plays the main role in service provision. The mayor's powers come from being directly elected as the 'recognised community leader'.[8] Indeed, while the role of the council manager and council are defined in New Zealand law, the role of the mayor is not.[9]

While the English mayor's powers and responsibilities in relation to the functions of the council, the services it provides and the legal responsibilities it has are defined in law, unlike the New Zealand counterpart, the role that the English mayor plays in being a political leader is less well defined; mayors must define that political leadership role for themselves and distinguish it from public service concerns. Moreover, elected mayors must also balance providing political leadership with organisational leadership of the council.

Elected mayors and organisational leadership

The English elected mayors view the role of a mayor and the focus he or she should take in very different ways. Lowndes and Leach found that they also approached the whole notion of political leadership in diverse ways: some emphasised long-term strategy whereas others operated with short-term 'disconnected priorities'; some prioritised external networking, while for others this had become marginalised in the face of other contextual challenges (notably CPA).[10]

The tension between external networking and running a council represents another balancing act the mayor must undertake: how much of the leadership process is political and fixed outside the council, and how much is organisational and fixed on a form of political–managerial leadership? Moreover, do mayors want to be seen as in control of a large public bureaucracy and managing its activities, or do they want to be seen as a politician in control of, or at least influencing, broader events on a local, regional and even national stage? As Lowndes and Leach identified, the answer is complex and not necessarily the mayor's alone to develop – as external pressures and context will influence the allocation of mayoral time and focus. Mayors, however, need to guard against becoming the prisoner of organisational demands and externally imposed contexts if they are to develop their own policy and initiatives.

The English mayor does have a dual leadership role to play, and political and organisational factors will interact to influence how the mayor acts in these two distinct but interrelated capacities. English mayors are placing varying degrees of emphasis on each to suit their own political and personal agenda. One way of identifying the organisational leadership role and control of the public bureaucracy is to see whether the mayor instigates or presides over any major reorganisation of the council officer structure. To indicate mayoral power over that officer reorganisation, it must be controlled by the mayor and rest on high levels of mayoral involvement, rather than be a restructuring instigated by the chief executive to suit officer convenience within the new governance arrangements.

Reorganising the machine

The English mayors have shown different levels of interest and involvement in stamping their control (by restructuring) over the organisation that is the council. Three trends have emerged in relation to structural reorganisations in mayoral authorities: those instigated and controlled by the mayor; those occurring as a result of officer initiative, with the mayor playing a minor role in the process; and those contingent reorganisations driven by circumstances with control shared by mayor and chief officers. The discussion here focuses on the three mayors who have strongly felt a need to stamp some form of political authority over the council: these three admitted to being determined to pursue a reorganisation of the officer structure to suit mayoral policy and priorities, and to tie that structure into the council cabinet. One stated:

> From the very outset I wanted to get this [council structure] right. I sat down with the chief executive a few days after the election and told him what I wanted; he filled in the details and we had a series of meetings with senior officers and cabinet members to make sure that we were supported by the council and not working at a tangent. I've pulled the political and managerial sides closely together. Also, it puts my mark down; we have a chief executive, but I'm the mayor and I head the entire council.

These mayors, sensing that council officers needed to be made aware of mayoral authority, and recognising the importance of supporting structures to achieving success in policy initiatives, sought to review council structures. They instigated, headed and gave approval to a reorganisation, but resisted temptation to become immersed in the details of departmental arrangements. As one mayor commented: 'If I'm going to take a strategic and long-term approach, I need a council that does the same, but I don't have to dot every i'. Yet mayors controlling the process also reported working very closely with the chief executive and negotiating with senior officers. Organisational leadership for the English mayor is built on compromise and leverage.

In addition, the mayor launching an organisational restructuring needs a clear and well defined set of political objectives, objectives which stretch beyond the short and medium term. Drawing together those objectives and structuring a council organisation specifically to support and pursue these secures three things for the mayor: first, it strengthens the likelihood that mayoral policy will be implemented and achieves a degree of success; second, it emphasises to council officers that the mayor provides organisational leadership alongside the chief executive; and third, it reduces a barrier between the political and managerial dimensions of local government.

In some cases mayors have questioned the need for a chief executive officer at all, realising that the office of elected mayor provides an electoral mandate not only as a political leader of the community but also as an organisational leader. The mayor, if he or she so chooses, can take on an organisational leadership role beyond that taken on by the most tenacious and administratively minded of council leaders – simply because the mayoral mandate can be interpreted, by a mayor, to grant that role. One mayor commented: 'I am seriously considering the future of the chief executive post; I am not convinced we need a chief executive with an elected mayor. We must have someone to be head of paid service, but I, as mayor, run this organisation.'

Three mayors reported that, as the council's chief executive had left shortly after the mayoral elections (stressing it was not because of those elections), they had been handed a very early opportunity to reconsider the role of the top officer post and to reconfigure relationships between officers and councillors and to develop something that matched the new political environment that an elected mayor creates. In one council the chief executive had been redesignated a 'managing director', to emphasise a subservient role to the elected mayor. In another council the title 'head of paid service' was being considered as a replacement for 'chief executive'. In another authority, where the mayor admitted to being 'consulted' rather than in control of the process of reorganisation and after years of the council working without a chief executive (under the previous leader and cabinet system), a chief executive was reintroduced. Mayors adopting a strong organisational leadership role are signalling to the council bureaucracy and the senior officer with whom they work day to day that there is a new and legitimate organisational leader in place and one that the electorate have appointed.

However, mayors – though they may conduct a structural reorganisation and review the position of the chief executive officer – do not have the power to appoint the chief executive: that is the council's role. The mayor cannot guarantee that any favoured candidate will be appointed to the post. Contrast this with the elected Italian mayor, who has the power to select and dismiss heads of offices and services and managers of the council as well as any representative on external agencies, and with the elected mayors of the two German *Länder* of Baden-Wurttemburg and Bavern, who perform the role of a powerful chief executive. Indeed, the south German elected mayor has been referred to, rather tongue in cheek, as 'an elected monarch'.[11]

While some of the English mayors have shown a marked determination to lead the council organisation, others have been less inclined to take on this role. Moreover, some do not see their role in relation to the institution that is the council at all. Intriguingly, this approach is not a result of standing for election on an anti-council platform; rather, it stems from a very clear vision that mayoral leadership should be 'political' and based on forging either temporary, single-issue alliances or broad governing coalitions outside the council. A mayor who looks beyond the confines of the council for what he or she can do does not want to be constrained too much by matters of organisational leadership. But the mayor must recognise the need to play the two roles to one degree or another. As one mayor commented:

> For the mayoral model to work it has to be more than just a super-manager of council services.... I spend a lot of time getting out and about and a lot of time working out how best to relate to my constituents. I can't do that if I'm always at the town hall.

The same mayor also admitted that when it came to the officer structure, no major changes had been instigated since the mayoral election. Rather, a realignment and a few 'minor changes' had been made to recognise the realties of the new mayoral office. He went on to suggest that major reorganisations should be avoided unless absolutely necessary, because they 'suck energy out of the organisation and distract people'; for this mayor other ways were needed to stamp authority on the council as an organisation, rather than undertaking costly and time-consuming reorganisations.

Some English mayors clearly see leadership of the council as an organisation, and a correct alignment of mayoral priorities and organisational structure, as a resource for enhancing their restricted and legislatively constrained power. Moreover, these mayors see organisational leadership as an extension of political leadership, or a merging of the two distinct processes.

One mayor from a second-tier authority admitted that:

> Because we are a district the council itself must always be looking at the county, let alone the government. But, if I use the resources of the council properly and make sure they are backing what I want to do, I can make sure the council punches above its weight in the area. I have to make sure the structure of the council is in the right place.

Thus, there has to be some congruence between long-term mayoral political vision and the organisational set-up of the council. It is vital that the latter supports the former, rather than driving mayoral priorities, focus and vision. One chief executive of a mayoral authority admitted that the organisational restructuring that took place after the election of the mayor was at his instigation and control, as the mayor did not want to be overly distracted by the process. But that was because the mayor had a very strong external focus and placed great emphasis on his work within local communities and across the borough. Yet it was vital that the officer structure supported that approach. The chief executive commented in interview: 'The infrastructure has got to be changed to support the mayoral role; the traditional infrastructure can't do that. It doesn't work so we've created something that supports our mayor and his unique approach.'

There is no settled pattern among English elected mayors as to the relationship they develop with the organisation that is the council. Some use that organisation to enhance limited mayoral influence and power; others see organisational leadership as rightfully the role of an appointed, rather than elected, official and prefer to distance themselves from the council machine; others see their role as an elected leader as giving them a legitimate organisational leadership role. One thing is clear: that the English mayor's lack of power to appoint the chief executive and other senior posts undermines mayoral control of the council. If English local government is synonymous with service provision, then English directly elected mayors require greater powers over that machinery. Appointments made by the mayor, both to the political cabinet and of directors of departments, could of course be subject to a form of confirmation hearing by full council or overview and scrutiny, so as to hold such appointments to public account.

At the moment, the mayor chooses to focus on leading the organisation, to one degree or another, or to focus on broader political leadership focused outside the council, but not to the exclusion of some form of organisational presence or leadership role, albeit one shared with a chief executive. That dual leadership role maintains the uncomfortable and often precarious balance between politician and senior officer, both often competing for domination of the council organisation. There is little in the English approach to directly elected mayors that does anything to solve that competition.

Local Strategic Partnerships

Local Strategic Partnerships (LSPs) are the cornerstone of the government's drive towards community planning and the development of a community strategy for each council. Each LSP is a single body which brings together parts of the public, private, voluntary, community and business sectors to ensure mutual support for 'different initiatives, programmes and services'.[12] Stewart points out that LSPs emerged from the development of government policies designed to tackle social exclusion and he identifies the LSP as an 'overarching partnership to review the multiplicity of partnerships' at the local level.[13] The council need not chair the LSP but is responsible for its effective working whoever does act as the chair of the LSP.[14]

LSPs can bring together representatives from organisations such as the local authority, the health service, police and fire services, probation service, employment and benefits agencies, culture and sporting agencies, government departments and a range of quangos, as well as representatives from business and charities. LSPs are at the heart of the partnership networks that have developed in the localities and many are an extension of the council machinery. They are a method for securing the delivery of services and coordinating the activities of other service providers.

It would be tempting to view LSPs as the formalisation of a governing coalition and as providing structure and substance to what would otherwise be an amorphous collection of participants in the provision of services and governance through an uncoordinated network. To do this, however, would be to misplace an LSP within the framework of urban regime theory. While the LSP may, at first glance, give the appearance of some permanent governing arrangement, with a continuous existence and a defined set of members and purposes, it is not formed by a political governor, with a specific political vision already formulated and who is seeking to develop a coalition for government.

A governing regime is not just about those who are elected to political office, but is an informal arrangement and set of tacit agreements that bring together a range of policy actors across public and private institutions. Dowding set out a number of features exhibited by a governing regime:[15]

- a distinct policy agenda;
- a long-term regime life span;
- a bringing together of a coalition of interests which are not necessarily formally constituted or created as a formal structure;
- the crossing of a wide range of organisational and sectoral boundaries.

The LSP, on the other hand, is a formal, government-inspired institutional arrangement that is rule driven and codified and set within the broader institutional framework of the local council. It is also focused on the bureaucratic processes involved in the provision of services, the coordination of service arrangements and on the processes of community planning. None of this requires an elected element to work; it does, however, require an elected element to hold such a body to account. Although an LSP is an institutional arrangement with a bureaucratic purpose, it can be used as a political tool and can play a powerful role in developing mayoral governance, and some mayors have recognised it as such.

At the time of writing, three elected mayors chair the LSP. Mayors are using the area-wide remit and focus they have to demonstrate to their LSP that they bring a particular governing vision to its deliberations that extends beyond the services provided by the council into a much broader political leadership. Four mayors have taken this step further and moved outside the structure of the LSP to develop their own mayoral forums to bring together a range of partners as a mechanism for mutual influence. Most undertake a process of continual debate and negotiation with partners, individually and collectively, and this process, coupled to the formal LSP and to other public consultation and involvement, places the elected mayor in an important position within the governance network.

The mayor of Lewisham chairs the LSP and has developed the position to match his approach to mayoral governance, an approach which focuses on the political processes involved in negotiation, exerting influence, responding to attempts at influence by others, constructing compromises and agreements, developing coalitions of support for mayoral initiatives and maintaining a steadfast focus on the broad governance of the area. Moreover, it became apparent to this mayor that the importance of the LSP in the development of his own political leadership style and his focus on governing the area needed to be reflected in the council structure itself. Thus, an LSP support team reports to a head of service, to ensure that the mayor receives the support that he requires in the complex dynamics that are developing between LSPs and mayoral government.

The role mayors play within the LSP, however, is one they themselves decide upon, influenced of course by local circumstances, governing networks and the need to respond to one government inspection or another. The LSP also provides a mayor with a platform from which to integrate partners with mayoral policy and with the mayor's broader vision for the area. As the LSP is a formal structure, it cannot replace the informal coalition and alliance formation that is a vital part of mayoral governance, particularly for those mayors who recognise the importance of extending their activities beyond the confines of their political parties.

Conclusions

The chapter has explored how the English elected mayors have tackled the dichotomy between acting as a political governor and as part of a governing institution with a detailed interest in the running and quality of public services. Elected mayors are faced with playing a dual political and organisational leadership role and, while they may have a personal preference for one or the other, they must give attention to both. Organisational leadership of the council can affect the quality of public services and the mayor's electoral chances; political leadership and the pursuit of a broad governing agenda will have a consequence for the way in which a range of organisations meet the challenges of public service provision. What a mayor cannot do is spend time immersed in the minutiae of service management and the detailed aspects of services delivery.[16]

Yet English mayors are using public services as a tool for governing and have developed the organisational and service machinery of the council in such a way as to pursue mayoral policy. Two mayors in particular reluctantly reported that they were drawn ever closer into the detail of council activity, driven in that direction not only by the regulatory framework affecting all mayors but also by the specific results of the government inspection regime. English mayors are, in some regards, prisoners of the council and its functions, as councillors have always been. Indeed, one mayor reported to feeling 'like both a politician and a manager' and, moreover, that some chief officers were treating him as though he were the chief executive. Nonetheless, he also believed that the arrival of an elected mayor had stopped old-style chief executives from 'making all the decisions and disguising it'.

English mayors inhabit a system in which there are two dimensions to their positions and power. First, they are, within the council, politically strong but administratively weak, much like the Israeli mayor.[17] When it comes to the outside world, English mayors are politically and administratively weak and thus must accrue what resources they can to influence, not govern, the outside world. The two dimensions of mayoral power affect the way in which mayors have been able to deal with the competing tensions they face: those between focusing on governing an area and the provision of public services; and those between providing political leadership to the community and organisational leadership – of a kind shared with a chief executive – to a large public bureaucracy. Added to this is the problem for mayors of balancing direction of the council organisation with not being seen by the voters to be defending it and as having become part of the council machinery. The evidence so far indicates that certain conditions have emerged as being necessary for mayors to successfully balance the tensions described:

- the strength of the mayor's political vision;
- mayors providing broad strategic organisational leadership;
- senior officers who are aware of the organisational responsibilities of the elected mayor;
- a council structured to support and pursue mayoral policy initiatives and governance;
- the development by the mayor of a range of alliances and coalitions of interest within the wider community designed to strengthen political involvement by local communities;
- an organisational structure designed specifically to support and pursue mayoral policy.

With these conditions met, mayoral organisational leadership need not be managerial leadership. Rather, it can become a facet of political leadership and of the broad governing role for the mayor. Moreover, a set of organisational arrangements can be put in place which reinforce and support the mayor's political role by using the provision of public services as a support for the achievement of a political vision. But achieving a political vision also requires political as well as organisational power and resources, and it is to this matter that we now turn.

Notes

1 Jones, G.W. and J. Stewart, 1983. *The Case for Local Government*, London, Allen and Unwin; Stewart, J., 2003. *Modernising British Local Government: An Assessment of Labour's Reform Programme*, Basingstoke, Palgrave Macmillan.

2 Nickson, R., 1995. *Local Government in Latin America*, London, Lynne Rienner Publishers.

3 Audit Commission, 2004. *Mayoral Arrangements: Middlesbrough Council*, London, Audit Commission.

4 Audit Commission, 2003. *Comprehensive Performance Assessment*, London, Audit Commission.

5 On the details of CPA, see three documents published by the Audit Commission in 2002: *Delivering Comprehensive Performance Assessments: Consultation Draft*; *The Comprehensive Performance Assessment Framework for Single Tier and County Councils*; and *Guidance for Authorities on the Corporate Assessment Process: Consultation Draft*.

6 DETR, 1998. *Modernising Local Government: Improving Services Through Best Value*; DETR, 1999. *Local Leadership: Local Choice*, London, DETR.

7 Committee on the Management of Local Government, 1967. *Report of the Committee, Vol. I*, London, HMSO; Committee of Inquiry into the Conduct of Local Authority Business, 1986. *Report of the Committee*, London, HMSO; Young, K. and N. Rao, 1994. *Coming to Terms with Change: The Local Government Councillor in 1993*, York, Joseph Rowntree Foundation; Copus, C., 1999. 'The Attitudes of Councillors Since Widdicombe: A Focus on Democratic Engagement', *Public Policy and Administration*, Vol. 14, No. 4. pp. 87–100.

8 Local Government New Zealand, 2004. *The Council, Mayor and CEO: The New Zealand Way*. See www.lgnz.co.nz.

9 Hambleton, R., 2000. *Enhancing Political and Managerial Leadership: The Council Manager Model*, London, IDeA.

10 Lowndes, V. and S. Leach, 2004. 'Understanding Local Political Leadership: Constitutions, Contexts and Capabilities', *Local Government Studies*, Special Edition, Vol. 30, No. 4, pp. 557–575.

11 Wollmann, H., 2004. 'Urban Leadership in German Local Politics: The Rise, Role and Performance of the Directly Elected (Chief Executive) Mayor', *International Journal of Urban and Regional Research*, Vol. 28, No. 1, pp. 150–165.

12 DETR, 2001. *Local Strategic Partnerships*, London, DETR.

13 Stewart, J., 2003. *Modernising British Local Government: An Assessment of Labour's Reform Programme*, Basingstoke, Palgrave Macmillan, p. 22.

14 DETR, 2001. *Power to Improve Economic, Social and Environmental Well-Being*, London, DETR.
15 Dowding, K., 1999. 'Regime Politics in London Local Government', *Urban Affairs Review*, Vol. 34, No. 4, pp. 515–545.
16 DETR, 1998. *Modern Local Government: In Touch with the People*, London, DETR; DETR, *Local Leadership: Local Choice*; DTLR (Department for Transport, Local Government and the Regions), 2001. *Strong Local Leadership: Quality Public Services*, London, DTLR.
17 Dery, D., 1998. 'Elected Mayors and *De Facto* Decentralisation, Israeli Style', *Local Government Studies*, Vol. 24, No. 2, Summer, pp. 45–55.

5

Democracy and representation: the rights of mayors

Introduction

The arguments both for and against directly elected mayors, as they have been expounded during referendum campaigns by the 'pro' and 'anti' camps, fall far short of a robust analytical framework concerning direct election to executive political office. Indeed, the arguments have often ranged from the anecdotal and hysterical to the impressionistic and mundane.[1] Moreover, exploring the notion of directly elected mayors within the wider context of the modernisation agenda has distracted attention from developing a broader understanding of the purpose, role and power of local political leaders. Yet the very English experiment with the office of directly elected mayor can contribute to our understanding of political and democratic processes in a way that goes beyond the mere dry description of institutions, into more generalisable concerns about local democracy and the nature of local representation.[2]

It is clear from the discussion in the preceding chapters that English directly elected mayors have little to distinguish them from indirectly elected council leaders – save from the fact of direct election by the local citizenry. Thus, it is on this factor that we must focus if we are to learn lessons from the mayoral experiment about the conduct and dynamics of English local politics. The advent of directly elected mayors raises a wide but simple set of questions about the effect of direct election to executive office on local democracy and representation, as set out in Chapter 1 (see page 19). This chapter looks at three of these questions: whether the new office of directly elected mayor strengthens or weakens the nature of English local democracy; whether the separation of powers, set in an English local context, is viable or achievable in current circumstances and what impact it could have on the nature of local self-government; and the place in local government of a written constitution and how such a notion fits with current local government practice.

The chapter also considers how the arrival of directly elected mayors impacts on Whig-like concerns for political representatives (and the representative institutions of which they are members) to be free of those who are represented and governed, so that they are able to govern in the interests of the 'whole' rather than the particular.[3] Freed from too close a relationship to the voter and constrained by party loyalty and unity, governing becomes a far more convenient and easy task. Direct election of the mayor changes the nature of the council's and councillors' task, from representation as broad governing, into a check and balance mechanism on local political power and responsibility, and thus transforms councils into a body which can hold and voice numerous views at one time.

The discussion in the chapter is set within a deliberately normative framework, one which rests on the assumptions inherent in current practices and processes of representative democracy. Such an approach, at this stage in the mayoral experiment and debate, is thought to be the most useful for pursuing an understanding of direct election to executive office. A normative approach is particularly appropriate given that the debate is currently captured and controlled by local political elites and the local government establishment.

The following section of the chapter explores what the notion of a directly elected political head of a council and the introduction of a limited separation of local powers do to our understanding of local democracy. The next considers the separation of powers and mayoral government in the context of a written local council constitution. The chapter concludes by exploring how, in the English context, the direct election of a mayor can result in an office distinctive from the indirectly elected leader and what this does for our understanding of local democracy and politics at the local level.

Local democracy and the mayoral experiment

The direct election of an individual to local executive office needs to be placed in the broad context of the development of democratic and representative government. Those concerns which traditionally underpinned arguments about the nature and extent of democracy find a reflection in discussion about how political leaders should be chosen and by whom.

In England, throughout the Victorian period, the development of both the institutions of local government and the franchise itself were not experiments in the extension of representative democracy. Rather, they were attempts to design a system that enshrined respect for property and the protection of the interests of a minority proprietor class within the heart of the political system, and to protect property ownership from the 'tyranny of the majority'. Theorists of liberal democracy sought to balance minority property rights with political involvement of the non-proprietor classes. Much democratic theorising has been based on reconciling support for a system of popular democracy with protecting 'the haves (a minority), from the have-nots (a majority)' and avoidance of a majority turning the 'instruments of state policy against a minority's privilege'.[4]

The fear of an irresponsible majority acting tyrannically against the interests of a minority underpinned the foundation of American democracy.[5] The answer to such a threat was to turn from notions of democracy or any wide-scale direct involvement in political democracy to republicanism, or 'representation'. As Madison described it: 'in a democracy, the people meet and exercise the government in person: in a republic, they assemble and administer it by their representatives and agents'.[6] As Crick points out, the important question for America's founding fathers in designing a new political system was how strong the 'democratic element' should be.[7] Furthermore, republicanism was linked to a broader set of ideals, such as 'simplicity, civic virtue, and even small proprietorship as the typical estate of a true citizen' and thus protected the propertied minority from the 'majoritarian overtones of democracy'.[8]

De Tocqueville identifies the success of the American experiment in developing a political system that protects the individual holding of property from the 'omnipotence of the majority'. It succeeds to such an extent that it becomes part of a broader political outlook – not simply a set of institutional arrangements and constitutional safeguards to property ownership, but a deeper belief in the sanctity of private property ownership.[9] Here is the key element in the success of representative democracy: it produces the illusion of wide-scale political involvement and control without threatening certain fundamental political beliefs about the hierarchical nature of society.

While protection of the proprietor minority from popular exploitation and expropriation is no longer a central feature of British local politics, earlier periods were characterised by just such a debate. First, the local government franchise as it developed throughout the nineteenth century ensured that those exercising the vote, and the candidates from whom they could select, fulfilled some property qualification.[10] The franchise and the office of councillor were restricted to certain sections of the community and even radical candidates 'tended to be small masters, shopkeepers or publicans'.[11] Young[12] refers to mid-nineteenth-century attempts to reform county government as not a search for 'representative democracy' but the development of a 'form of ratepayer democracy'. Gyford emphasises the point that the relationship between the local electorate and councillor was primarily a fiduciary rather than a politically representative one. He comments that: 'the bodies which emerged from the 1835 Municipal Corporations Act were seen first and foremost as owners of corporate property'. Indeed, 'councillors as members of the corporation were trustees in a fiduciary relationship to the ratepayers within a system based upon the rights of property'.[13]

The development of municipal government as an integral part of the growth of the British state led to battles involving private commercial interests, particularly where those interests felt threatened by municipalisation.[14] Indeed, municipalisation and the pursuit of local redistributionary policies undermined the Victorian assumption that national politics were irrelevant to local government.[15] Moreover, the extension of the franchise during the Victorian period brought with it the notion that property ownership would require protection from infringement by either national or local government.[16] Liberal democracy, then, has traditionally portrayed liberalism, with its entrenchment of minority rights, both political and property, as a counterpoint to democracy.

Edmund Burke had of course earlier provided a justification and explanation of the need for the political representative to govern in the interests of the whole, rather than particular interests or concerns:

> Parliament is not a congress of ambassadors from different and hostile interests, which interests, each must maintain, as an agent and advocate, against other agents and advocates; but Parliament is a deliberative assembly of one nation, with one interest, that of the whole – where not local purposes, not local prejudices ought to guide, but the general good resulting from the general reason of the whole.[17]

Burke acknowledged that the representative owes the citizen his or her unbiased opinion, mature judgement and enlightened conscience; the representative is not bound to substitute the citizen's judgement for his or her own. Indeed, the representative 'betrays instead of serving' the citizen if he or she substitutes another's opinion for his or her own. Yet the elected representative is not a delegate of the electorate, but of the party which governs in the interests of the whole, as it perceives that whole to be. As Eulau and Whalke state: 'above all freedom from local connections and instructions was for Burke a necessary and very practical condition to work for a Parliamentary party, be its leader, and accept the commitments of a party man'.[18]

The eighteenth- and nineteenth-century concerns about minority rights within a representative democracy have echoes in the concerns that many today express about local government. The minorities attracting attention today are not the proprietor class. Rather, they are minorities of ethnicity, gender, age and sexual orientation. Such an interpretation of representation sees elected chambers, and the members of them, as necessarily a microcosm of the wider society. Concern for property rights was assuaged by the notion that the representative governs in the interests of the whole, which coincided with the interests of property ownership. The arguments of today's proponents of microcosmic representation and minority concerns move in the opposite direction: from the interests of the whole to the interests of the specific, and from the representative as a trustee to the representative as a delegate of the specific minority group. Indeed, for microcosmic representation to work in today's local government requires either: a form of syndicalism to be introduced into local democracy, with various groups electing their own representatives to pursue their own interests; or a form of proportional representation that allows voters to select not only from political parties but also from a range of political associations and single-issue/interest groups.

Microcosmic representation fails in the context of modern-day local representative government because of the power of political parties and their dominance over local politics. While councillors from minorities may have a greater insight into their own specific communities and have a network of contacts within them, merely securing a greater number of minorities elected to council chambers will achieve nothing if those elected are party representatives and place the party above all else. So, the concern for governing for the interests of the whole or for specific interests remains at the heart of the development of a political system. We need then to look at what the separation of powers and the elected mayor means for concerns about governing for the whole and the protection of minority rights, as well as for the inversion of past concerns about the role of a representative as a trustee or delegate of those who have elected them.

The architecture of local democracy and separating powers

The shape and form of English local government reflect the concerns of democratic theorists to protect property interests and the rights of minorities, and have underpinned the way in which local political decisions are made. They also reflect the beliefs of writers such as J.S. Mill, who saw local government as a collective endeavour with an educative effect on those involved that would make political participants less selfish and more aware of the interests and concerns of others.[19] Mill also saw local government as a unified though multidimensional institution, concerned with a range of local issues and services, rather like the national Parliament. Mill is worth quoting at length:

> The local, like the national Parliament, has for its proper business to consider the interests of the locality as a whole, composed of parts all of which must be adapted to one another, and attended to in the order and ratio of their importance. There is another very weighty reason for uniting the control of all the business of a locality under one body. The greatest imperfection of popular local institutions, and the chief cause of the failure which so often attends them, is the low calibre of the men by whom they are almost always carried on. That these should be of a very miscellaneous character is, indeed, part of the usefulness of the institution; it is that circumstance chiefly which renders it a school of political capacity and general

intelligence. But a school supposes teachers as well as scholars; the utility of
the instruction greatly depends on its bringing inferior minds into contact
with superior, a contact which in the ordinary course of life is altogether
exceptional, and the want of which contributes more than anything else to
keep the generality of mankind on one level of contented ignorance.[20]

Thus, there is a deliberative element to local government activity that
requires a collective involvement of all the membership of a council, not
least because, in Mill's analysis, such collective endeavour has an educative effect. Coupling this to the concerns about the fiduciary relationship
councils have to those who pay the local taxes, and the concerns of the
likes of Edwin Chadwick, Jeremy Bentham and James Mill for utilitarian
principles and centralised and efficient administration, we can understand how collective decision-making by committee came about. But, as
Stewart points out, collective decision-making in local government has
a simpler genesis:

> the committee system had been part of local government since the intro-
> duction of elected municipal government in the early nineteenth century
> and was based on the statutory precept that the council was a corporate
> body, responsible for all that happened in the authority. The council exer-
> cised that responsibility through a series of committees.[21]

Mill does, however, consider the executive aspect of local government and recognised that 'local business has its executive department'.
While not arguing for directly elected mayors, Mill equates the executive
responsibilities of local government with those of the state and argues
that the same problems and solutions emerge when it comes to the
activities of an executive. Much of his concern is with the weakening
of political responsibility that comes from collective, committee-based
decision-making and, thus, with accountability. Indeed, with regard to
collective activity, undertaken 'behind closed doors', Mill comments:

> Things are much worse when the act itself is only that of a majority – a
> board, deliberating with closed doors, nobody knowing, or, except in some
> extreme case, being ever likely to know, whether an individual member
> voted for the act or against it. Responsibility in this case is a mere name.
> 'Boards' it is happily said by Bentham, 'are screens.' What 'the board' does
> is the act of nobody; and nobody can be made to answer for it. The board
> suffers, even in reputation, only in its collective character; and no indi-
> vidual member feels this further than his disposition leads him to identify
> his own estimation with that body.[22]

While Mill is concerned with the activities of the central executive and
with administrative aspects of the executive process, he has provided
a devastating criticism of collective, committee-based decision-making
in local government. This criticism is particularly apt today, since the

party group has replaced the committee as the place in which the real political decisions are made. Mill goes on to argue that in local government each 'executive officer should be single and singly responsible for the whole of the duty committed to his charge.'[23] He is of course talking here of appointed officials, not elected members, but the principle is established of individual responsibility for actions taken at the local level. Mill also goes on to equate the local 'mayor or chairman' as 'occupying a position analogous to that of the prime minister in the state, and under a well-organised system the appointment and watching of the local officers would be the most important part of his duty.'[24]

None of this can by any means be taken as Mill arguing for directly elected mayors, but he does provide an argument for moving in that direction. Indeed, Victorian England experienced direct election to a form of executive political office with elections to bodies such as boards of Poor Law Guardians, street improvement commissions and school boards. The elections to these boards, at various times and various places, provoked intense political and party political campaigns.[25] Yet this does not compare to the English medieval experience of elections to the offices of reeve, sheriff, bailiff and mayor.[26]

In his 'Constitutional Code' of 1830 Jeremy Bentham set out a completely reformed political system of government for Britain. Underneath an annually elected legislature he proposed a series of rationally designed districts and sub-districts, which were further subdivided into the smallest level of local government: the 'bisdistricts'. The bisdistrict included a political office to be known as the 'local headsman', which was to be an executive office directly elected by the majority of local voters but which reported direct to ministers. Bentham gave this office substantial local power over a range of areas – not all of which were traditional local government concerns. The notion of a 'local headsman' rests on the concentration of wide executive and administrative powers and responsibilities in one office.[27] What Bentham provides us with is an intellectual underpinning for the direct election to executive office of a powerful local representative and governor, an intellectual underpinning that is far more rigorous in its analysis than the vague conceptualisation of local political power and accountability set out in the current government's modernising agenda.[28]

The separation of powers: a new framework for local government and democracy

The desirability of a separation of powers at any level of government and the degree that separation takes will depend on the beliefs held about the use and purpose of political power, how and where it is concentrated and whether government should be a politically restrained or unrestrained process. It also rests on how far periodic electoral contests are seen as a sufficient restraint on government, and whether institutional arrangements are required to limit or delay governmental activity. In addition, the separation of powers becomes more or less desirable, and effectual, depending on attitudes towards the existence and activities of factions, groupings and parties within the political system and whether one such party or faction, or a number of them, will have an almost permanent dominance of the political and governmental processes; representative institutions alone do not protect against such political dominance.

Locke argued for the distinct nature of the separate elements of government and the need to balance those elements by placing responsibility for them with different people and institutions; he saw the legislature as the more powerful tool of government, but behind it rests the ultimate political power of the 'people'.[29] The separation, for Locke, need not be complete, but it must be a separation that is clearly identifiable and obvious to all.

It is in the development of the constitution and governmental system of the United States that we see the separation of powers taken much further than in the British context, and specifically designed to prevent, as far as possible, government becoming dominated by any one party or faction. Madison complained in the *Federalist* that some state constitutions had violated that sacred maxim of free government (the separation of powers) by 'too great a mixture, and even an actual consolidation of the different powers'. Indeed, for Madison:

> The accumulation of all powers, legislative, executive and judiciary, in the same hands, whether of one, a few, or many and whether hereditary, self-appointed or elective, may justly be pronounced the very definition of tyranny.[30]

While the ability of an English council to tyrannise the population is remote, those faced with an unpopular council decision and campaigning against it may see the 'steamrolling' through of a particular decision about which they disagree in an undemocratic light. If a council speaks with one voice then the possibility of holding that council to account, or for it to articulate views in opposition to its own, is negligible. A clear separation between an executive responsible for a decision and a representative chamber responsible for holding that decision-maker to account provides a form of solution to local citizens seeking to build a political alliance with elected representatives to pursue a particular course of action. Moreover, if that executive is directly elected then the separation of powers becomes more acute and thus those seeking to influence political decisions have two avenues of approach: the executive mayor himself or herself; or the wider elected local chamber.

If the intention of a separation of powers is to prevent any one party, grouping or faction from securing a more or less permanent dominance of the offices of government, then in the English local setting a problem emerges. The rigidity of party boundaries and the loyalty which party representatives grant to their party can, in the English context, result in party loyalty crossing the institutional boundaries of a local separation of powers. Party loyalty may serve to prevent the elected chamber from challenging and holding to account an executive mayor of the same party, at least in public; and opposition parties may seek to undermine an executive mayor regardless of the validity of any policy initiative he or she announces and pursues.

The direct election of an individual to executive office provides the electorate with the means to hold the mayor to account for past actions or inactions. Such closeness of the accountability relationship is currently lacking from the existing leader and council model, where, unless voters live in the leader's ward, they have no electoral means by which to hold him or her to account – save for voting against the governing party and hoping for the best. But local elections and campaigning or political action through political associations do provide the local citizenry with limited mechanisms and processes of control, or at least influence, over local political decision-makers collected in the council.[31]

Yet, certain political concerns are assuaged by indirect democracy. Those concerns are that: political decision-making must be certain and constant; distance is required between the represented and representatives so that populist pressure does not drive the response of the political elite to policy problems; government must be, as far as possible, a convenient process for the governor; and the electorate do not share the liberal view of politics held by the political elite and may elect candidates to office from the political extremes. Thus, indirect election of the executive acts as a safeguard against the voters doing the wrong thing.

It is indisputable, however, that direct election to executive office enhances local political accountability. It does this by providing an opportunity for the electorate to cast a judgement on the individual responsible for decisions; it also provides political associations with a clear and present target for political activity. Moreover, separating the executive and political head of the council from the rest of the representative body fundamentally recasts the nature of the internal dynamics of the council. With control over who is the head of the executive placed in the hands of voters, a direct link of accountability is made between governors and governed, a link which is far more powerful than the link between voter and council in the effect it can have on governing decisions. It is important to strengthen the link between local politicians and citizens because this will address a myth of liberal democracy, that electors choose representatives to control local administrators, rather than to govern or to take governing decisions.

A local separation of powers, however limited, relies on each element of the separation acting as a check on the other, and with each element playing a different role: the executive governing; and the chamber representing, deliberating and holding the executive to account. Moreover, the relationship between the elements of local government will not always be conflictual; rather, they will also be cooperative, as many local political problems can be solved by negotiation, compromise and developments in policy initiatives. Where conflict does occur, the role of the council is vital in providing a counterbalancing voice and real checks on what elected mayors may wish to do. Thus, it is necessary to construct the right balance of power between mayor and council, using overview and scrutiny to explore mayoral activity, challenging and delaying mayoral initiatives, and articulating a wide range of opinions in council to explore mayoral policy and direction and act as a safeguard to politically contentious and conflictual decisions. With the powers of elected mayors as they are currently constructed, those concerned about mayoral power have little in reality to worry about.

Yet it is clear that there are clear democratic benefits to be gained from a separation of powers at the local level and more to be gained from a more acute separation than currently exists. The separation could be further developed in two ways: first, by allowing the elected mayor to appoint a cabinet from beyond the membership of the council; and second, as well as electing a mayor by popular vote, electing the cabinet with the mayor. Indeed, the Local Government Act 2000 has as one of its provisions the following:

> A form of executive some or all of the members of which are elected by the local government electors for the authority's area to a specified post in the executive associated with the discharge of particular functions.

> A form of executive some or all of the members of which are elected by those electors but not to any such post.[32]

Giving the electorate the ability to elect not only the mayor but also the entire executive extends the process of direct election to its logical conclusion. Yet it is important here not to lose sight of the overriding factor of political accountability underpinning the elected mayor: that the individual is directly elected and cannot take cover from accountability or disperse accountability among a collective body. A directly elected cabinet would add to the potential for the dispersal of accountability in much the same way as electing a council currently does; yet it would be an executive that was elected and not a representative chamber, so the potential for hiding from responsibility – collectively or individually – is still reduced.

However, England has two types of mayoral government, and the discussion here has centred on that of the mayor and cabinet rather than the mayor and council manager. The latter arrangement has an appointed official as the most powerful element of the executive, yet the elected element is politically weak in relation to both the manager and the rest of the council. Despite two mayoral models existing, the legislation, and as a consequence the local electorate, lacks a wider choice of how to configure the form of directly elected political leadership, to take into account the powers and responsibilities it has, or to develop a system of unique local political leadership that redresses the constitutionally inferior position of local government relative to the centre.

The direct election of a separate executive, either individually as the mayor or collectively as an entire executive, is in itself a powerful enough argument to prefer this approach to local government over any indirectly elected or an undifferentiated political system of decision-making. However, other factors need to be considered: the way in which the separation of powers is set out and described locally, within a council's own constitution; which of the mayoral models are selected and why; and, more widely, the constitutional position that local government has in relation to central government and the broader network of governance. Directly elected mayors have a compelling argument in their favour only if they can be distinguished from any other form of executive and if they can 'govern' in a fashion that is not currently available to any council and its indirectly elected leader.

A written constitution

English local government has, as a result of the Local Government Act 2000, adopted written constitutions, mostly based on the model constitution produced by the Office of the Deputy Prime Minister (ODPM). As a consequence, local government generally has shown a marked reluctance to treat the exercise of producing a constitution as anything other than yet another centrally imposed task. Moreover, the involvement of councillors in the constitution drafting process has varied greatly across the country. In some areas members were immersed in constitution drafting, forming working groups, both cross-party and single-party, and producing a number of versions of the constitution before a final version was adopted by the council. In others, however, members all but abdicated responsibility for drafting the constitution to council officers.

The council constitution that opens with a bold preamble of political intention – perhaps beginning 'We the people' or any such declaration and that sets out the vision and intention of what is to follow in the constitution – will be placed to send a clear message about the importance of the constitution to governing the area. At the moment, any reader of a council constitution is faced with a rather dense and impenetrable document, more concerned with standing orders for meetings and financial regulations than with political considerations about democracy, representation, the balance of political powers and the rights of local citizens.

In the constitution drafting process some English councils lost an opportunity to fundamentally assess the nature of political decision-making in each and every area, to construct a system of local political rights, duties and responsibilities for council, councillors and citizens alike, and to review the state of local democracy and respond accordingly. Working out abstract concepts to meet local circumstances requires a dry-run and a reassessment based on experience. Many councillors and councils are now recognising the importance of the constitution and are already reviewing and revising those documents, to turn them into a meaningful statement of political intention. In contrast, many other authorities clearly thought long and hard about the relationships between the executive and council and about the relationship these have with the outside world.[33] Moreover, many, including mayoral councils such as Hackney and Lewisham, invested considerable time and effort in developing the constitution in such a way as to 'improve local democratic activity'.[34]

The drafting of council constitutions needs to recognise that councils are based on a separation of powers, albeit a limited one, and that this is also the case in mayoral authorities. But, at the same time, the constitution must make clear the connections between the elements of the modernised council and the connections with a range of formal bodies of governance and stakeholder groups outside the council, as well as with informal political associations of local citizens and citizens individually. Thus, the constitution should be much more than an internal rulebook for the conduct of council business: it should be a document that addresses the nature of political processes and the use and limitations of political power within the council and beyond.

A constitution is a document around which the boundaries of the political and legal worlds meet with the principles and practices that drive those worlds. It is a mistake to view a council constitution as a legal document requiring only interpretation by council solicitors and as something that can be seen only as a legal construct. Rather, it is a politically dynamic document that speaks of political principles and realities that are not subject to accurate legal interpretation. Allowing lawyers alone to be the guardian of the constitution is an error. Yet constitutional law is a powerful force in the interpretation and implementation of the principles of any constitution and constitutional arguments will be settled through a legal process. However, as MacCormick argues, the 'legal and political can and should be held conceptually distinct' and, further, that a constitution and constitutionalism are the:

creed according to which political power ought only to be exercised under constitutional provisions and subject to constitutional restrictions ... it is also a virtue – the virtue of exercising power and of conducting political debate in terms which fully respect and honour the constitution.[35]

Yet, despite a constitution addressing issues of political power and its use, disputes about its meaning and interpretations of power to act will require legal rather than political resolution. Nonetheless, councillors and local citizens must take ownership of the content and interpretation of the constitution and not abdicate them to lawyers, however tempting and secure that might be. While what a council does must adhere to a legislative source, what a council constitution then does and how it addresses the use of political power can be placed in the hands of local communities and their representatives.

A council constitution is the framework within which local political power is understood and exercised, rather than a set of legal restraints requiring legal interpretation during the heat of political battle. But how does a written local constitution based on a separation of powers help us to understand the nature and processes of mayoral local government within the English context? To answer these questions we must move beyond what mayoral council constitutions currently are and what they say to a broader consideration of mayoral government in a constitutional framework.

Local constitutions: 'We the people', 'We the council' or 'I the mayor'?

At the local level, council constitutions should display all the hallmarks of what would be expected from the processes of drafting and adopting a constitution of a nation state. Control and possession of the constitution rests with local citizens – not the council. But, as Tom Paine described it, 'a constitution is not the act of a government, but of a people constituting a government and government without a constitution, is power without a right.'[36] In the English local context, of course, not all this applies. Citizens do not constitute their councils (as is possible in the United States). Rather, central government constitutes local government and councils have constitutions only because Parliament requires it; it is Parliament that is the sovereign power, not local citizens, and it is a council, through parliamentary instruction, that reconstitutes itself in drafting and adopting its local constitution.

Yet much of what Paine argues does apply in the context of English local government. The act of drafting a constitution is one which councils should share with local citizens and is a process by which people can be engaged in deciding upon the shape and nature of local democracy. If citizens must grant approval to the arrival of an elected mayor through a referendum, then public involvement in designing and configuring the powers of the mayor, the checks and balances in the system, the political relationships between elements of the separation of powers, and the relationship that a mayoral authority and the mayor have with local citizens, ensures that council constitutions are not an 'act of government, but of a people constituting a government'. The latter is secured of course only as far as statute allows and takes place within statutory confines and government regulation – the local citizen may be involved, but does not constitute the local government, yet with the referendum provision citizens do have the final say on whether local government will be mayoral or not.

Any council constitution – mayoral or otherwise – that commences with the preamble 'We the people' must not merely have consulted the people but also have placed local citizens in a position to have real control over the content and structure of the constitution, perhaps placing the constitution itself before the people for approval in referendum. Practice among the mayoral authorities in engaging the public in the constitution drafting process varied. The common view from mayoral councils was that the referendum which sanctioned the introduction of the mayor was indeed 'constituting' the council's political decision-making structures. However, linked to this, the consultation under the provisions of the 2000 Act, the mayoral referendum campaign and vote, and the campaign and election of a mayor had all politically exhausted local citizens, to the extent that further engagement in the details of a constitution would have been untenable. However, future mayoral constitutional reviews will be more conducive to citizen involvement.

Many council constitutions can only, in all honesty, contain an opening to a preamble along the lines of 'We the council', as little or minimal citizen engagement in the process has been generated. Indeed, any constitution with such an opening statement is, in Paine's consideration, not a constitution at all, but rather an act of government. Furthermore, it implies an inward-looking document, concerned only with the processes and structures of the council itself; a council speaking to itself about itself. A constitution, on the other hand, must bind a community together and draw upon common themes and threads. In Aristotle we find the strength and importance of commonality and cohesiveness of constitutional government:

> The members of a state must either have all things in common or nothing in common, or some things in common and some not. That they should have nothing in common is clearly impossible, for the constitution is a community, and must at any rate have a common place – one city will be in one place, and the citizens are those who share in that one city.

In his survey of ancient constitutions and constitutional government, Aristotle concluded:

> It would seem also to be a bad principle that the same person should hold many offices ... for one business is better done by one man ... hence where the state is large, it is more in accordance both with constitutional and with democratic principles that the offices of state should be distributed among many persons.

So, here we find the need for constitutions to recognise and accommodate the factors that create and sustain recognisable communities, at least of place. Yet Aristotle also warns of the dangers of a 'state' becoming over-unified: 'so we ought not to attain this greatest unity even if we could, for it would be the destruction of the state. Again, a state is not made up only of so many men, but of different kinds of men; for similars do not constitute a state.'[37] Taking a huge leap into English local government, we find the need for: a recognition not only of what binds, but of the differences of political need and different relationships that different citizens may have to political institutions and processes; and for political institutions to be, if not separate themselves, in separate hands.

While it is clear that constitutional theorists and writers have had little impact on the development of council constitutions in English mayoral authorities, the fundamentals of constitutional government and the drafting of constitutions – resting on the involvement and approval of the governed – apply in the English local context. Moreover, within mayoral authorities, where there is a sharper separation powers than under the indirectly elected leader executive, and where the mayor comes with a separate mandate, the constitution needs to provide the mayor with the legal and political resources to carry out his or her role.[38] Indeed, it is vital in mayoral authorities that the constitution reflects the uniqueness of both the mayoral office and the locality which chose to use it.

If these constitutions fail to reflect the political traditions, histories and cultures of the communities constructing them, and the special nature of the specific geographical location within which the mayor exists, and fail to recognise what it is that makes that area unique, they become no more than a dry and pointless council document. More importantly, the constitution and the new mayoral office become no more than a convenient new form of government, rather than the accommodation of political leadership into a new set of institutional arrangements located in the context of a particular location and its communities. It is in reflecting the uniqueness of the institution of elected mayor and the uniqueness of the communities and citizens mayors represent and govern that the constitutions of mayoral authorities largely fall down – but they were pushed by central government. Indeed, in looking at mayoral constitutions, if the name of the council were removed it would be impossible, in most cases, to identify the part of country concerned.

It is not surprising that the constitutions of mayoral councils largely reflect the articles and provisions of the model constitution produced by the government.[39] Even in relation to the basic roles that the mayor performs, most constitutions repeat and amend only slightly the roles provided in the model. These state that the mayor will:

- be the local authority's principal public spokesperson;
- give overall political direction to the council;
- appoint the cabinet and deputy mayor;
- decide on the scheme of delegation for executive functions;
- chair meetings of the executive;
- represent the local authority on such external bodies as the mayor decides.[40]

Some mayoral authorities have nevertheless given greater thought to the role an elected mayor may play and have set out those roles within the constitution. The mayor of Hackney, in addition to the roles set out in the model constitution, is also expected, by article 4 of the constitution (among other things):

- to represent the interests of Hackney to government and other part- ners and stakeholders;
- to promote and improve the economic, social and environmental well-being of Hackney and its inhabitants;
- to have regard to the principles of sustainable development;
- to have regard to equality of opportunity;
- to lead and speak up for Hackney as the principal public spokesperson and to act as a champion for the whole borough;
- to be accessible to citizens;
- to promote the rich cultural diversity of Hackney, which is one of its key strengths as a borough.[41]

The above is not a complete list of the constitutional requirements and expectations of the mayor of Hackney, but those presented do indicate the initiative and imagination that one authority has taken in extending the mayoral role beyond the very basic premises of the model constitu- tion.

There are here, however, as with any constitution, some carefully placed political and ideological underpinnings to the role of the mayor. A mayor elected from a place on the political spectrum that did not accept sustainable development as a policy preference and who was more growth oriented, or a mayor who did not believe in equality of opportunity or that diversity was a strength and who wished to pursue a different political direction, would be somewhat bound by the constitution or open to accusations of acting unconstitutionally. Or would he or she simply ignore the constitution and accusations of acting unconstitutionally?

The constitution of Hartlepool council has granted the mayor an interesting ceremonial role to play. As well as acting as the political head of the council the mayor of Hartlepool is also to attend the following civic and ceremonial functions:

- an annual civic service to be held in conjunction with the chair of the council;
- an annual charity event (formerly know as the mayor's charity ball), to be held at the discretion of the chair of the council and the mayor;
- the annual remembrance day service.

The mayor will also act as the representative of the council at:

- official openings (in consultation with the chair of the council);
- ministerial visits;
- any other events, as determined by the council.[42]

The role of the mayor of Middlesbrough, in addition to the model's roles, is also to propose the budget and policy framework and any amendment thereof, and to promote LSPs.[43] The mayor of Stoke-on-Trent (England's only mayor and manager authority) also has the roles of advising the council manager on the implementation of the budget and policy framework and decisions in accordance with them. That mayor can also appoint such executive advisory committees and the membership of those committees as he or she may require.[44]

Yet, despite some attempts to localise mayoral council constitutions, the provisions and requirements of the model constitution produced by the ODPM are the dominant and dominating factor when it comes to their drafting. While the council constitution can specify the nature of the relationship between the mayor, the council and the citizen, it cannot alter the fundamentally subservient relationship English local government has with the central political authority at Westminster and Whitehall. While the intensity of central control over local self-government has waxed and waned over the centuries, the powers and responsibilities of local government are themselves a product of the development of parliamentary democracy and the relationships between Parliament and the monarch.[45] English elected mayors cannot act from powers granted to them by a sovereign local citizenry contained and restrained within a local constitution but only from statutory provision, which itself is subject to judicial interpretation. For this to change and for communities to grant their mayors the powers and responsibilities they wished them to have locally would require a fundamental recasting of the nature of the English state and its unwritten constitutional basis, along with the supremacy of Parliament.

The special nature of the political relationship that the mayor has with the local citizenry provides a clear political justification for mayoral constitutions to be far freer from central control than the constitutions of authorities with an indirectly elected leader. As the mayor holds office by virtue of the public vote, the local citizenry should have a far wider range of powers available to them to grant to the mayor than those granted to a council leader, who comes to office with no direct mandate other than an assumed one granted by the majority group on the council. Again, however, we see that a written mayoral constitution and mayoral government have no real features or powers that distinguish mayoral from non-mayoral councils (a subject to which we return in the Chapter 9).

Yet mayoral constitutions do provide a very clear framework within which a mayor can operate and set out the powers and checks and balances of the system. Despite the limitations on English council constitutions, and local government more broadly, a written local constitution is a vital element of a thriving local democracy that England has lacked for too long.

Conclusions

The direct election of an individual to local political executive office is the distinctive and defining feature of elected mayors. Indeed, within the English approach it is the only clear defining point between mayors and indirectly elected council leaders, as they hold broadly similar powers and responsibilities, set within a local separation of powers. Granting the mayor a direct mandate was not seen by the government as an opportunity to experiment with the role and responsibilities of the local political leader; mayors are just expected to act differently. Even if the government had granted mayors powers and roles far in advance of council leaders, such powers granted would be redeemable by government and would not provide mayors with an autonomous political existence. The direct election of the English mayor is all that distinguishes the office from other political posts with executive powers.

It is also clear that the separation of powers in English local government is limited in nature but that their separation nonetheless reflects long-standing concerns about the nature of English local democracy and politics, about the purpose of local government and about the nature of its relationship with local citizens. Setting out the structure and dynamics of political decision-making in the form of a written constitution provides an opportunity for councils to debate with citizens how they wish to be governed and by what processes. Moreover, the constitution acts as the framework for a series of checks and balances between elements of the separation of powers and sets out the relationships between them. Yet mayoral councils are bound in the same way as non-mayoral authorities when drafting a constitution, and citizens have no discretion in the powers they wish to grant to their mayor through the constitution.

Despite these limitations council constitutions can set out a framework within which develop the relationships between the mayor and political associations, community groups and citizens outside the council. The council constitution is a vital source of direction to a mayor in what he or she is expected to do in relation to the citizens served and governed. Moreover, a constitution provides the citizen with a set of political rights in relation to local politics and local government, and identifies a framework within which political decisions are made and can be challenged. Council leaders have long existed without council constitutions, but it is inconceivable that elected mayors could operate without such political authority set out in a written local constitution. The need for a codified political structure, a clearly defined set of interactions and a written source of powers and responsibilities for elements of the political system is another aspect that distinguishes the English elected mayor from an indirectly elected council leader.

The direct election by the local voters of the political head of the council and the political leader of the community provides that politician with a clear mandate. Such community support is, however, only a resource for political power and influence, not a guarantee of it. An indication of this is how English mayors have yet to become important political players on the regional and national political stage. They are constrained in this not only by local government's relationship to central government but also by the small number of elected mayors in England, as well as by England's big and powerful cities lacking the political bravery and imagination to adopt the mayoral model. As Stoker and Wolman found, the ability of mayors to rise above the local area for which they are elected depends on the nature of the areas they represent, and on their ability to forge coalitions and to take collective action with other mayors.[46]

To develop English mayoral government into a distinctive feature of the political landscape, with powers and responsibilities to govern locally and make an impact in broader networks of governance, requires a system based on more than the political skills and acumen of the individual office holder. It requires reforms of the existing system that acknowledge fundamental principles about mayoral government, namely the following:

- A direct mandate from the voters, rather than an assumed collective mandate to a council, grants the mayor the ability (with the requisite powers) to take political action, to introduce political initiatives and to govern in the broader sense.[47]

- A separation of local political powers and institutions allows mayors and councillors to specialise in aspects of the political processes, which requires them to have appropriate powers.
- A separation of local political powers and institutions in English local government should more accurately reflect the political needs of local citizens, and demands a responsive political system with high levels of accountability.
- The drafting of mayoral council constitutions must be a cooperative process between councils, councillors and citizens, and developing and sustaining wide-scale citizen engagement and involvement in the drafting and workings of the constitution are a vital responsibility for any council as a politically representative body.
- A mayoral council constitution must be drafted to reflect the unique nature of the directly elected office.
- A mayoral council constitution must be drafted to reflect the unique nature of the area in which it is located.
- The limited political power and responsibility held by English mayors need to be increased relative to those of council leaders.

If the local citizenry are to be given a choice of how they wish to be governed, as well as by whom they wish to be governed, and if they select an elected mayor as the preferred form of local government, there must be a purpose to that choice. Voting 'yes' in a referendum is purposeful only if the resultant new office can do more than the old indirectly elected leader, and this demands that the powers of elected mayors, the councils they lead and the relationship both have to governing an area need to be developed. Before setting out any suggestions for such reforms to the English approach to elected mayors, we need to examine the English elected mayors in action, and this is explored in the next chapter.

Notes

1 Orr, K., 2004. 'If Mayors Are the Answer Then What Was the Question?', *Local Government Studies*, Vol. 30, No. 3, pp. 331–345.
2 Birch, A.H., 1993. *The Concepts and Theories of Modern Democracy*, London, Routledge.
3 Birch, A.H., 1971. *Representation*, London, Pall Mall Press.
4 Held, D., 1993. *Models of Democracy*, Cambridge, Polity Press, p. 66.
5 Beloff, M. (ed.), 1948. *The Federalist, or the New Constitution*, Oxford, Basil Blackwell, pp. xvi–xvii.
6 Madison, J. (M. Beloff, ed.), 1948, first published 1787. Paper No. XIV, in *The Federalist, or the New Constitution*, Oxford, Basil Blackwell, p. 62.

7 Crick, B., 1982. *In Defence of Politics*, Harmondsworth, Penguin Books, p. 58.

8 *Ibid.*, p. 68.

9 De Tocqueville, A. (J.P. Mayer, ed.), 1994, first published 1835, 1840. *Democracy in America*, London, Fontana, p. 260 and pp. 638–639.

10 For a comprehensive discussion of the property qualification for the franchise and council candidacy, see Keith-Lucas, B. 1952. *The English Local Government Franchise*, Oxford, Basil Blackwell.

11 Hennock, E.P., 1973. *Fit and Proper Persons: Ideal and Reality in Nineteenth-Century Urban Government*, London, Edward Arnold, p. 10.

12 Young, K., 1989. 'Bright Hopes and Dark Fears: The Origins and Expectations of the County Councils', in K. Young (ed.), *New Directions for County Government*, London, Association of County Councils, pp. 4–21, at p. 6.

13 Gyford, J., 1986. 'Diversity, Sectionalism and Local Democracy', in Committee of Inquiry into the Conduct of Local Authority Business, *Research, Vol. IV: Aspects of Local Democracy*, London, HMSO, p. 128.

14 Davis, J., 1989. 'The Progressive Council, 1889–1907', in A. Saint (ed.), *Politics and the People of London: The London County Council 1889–1965*, London, Hambledon Press, pp. 27–48, at p. 28; Young, 'Bright Hopes and Dark Fears', p. 17.

15 Davis, 'The Progressive Council', particularly, pp. 32–35. For a further discussion, set between the wars, see J. Gillespie, 1989. 'Municipalism, Monopoly and Management: The Demise of Socialism in One County, 1918–1933', in Saint (ed.), *Politics and the People of London*, pp. 103–125.

16 Soldon, N., 'Laissez-Faire as Dogma: The Liberty and Property Defence League 1882–1914', in K. Brown (ed.), *Essays in Anti-Labour History: Responses to the Rise of Labour in Britain*, London, Macmillan, pp. 208–233.

17 Edmund Burke's address to the electors of Bristol, 1774, cited by Birch, *The Concepts and Theories of Modern Democracy*, p. 75.

18 Eulau, H. and J. Whalke, 1978. *The Politics of Representation*, Thousand Oaks, CA, Sage, pp. 43–48.

19 Mill, J.S. (R.B. McCallum, ed.), 1948, first published 1861. *On Liberty and Considerations on Representative Government*, Oxford, Basil Blackwell.

20 *Ibid.*, p. 283.

21 Stewart, J., 2003. *Modernising British Local Government: An Assessment of Labour's Reform Programme*, Basingstoke, Palgrave MacMillan, p. 55.

22 Mill, *On Liberty*, p. 264.

23 *Ibid.*, p. 285.

24 *Ibid.*

25 Keith-Lucas, *The English Local Government Franchise*; Hennock, *Fit and Proper Persons*; Owen, D., 1982. *The Government of Victorian London 1855–1889: The Metropolitan Board of Works, the Vestries and the City Corporation*, Harvard University Press.

26 Tait, J., 1936. *The Medieval English Borough: Studies on its Origins and Constitutional History*, Manchester University Press; Redlich, J. and F.W. Hirst, 1958. *The History of Local Government in England*, London, Macmillan; Jewell, H., 1972. *English Local Administration in the Middle Ages*, Newton Abbot, David and Charles.

27 Redlich and Hirst, *The History of Local Government in England*, p. 101.

28 DETR, 1998. *Modernising Local Government: Local Democracy and Community Leadership*, London, DETR; DETR, 1998. *Modern Local Government: In Touch with the People*, London, DETR; DETR, 1999. *Local Leadership: Local Choice*, London, DETR.

29 Locke, J. (P. Laslett, ed.), 1992, first published 1690. *Two Treatises of Government*, Cambridge Texts in the History of Political Thought, Cambridge University Press.

30 Madison, J. (M. Beloff, ed.), 1948, first published 1788. Paper No. XLVII, in *The Federalist, or the New Constitution*, Oxford, Basil Blackwell, pp. 245–252.

31 Parry, G., G. Moyser and N. Day, 1992. *Political Participation and Democracy in Britain*, Cambridge University Press.

32 Local Government Act 2000, Part II, section 11, sub-section 6.

33 ODPM, 2003. *Strengthening Local Democracy: Making the Most of the Constitution*, London, ODPM.

34 *Ibid.*, p. 19.

35 MacCormick, N., 1993. 'Constitutionalism and Democracy', in R. Bellamy (ed.), *Theories and Concepts of Politics*, Manchester University Press, pp. 124–147.

36 Paine, T., 1985, first published 1791–92. *Rights of Man*, Harmondsworth, Penguin, p. 185.

37 Aristotle (S. Everson, ed.), 1992. *The Politics*, Cambridge Texts in the History of Political Thought, Cambridge University Press, p. 21 and p. 49.

38 Harrigan, J.J., 1991. *Politics and Policy in States and Communities*, London, Harper Collins, p. 202.

39 Although discussion of council constitutions is ongoing and they will change over time.

40 DETR, 2000. *New Council Constitutions: Modular Constitutions for English Local Authorities*, London, DETR, p. 48.

41 London Borough of Hackney, 2000. *The Constitution of the London Borough of Hackney*, London, London Borough of Hackney Council, article 4.

42 Borough of Hartlepool, 2002, *Hartlepool Borough Council Constitution*, Hartlepool, Hartlepool Borough Council.

43 Borough of Middlesbrough, 2002. *Middlesbrough Council Constitution*, Middlesbrough, Middlesbrough Borough Council.

44 Stoke-on-Trent Borough Council, 2002. *The Constitution of Stoke-on-Trent Borough Council*, Stoke-on-Trent, Stoke-on-Trent Borough Council, p. 13.

45 Redlich and Hirst, *The History of Local Government in England*.

46 Stoker, G. and H. Wolman, 1992. 'Drawing Lessons from US Experience: An Elected Mayor for British Local Government', *Public Administration*, Vol. 70, Summer, pp. 241–267, at p. 262.

47 See Copus, C., 2004. *Party Politics and Local Government*, Manchester University Press.

6

Elected mayors: a new style of English local politics?

Introduction

The English directly elected mayor inhabits a legislative and regulatory framework that carefully prescribes the duties, powers and responsibilities of that office and provides for the political structures of the council in which they will be enacted. While the government has made much of mayors' separate and distinct mandate, the mayoral office operates within the same political structures as the council leader, with broadly similar powers and responsibilities. While the internal political dynamics of mayoral councils are developing a shape and motion of their own, it is how the office of elected mayor develops the external dynamic of a political leader and governor which will help distinguish the office from that of the indirectly elected council leader.

In Chapter 3 the concept of political leadership as it attaches to English local politics was considered, as was the government's thinking in this regard. Yet academic work has shown that it is important not to define political leadership solely by what politicians do or do not do when faced with political problems. Political leadership has been placed in a much broader conceptual framework by Leach and Wilson, Svara and Clarke *et al.*, for example, but much of our understanding of what political leadership is comes as a result of what political leaders do.[1] Our understanding of political leadership will be further informed by what these new English mayors do in the complex local political environment beyond the doors of the town hall.

In addition, political leadership should be understood as a combination of systemic factors arising from the political, constitutional, cultural and legislative framework within which the mayor is located, and in terms of how the mayor uses those systemic resources and other personal and political resources. Moreover, how any elected mayor accrues additional resources and power, by the force of his or her own efforts, political skill, good luck and reputation, provides a Hobbesian foundation to understanding how individual mayors can develop as political leaders to wield political power either granted to them by the system or absorbed from other sources.[2]

This chapter explores how English directly elected mayors have been developing the role of political leader – as distinct from the political head of the council – as an office with the responsibility for making governing decisions. The chapter examines, through three case studies, how mayors have controlled, or been driven by, the dynamic of local politics. The purpose is not to decide on which mayor was effective and which not. Rather, it is to assess the political forces with which individual mayors were confronted and how they acted in a very specific set of political circumstances and context. As a consequence, the chapter assesses just how powerful the English elected mayor is when it comes to the governance of the locality.

The case studies explore the interactions between the mayor, the council and councillors, the community and other interested agencies and bodies in each of the issues. As such, they do not present all the intricate and complex details of the issues concerned, but rather they present those matters which aid an understanding of local political dynamics.

Hartlepool: the ghost ships

The Hartlepool 'ghost ships' issue displays all the tensions and difficulties involved in any conflict between environmentalism and economic development. It also displays the problems inherent in governing in the interests of the whole of a locality and at the same time representing the clear interests of very specific communities. It also rests on the complex political dynamics between local government and politics and central government and politics, the role of quangos in the governance process, and constitutional and legal arguments. The issue here is not confined to a local context alone, but spills beyond that. As a result, the issue is a test of how an elected mayor not only can act as the head of any one council, or as the political leader of a defined locality, but also can use the office to influence the activities of other regional and national agencies and government.

In 2003 a Teesside company won a contract to dismantle thirteen former US naval ships from a fleet of around 100, moored on the James River in Virginia. The ships were to be towed some 4,500 miles across the Atlantic, first to the Scottish coast and then to a dry-dock in Graythorp, Hartlepool. The US government had paid around £1 million per ship for past contracts of this nature. It was estimated that the contract would lead to the creation of around 200 permanent jobs; the local newspaper, the *Evening Gazette*, estimated the contract to be worth some £11 million.[3] Unemployment in the Teesside area at the time stood at around 16,000.

The company concerned promoted the contract on the basis of the ship-building and industrial capacity and traditions of Teesside, coupled with the quality and expertise of the local workforce. The dismantling of the 'ghost ships' was seen by supporters of the project as a way of assisting in the economic regeneration of the area and of enhancing the area's reputation as a major regional centre for dealing with complex marine decommissioning projects. The contract not only linked with the industrial past of the area, but was also seen as a major re-establishing of its economic base. The project allowed for private boosterism for the area, with claims made that the US government decision to grant the contract to a Teesside company was recognition that the area's dry-dock facilities were among the best in the world.[4]

The contract was supported by major economic interests in the area, not solely the company concerned, in particular the Tees Valley Development Corporation, whose chief executive commented publicly on the importance of the deal to economic regeneration. The North East Chamber of Commerce also supported the 'ghost ships' contract as a way of bringing employment to a specific area and having a positive cumulative effect on the region; also in support was the Tees Valley Partnership, whose chair promoted the deal. Thus, powerful economic interests lined up behind the proposed decommissioning of the ships. The company that secured the contract also planned to develop a £1.2 million landfill site in the area, to convert hazardous waste into 'concrete blocks', which would then be 'built into impervious cells' for landfill – an approach that would enable the site to meet new European waste restrictions, which came into force in 2004. The new landfill site would be used to dispose of the hazardous waste onboard the 'ghost ships'.[5]

Against these powerful economic interests were ranged: Friends of the Earth, a local protest group entitled IMPACT, local residents, the Royal Society for the Protection of Birds, wildlife experts and, taking a cautious role, English Nature. In addition, and involved at various points in the development of the issue, were: the Department of Transport, the Health and Safety Executive, the Coastguard Agency, the High Court, MPs, local governments in the US and a US-based 'toxic export' protest group called Basel Action Network. Coupled to this, local councillors of all parties and independents, and the mayor, all voiced opposition to the scheme at some point. The concerns of the opponents of the project were based largely on the possible damage to the health of local people arising from the presence of asbestos, oil and carcinogenic PCBs, which were part of the fabric of the ships, and on the likely damage to the local natural environment from the same sources. Hartlepool and Teesside traditionally thrived on ship-building and chemical asbestos, and as a consequence the area has a very high level of people suffering from asbestos-related diseases. As one campaigner said, 'Importing asbestos is importing death'.

As well as concerns about the health of the local population and about the environmental degradation of the area, concerns were also raised about the safety of the ships on the journey across the Atlantic and whether the ships would survive the trip. Thus, very local environmental concerns joined hands with broader concerns for the global environment. As well as the environmental matters at stake, protestors also voiced anger at being seen as a dumping ground for the waste products of other nations and at the fact that Hartlepool was being treated as the world's dustbin. As one local campaigner said in interview: 'Hartlepool is a very proud but insular area; emotionally we are an island surrounded by land.'

Thus, local civic pride also played a part in the way in which the issue developed. Such civic pride is a vital element that eases the task of local political leadership, as the leader can build upon an existing psychological critical mass among local citizens that makes them amenable to a leader who not only supports and understands local traditions and strengths but also has a clear vision of short- and long-term objectives. Civic pride, emerging from the history and traditions of the area, its regional and national standing, the cohesiveness of its local communities (of whatever shape or size) and the resonance and salience that the locality has for citizens, is crucial if local political leadership is to have any real meaning – but it is also a factor the successful leader can stimulate if it is lacking. The place where the mayor is located matters and affects the development of mayoral government.[6]

The role of the council in the issue of the 'ghost ships' was twofold: it was a recipient of citizen protest and played the role of a representative institution in that regard; and, while the council and mayor had no power over the decision as to whether the ships would come to Hartlepool at all, they were the planning authority that would make the decision as to whether the required dry-dock facility could be developed. Not surprisingly, the conflict between the council's representative and regulatory roles became acute as the issue developed. It is the tension between these two often conflicting roles that sat at the heart of the way in which the mayor and councillors were able to respond to the issue. Yet regulatory powers and the representation and articulation of local opinion are not always mutually inclusive, as will be seen.

After the announcement that the contract to dismantle the ships had been won and that the work would be carried out in Teesside, the environmental group Friends of the Earth and a local action group began to organise protests. Although these were focused on the company concerned and aimed at attracting media attention Hartlepool Borough Council was also a target, and an expectation soon emerged that the council and the elected mayor would act in support of local residents and protestors. Friends of the Earth called on the council to launch a full environmental investigation into the matter. Local councillors for the areas most affected soon entered the fray and supported the protestors. Councillors across the political spectrum made public statements in opposition to the 'ghost ship' project; an informal single-issue cross-party alliance developed as councillors put party affiliation to one side to campaign on the issue – though not in a formal cross-party sense. Public pressure mounted on the council and mayor to prevent the ships from arriving. In October 2003 a public meeting was organised by Friends of the Earth, at which the project was condemned. Also in October one of the council's neighbourhood committees considered the issue; the meeting attracted a large attendance by the public and from people across the region, not just Hartlepool; the scheme was vociferously condemned at the meeting.

The council's position was made all the more complex by its role as the planning authority which had to consider the company's application for permission for the construction works it needed to undertake to ensure it had the correct facilities to dismantle the ships. English councils, however, cannot use the planning regulatory functions to govern; they must, as was pointed out by the then MP for the area, Peter Mandelson, make a decision based on the merits of the planning application and not other extraneous concerns – such as what local people think! The company argued that it had planning consent going back to 1997 for the dry-dock; the council argued that the planning consent was not valid. Confusion, claim and counter-claim surrounded the issue of planning consent. The matter was made all the more difficult when an extraordinary council meeting, called to consider the issue in November 2003, voted unanimously to oppose the project and to pressure the government into action to prevent the ships from arriving. That decision led Peter Mandelson to question whether, as the council had made such a public statement, the planning application would receive an objective hearing and be considered on its merits. He accused the council of having 'compromised its position' by taking a policy position on the matter.[7]

The issue was also considered by the council's cabinet and by an overview and scrutiny committee investigation. At the day-long overview and scrutiny meeting, called to consider the environmental and economic regeneration aspects of the contract, the company was present, represented by a barrister, alongside protestors, and all where given time to address the meeting. The Environment Agency, Port Authority, the Regional Development Agency and the Health and Safety Executive, among others, were in attendance at this first meeting; four meetings were held at which the overview and scrutiny committee considered the issue. Indeed, a council report that went through cabinet and the overview and scrutiny committee assessing the issue was then sent to the Environment, Food and Rural Affairs Select Committee of the House of Commons. Cabinet and the overview and scrutiny committee played a part in solidifying the position of the council on the matter – which was to oppose the 'ghost ships', a position complicated by the council's planning powers and the way in which those powers had to be used. But what role did the elected mayor play?

The 'ghost ships' saga is interesting not only because it arose in an area governed by an elected mayor but also because it affected an area in which two elected mayors – both independent – held conflicting positions on the issue. Stuart Drummond, mayor of Hartlepool, opposed the arrival of the ships, but Ray Mallon, mayor of Middlesbrough, supported the contract to dismantle the ships in Teesside. Campaigners in the area recognised that when the mayor of Hartlepool opposed the dismantling of the ships, as one campaigner put it, 'an important friend was won for those protesting against the ships'. It appeared, however, to those outside the council that the mayor had 'waited to see what happened with councillors and officers before making his mind up'. Once deciding upon his position, the Hartlepool mayor made a series of press statements in which he voiced opposition to the ships' arrival. He was quoted in one local paper as saying:

> It is absolutely critical that the ships turn around and head back to the United States to bring an end to this farce … there are at least five permissions outstanding between the Environment Agency, Hartlepool Council and the Department for the Environment, Food and Rural Affairs, so I don't see how these ships can enter British waters…. We must prevent a situation whereby these ships are floating around off the coast of Hartlepool with nowhere to go. This situation can be prevented if they return to the USA now.[8]

In an interview the mayor commented:

> The council as a body had no real control over the whole thing, other than the planning consent, and it was our view all along that the company didn't have the consent it needed. The ships were still sent over; the matter went to court and we were proved right. I was not going to have the ships here and the burying of the toxic waste and asbestos in Hartlepool. I went on record in council as saying 'I don't want Hartlepool to be a dumping ground for other people's rubbish'.
>   I follow my conscience on such issues; it was good that the council and I took the same position; I make the decision I think is best for all, but you can't please all the people all the time.

The mayor also held a number of meetings with the company, local MPs and government agencies to negotiate a solution. He used a network of contacts and the office he held to exert political pressure on those who could prevent the ships arriving – but had no power to decide the matter.

Ironically for the mayor and for the office of elected mayor, one campaigner made the following comment: 'Thank God we have a few councillors who have pushed this issue forward into the public arena'. The individual making that comment went on to be elected as an independent candidate for the ward most affected by the project.

The elected mayor of Middlesbrough took a different view of the matter, one which saw the cumulative economic effects of the project as overriding environmental concerns. In this the mayor was absolutely consistent with the emphasis he had given to economic regeneration and in recognising the importance of a regional dimension to his mayoralty. The mayor had a vision that extended beyond the locality from which he was elected and had worked to forge better relationships with neighbouring authorities, where relations in the past had traditionally been 'strained'.

The Mallon mayoralty was not constrained by the boundaries of Middlesbrough Council and he had worked to develop political and business networks, which had made him a very powerful player in the region. Thus, the holder of one particular mayoralty had extended the influence of the office far beyond the council as an institution and area. While not yet displaying the characteristics of an urban regime, as the political and economic network involved had not yet developed a consistency of membership or policy, the Middlesbrough mayor had created and worked towards a clear policy agenda and long-term vision, which made his position on the 'ghost ships' understandable to, if not popular with, environmental groups and protestors.

On the issue itself Ray Mallon signalled his support for the project on a high-profile visit to the company's site, where he commented:

> The Americans should be applauded for putting this contract on the free market and the company applauded for winning it. Friends of the Earth object to this. I am a supporter of Friends of the Earth but on this occasion they have got it wrong.... We have to deal with these ships somewhere and the company is a world class one and are experts in this field.

He was also reported in the local press as accusing opponents of the contract of 'talking fiction and scaremongering' and as saying that 'the whole issue is nothing compared to what happens on the roads of Teesside every day of the week with the number of chemical tanker journeys being made'. The chair of Hartlepool council replied saying: 'The ships should go back ... about 90 per cent of the town want the ships to go back and that is reflected in the views of the elected councillors'.[9]

Thus, the two sides of the argument found a champion in a different directly elected mayor. It is at this point that the political and personality characteristics of the individuals and their respective approaches to governance come into play. These characteristics include how quick they are to develop a position on any issue and how they then deploy the personal, political and institutional resources they have at their disposal to pursue the position they favour. The process is made easier if a mayor has a defined and clear vision for the governance of the area and a set of policy initiatives which can act as criteria against which all other issues can be judged.

Ultimately, the protestors, Hartlepool council and the Hartlepool elected mayor were unsuccessful in their campaign and the first ships arrived in December 2003 and are still moored, at the time of writing, at Graythorp while the legal arguments around the issue are decided and planning permissions resolved. Yet it would be far too simplistic to conclude that one mayor succeeded and another failed. Neither had the power to make the final decision and the legal environment within which local politics is conducted makes it difficult, in these circumstances, to judge the relative success or failure of these two English mayors.

More than anything, the Hartlepool 'ghost ships' issue illuminates the lack of political power held by an English mayor when compared with that of some mayoral counterparts across the globe. The mayor of New York or an Italian mayor would simply close the ports to such ships, or even dispatch the coastguard to fend them off – much as the Portuguese government did when the ships sailed close to Portuguese waters. (The New York mayor does not have control of the ports – that is a state responsibility – but it is difficult to imagine a Mayor Giuliani type being constrained by that detail!)

Outside the granting or withholding of planning consent and the messy argument about whether existing consents were valid, Hartlepool council, as well as the mayor, lacked the power to make the final decision about the ships. Even the use of its planning regulatory powers is constrained by planning law and case-law, and we find no tool for government in them. Thus, the two main representative institutions, the elected mayor and the council, could not govern in this case and had no power to alter events, being able only to negotiate with interested parties and agencies, bring pressure to bear and attempt to influence the outcome of an important local issue. Or, rather disappointingly, the mayor and other politicians are sidelined while the courts resolve the matter.

North Tyneside: a public baths controversy

The closure of Killingworth public baths in North Tyneside is the type of issue which dispels myths about public apathy. While the public may not always be stimulated into turning out to vote at an election, this does not imply that voters are always uninterested in local affairs. Rather, when an issue that stimulates public concern arises and sections of the community are stimulated into action, what we see is that public engagement in local affairs is an episodic process, driven by important local concerns. Councillors, and of course elected mayors, are continually engaged in these political processes, in balancing competing political pressures and in governing and representing locally. The broad and continual interest in political affairs had by local politicians is distinct from the often (but not exclusively) narrow and episodic interest in local affairs expressed by citizens and stimulated by important local issues: Killingworth public baths in North Tyneside is just such an issue.

Killingworth public baths, constructed in 1973, were one of the last remaining buildings of the original Killingworth new town development and, as such, the baths had a local impact beyond what might normally be expected, being a prominent part of the town's recent history. The baths had suffered a series of maintenance problems and so had required frequent remedial work; there were serious concerns that the floor was on the verge of collapse. In December 2003, the Conservative elected mayor, on receipt of a report from the council's Directorate of Education and Cultural Services concerning the physical condition of the baths, ordered a temporary closure and a health and safety investigation by an external consultant. The mayor wanted to consult local people on the future of the baths before acting, but the independent report stressed the serious nature of the baths' condition and that they should be closed immediately, without consultation; the mayor took just such a course of action, supported by the cabinet, and ordered the baths closed for safety reasons. Announcing the closure, the mayor was reported as commenting: 'Our first and foremost priority must always be for the health and safety of our staff and the public. Now we have received further reports which make it clear that the building is no longer fit for purpose'.[10]

In an interview the mayor commented:

> As mayor, closing the baths was the first unpalatable thing I had to do; I really wanted to consult the residents before taking any action because there would be a reaction to this and people would want to know why such a decision had been made. I ordered a health and safety report and we went through everything that was wrong with the pool and when the crunch came, we had to close it; I wanted to tell people first but the consultant impressed on me the urgency of the situation; the pool just had to be closed.

The mayor's strongly expressed desire to consult local people before taking action indicates that her political antenna had made her aware of the likely public reaction. She also knew that informing people before a decision was taken and why it was to be taken could reduce much of the intensity of that reaction. In this case, however, the mayor was not able to act on her political instincts. Health and safety concerns overrode those and the reaction to the decision was very much as she had expected: a public outcry. Indeed, one resident described local people being 'stunned' by the closure and saw it as something which had come 'from nowhere'. There were no similar facilities in the nearby area, with the nearest public baths being eight to ten miles away from Killingworth, either in the centre of Newcastle or in Whitley Bay.

The mayor defended her decision thus:

> There's no doubt that the closure of the old leisure centre in the interests of health and safety has been a big disappointment to many people. It was a tough decision but it was also the only decision that could be made. No one is in any doubt that the building was rapidly approaching the time when the public and staff alike would have been at serious risk of injury. Now we must work for a future in which Killingworth has the best possible leisure facilities.

Some local campaigners were suspicious that a health and safety issue was being used as an excuse to close the baths as a way of reducing expenditure and that the consultant's report had simply provided the ammunition with which the closure could be made with minimal difficulty. Campaigners were also concerned that once the baths closed there would be no replacement made; many remembered the closure of the public baths in Wallsend by the then Labour administration (before the 2000 Act) and that the local community had been waiting some ten years for a replacement.

Local Labour councillors from the wards most affected were at the centre of the campaign to keep the baths open and applied pressure on the Conservative mayor in this regard. Indeed, much of the stimulation of public opinion and activity around the issue came as a result of the local councillors. A local Labour councillor put forward the view that the centre should not be replaced but rather refurbished, which was calculated as being cheaper than the cost of demolition. The usual methods of protest were employed by local people, such as meetings, leaflets, use of the press to publicise the issue and the collection of a petition, which secured some 2,000 signatures. Indeed, even North Tyneside's MP, former cabinet minister Stephen Byers, became involved. He made a public request for sports minister Richard Caborn to visit Killingworth to see the facilities available and to view, at first hand, what had been lost to the local community. Byers was reported in the local press thus:

> Three years ago the plans were in place to build new sports centres at Killingworth and Wallsend and these were scrapped when the Conservative Mayor was elected [referring to the first elected mayor of North Tyneside]; we are now seeing the fall-out of that decision. What Killingworth needs is a modern sports and leisure centre for the 21st century.[11]

There was, on the one hand, no doubt that a party political dimension existed in the responses and campaigning around this particular issue. Labour councillors and the local Labour MP were presented with an opportunity to be at the forefront of a high-profile public campaign against the decision of a Conservative directly elected mayor, a mayor who, at the time, had a minority Conservative group facing a majority of Labour and Liberal Democrat councillors. The mayor, on the other hand, was able to use the rejection of a funding bid put to government to build a new leisure centre in the locality as a way of indicating that responsibility for the lack of replacement facilities rested with the Labour government, not her administration. Thus, at the time, a chance existed for all combatants to draw some party political advantage from the issue.

On the other hand, of course, the role of the local ward councillor in such cases, and under a mayoral system, is to represent and articulate the views of the local community, and the councillors concerned (all Labour) carried out just that role. Indeed, the councillors went further, by organising and taking part in the popular local campaign around the baths' closure. Moreover, the campaign was not just a party political one. Rather, it attracted support from the immediate local community and beyond. Here the mayoral system was seen to be working partly as it should: the mayor took the governing decision and the responses of the electorate to that decision were represented and articulated by local councillors acting as advocates of the areas they represented.

Yet the mayor did not simply act as the target for and recipient of community protest. She also acted in a way that saw her respond to the initial public reaction and the on-going campaign by attempting to negotiate and develop a compromise solution with local people. The mayor's approach in wishing to negotiate and involve local people appears to be a stylistic choice, rather than making a virtue out of the necessity of facing a public campaign. In interview the mayor made it very clear that she wished to involve as many local people in a wide-based consultation about the future of leisure facilities in the area, but that she could not and would not back down from the original decision, which was largely out of her hands and based on health and safety advice. The mayor commented:

> We organised a half-day consultation event at which we listened to different views on the pool and what people wanted from it; we distributed questionnaires to find out what people thought. I wanted to take the best ideas and work from them. The event lasted from about 3 p.m. to 7 p.m. and about 700 people turned up during that time; it just never seemed to stop. We had set out photographs of the pool to show people what we were dealing with and what we were talking about and it came to a point where about seventy people wanted a one-to-one with me as their mayor – which they all got, but I managed to get through it.

Despite the continuing protest campaign, the mayor was effusive about the success of the consultation event; not only did it enable her to speak directly to those involved, but it did so within a consultative structure through which people were provided with information and given the opportunity to respond to proposals and have an input into developing the plans. It also diffused much of the anger and resentment at the speed of the original decision to close the baths and took the sting out of some of the criticism of the decision. Consultation is double-edged: it is useful for the consulted and for the consulters.

The mayor followed the consultation event with the formation of a steering group designed to explore the issue of leisure facilities within the Killingworth area and to consider options for the replacement of the old baths. The steering group was open to local people and to members of various interest groups. The mayor commented in interview:

> I put one councillor on the group, not all three [ward councillors] but the one who was interested, and I added the cabinet lead member on leisure and that's it from councillors. The rest of the membership is sixteen other people: eight directly from Killingworth and the others from the surrounding area. I took a cross-section of people and ages when setting up the group. Local children can also input their views through the schools. It is a really good group and it has worked extremely well. People are happier because they are included.

At the time of writing, final decisions were still to be made about the future of leisure provision in the Killingworth area and in the 2005 mayoral election the Conservative incumbent was defeated by the Labour candidate. There was most definitely a party political dimension to the way in which the issue developed, with both Labour and the Conservatives able to exploit the issue for party political advantage. But, at the same time, by their trying to secure party advantage, the public had their local champions: in this event, the champions turned out to be local Labour councillors, the Labour MP and the Conservative mayor, who had made the decision in the first place. It is easy to be sceptical about the way an issue like the closure of the Killingworth baths develops and is exploited by political parties, but in this case the party differences between mayor, councillors and MP probably led to the development of a political dynamic through which the mayor was challenged in just the way the mayoral system encourages. If all political players had been from the same party it is likely that a certain degree of closing of ranks to protect the party would have been evident. In this case local politicians generated a powerful dynamic to drive and shape community engagement but because it suited party politics.

The mayor acted variously as the public face of the political decision-making process, the target for public protest, a mediator and as a negotiator of a resolution to the issue. The use of a steering group has echoes in mayoral commissions and boards that are common across the

United States and are used to advise and support the mayor. The task of the new mayor is to respond to the outcomes of the steering group's deliberations in such a way as to display publicly how the final resolution to the question reflects those deliberations, and to show how the work of the group links into the wider political policy-making process.

Again, it is easy to be sceptical. Would the mayor have gone down this route of consultation and public engagement if there had not been a public reaction against the decision? Did the mayor have plans to reduce council expenditure and use this as an opportunity to close a council facility? Would the Labour councillors and MP have been quite so assid-uous in their opposition to the decision and their pursuit of improved facilities had the mayor been Labour at the time? While it is enjoyable to consider these points as a background to the political dynamic around the issue and while such conjecture may add some depth to the initial view of the issue, it is difficult to prove how people might have acted in different circumstances or what their motivations were for acting as they did in the actual circumstances. Suffice to say, with the political party as such a dominant force in local politics, all issues are party political to some degree and the Killingworth baths issue is no different.

The personality and political style of the individual mayor does make a difference to the way in which issues are dealt with and in this case the mayor was very open to consultation and involvement. Moreover, she gave an impression of an arms-length relationship with the Conservative group on the council and party politics in general. She commented in interview:

> I can rise above party politics and I recognise that I have risen above party. Although I stood on a Conservative ticket I feel very much as a managing director of a company, a public company, and the people I think are my shareholders are the people outside: the residents. I've huffed Conserva-tives, Liberal and Labour because I won't do what they want me to. I'll do what is right and I have had had some ups and downs with my own party.

She added, 'I think you realise as mayor that you can't always be party aligned'. The comment is enlightening because it suggests this mayor has a fractured relationship with her party. The fracturing, but not severing, of the relationship between mayor and party enabled her to step outside the narrow party view on political issues and embrace wider concerns. It also enabled the mayor to build coalitions and to negotiate with a wide range of political associations and interest groups. The mayor did not jettison her political beliefs, which had sustained her interest in politics for many years. Rather, the party was relegated in the eyes of the mayor when balancing the competing pressures involved in political decision-making, and as a result it was easier for her to engage a wider public debate concerning the resolution of a local issue.

Watford Borough: a hospital development and a link road across green space

One would have thought that the redevelopment and extension of a local hospital would have caused no problems for local policy-makers and would have met with general enthusiasm. But local politics is a complex business and local issues are rarely, if ever, straightforward, as the proposal to develop Watford General Hospital shows. The redevelopment of the hospital is part of a government initiative to provide fifteen new hospitals across the country, at a cost of £4 billion, to be funded largely through Private Finance Initiative schemes.

Six 'partner organisations', working with varying degrees of interdependence, drew up three options for the development of the existing hospital in Watford. The six partners involved in the scheme were: West Hertfordshire Hospitals Trust, Watford Football Club, Hertfordshire Partnership NHS Trust, East of England Development Agency, Watford and Three Rivers Primary Care Trust, and Watford Borough Council. The three options set out various alternatives concerning the nature of the care to be provided, the facilities available, the scale of the site and whether the health facilities would link with other services, such as leisure and recreation and commercial activity. The options thus moved from a straightforward medical care facility to a much broader community and commercial focus on an extended site. Each of the options, however, included the building of a link road across existing green open space at Oxley Park playing fields, to enable traffic to exit the M1 and travel direct to the hospital. The link road indicates that the nature of the hospital would change under any of the options from a local to a regional hospital, acting as a specialist centre; it was the link road that was the problem!

A backdrop to the issue was that the proposal to develop a link road from the M1 had been considered for some years before the proposed development of the hospital. Moreover, the various sites that would be encompassed by the development had non-health-related uses, and other potential future uses – leisure, commercial or other forms of development. Some local campaigners saw the development of the hospital as a way in which those pressing for the link road could tie it to a socially acceptable project and thus dissipate local opposition. Opposition also existed to the road running through the hospital site, as it could then be used by traffic to cut through the town; for many local people, if a road was to be built, it must be only to the hospital and not through it.

So, the proposal to develop a hospital site and provide a vastly increased range of health care facilities to local people as well as a specialist regional health centre was neither simple nor unanimously supported. Rather, different aspects of the various schemes attracted partial support and partial opposition from the public, local campaigners and local politicians alike.

Any development of the hospital would entail the transfer to Watford of the accident and emergency services located at Hemel Hempstead Hospital. The Strategic Health Authority (SHA) indicated that without the link road the new site would be difficult for people from Hemel Hempstead to gain access to, as they would have to leave the M1 and travel through Watford town centre. As one local campaigner interviewed for a local paper commented: 'These options are a joke. People are being asked "Would you like a road, would you want a road, or would you love a road?" That's not a real choice: anyway, you get a road'. She added that 'People need more than hospitals to keep them fit and healthy. Children need open space and fresh air to run around; that is important for health too'.[12] But, despite the importance of the link road to the SHA's plans, funding for such a road was not a certainty. Nor did the road form part of either Watford Borough Council's local plan or Hertfordshire County Council's local transport plan (in fact it had been rejected during the production of those plans).

Local people were being offered the prospect of considerable development and extension of their health care facilities, including what was termed a 'health campus'. This was set out on the borough council's website and would include:

- the location of community, intermediate and acute care facilities alongside leisure, recreation, education and fitness facilities;
- opportunities for outdoor recreation such as allotments, walking and cycling;
- businesses, medical education and research facilities.

Furthermore, environmental sustainability would be promoted through:

- a green travel plan that would encourage access to the site by public transport, walking or cycling;
- minimising the carbon impact of the scheme through the use of renewable energy;
- a waste-minimisation strategy to emphasise recycling, reuse and re-engineering of waste.

All this was set alongside the 'promotion of social inclusion and community cohesion' through:

- community involvement in the development process;
- social and economic measures to improve access to training and employment;
- the creation of an enterprise culture within the neighbourhood.

The website included a quote from the chairman of Watford Football Club: 'There's no question that working in concert, rather than as individual organisations, will result in improved amenities for the people of Watford'. The site also included a feedback sheet for responses to the proposal and, among other things, asked respondents to indicate (on a scale of one to five) whether they 'agreed' that the link road was 'crucial to the project's success … to cope with visitors, patients, emergency vehicles and public transport'.[13]

Powerful private, commercial and public organisations supported the proposed development of the hospital and the hospital site, which would have an effect on the social, economic and commercial environment beyond its provision of health care. But, as the local branch of Friends of the Earth and other local campaigners argued, the development would also have an impact on the environment: an impact that they considered would be detrimental. While the decisions about the development were not the borough council's alone, the elected mayor soon became a key player in the issue and a vital target point for public protest and campaigning activities around the proposed development. The mayor was also seen by those agencies and interests supporting the development as vital to their final success in obtaining approval for the scheme. Thus, both 'pro' and 'anti' interests recognised the central role a directly elected mayor could play in securing the decision they wanted, even though that final decision was not the mayor's alone to make.

In this case the Liberal Democrat elected mayor had taken a very careful and subtle approach, as she recognised the value to the area of the development of the hospital and health care facilities; yet she also had concerns about the need for and impact of the road on environmental and social grounds. In an interview the mayor said:

> The SHA have taken the road as a given; it is at the heart of the scheme for them, but that is just not the case for us. When the site looked as though it could go for industrial use I was sceptical about the road but things were evenly balanced; if pushed though I was not enthusiastic about it. The health campus idea seems to me to tip the balance in favour of the road. Particularly as the hospital [Watford General] would then retain its acute status.

She added:

> The way in which the scheme has developed and the options given mean that I have to look at this again with the council. I want an assessment of the environmental and traffic impacts on the scheme and I want to see those assessments before making my mind up. I will do what I think is best for the town: as mayor I have to. There are real differences of opinion in my group [Liberal Democrats] with some in favour of the road, but because it will improve the hospital facilities; others are vehemently opposed to the road and have been for a long time; and others are waiting to see before making their minds up – publicly anyway.

The mayor gave an insight here into the tensions within her party group of councillors and frankly admitted to 'holding the line' between those for and against within the group until 'we had all the evidence on which to come to a position'. She also commented that other party groups were 'watching how things developed' and that they were in the same position as her own group – with varying opinions among councillors of the same party. While the mayor was an obvious recipient of public pressure in this case, she maintained in public a balanced and, indeed, almost neutral stance. Yet she had been reported in the press some years previously as being in opposition to a road across the area concerned. When the issue re-emerged, however, and was linked directly to improved health care facilities, the mayor, by taking a publicly neutral stance, placed herself in an ideal position to negotiate and to be seen as willing to assess all views and evidence before coming to a decision.

There was little room, however, for a negotiated compromise brokered by the mayor between campaigners and the SHA and developers, as the SHA insisted that any development rested on the construction of the link road and that without it the future of the hospital itself could be in some doubt. The campaigners seemed less intransigent in their views, with one commenting that he was 'keeping an open mind' about the road but was insistent that 'those involved need to look at alternatives to the road'. It was clear to the mayor that much was at stake and not just the building of the link road. Moreover, the mayor certainly wanted the hospital development to progress and was an enthusiastic supporter of the health campus initiative. While her favoured position was the achievement the health campus without the new road, she was not prepared to allow the question of the road to destroy the possibility of what appeared to be a vastly improved health care facility located within Watford, which would be of regional and possibly national importance – a major coup for the borough would be secured by such medical facilities being located within its boundaries.

Watford and District Friends of the Earth recognised that it was not the mayor alone who would make the final decision and were careful in much of the press publicity they generated to associate mayor and borough council together. Mayor and council were targeted by the group, and by local campaigners more generally, because, although not the final decision-makers, they were the elected representatives of the area and mayor and council had separate and distinct electoral mandates and representative roles to play. Environmentalists went as far as to threaten a 'Swampy-style protest' if the council supported, or gave the go-ahead for, the scheme (Swampy being a now almost legendary environmental campaigner involved in direct-action campaigns against the Newbury by-pass). The usual high-profile campaigning techniques were employed by campaigners, designed to apply pressure on the council and mayor to oppose the link road aspect of the proposals and designed to raise public awareness of the issue and involvement in the campaign. Friends of the Earth needed to be careful that, while campaigning against the road, they would not be held responsible should the SHA decide not to develop the hospital facilities or, worse, reduce or close what was already in existence.

At a cabinet meeting held on 8 November 2004 a report was received from council officers which set out the 'master plan' for the Watford health campus and which was to act as 'a context for the preparation of the future local development framework'.[14] The plan was endorsed by the cabinet but a decision was not made on the construction of the link road. Indeed, at that cabinet meeting the mayor expressed the view that, despite the SHA seeing the road as a 'given', the council would need 'strong evidence of access problems to justify the road being built' and that it would in any case be 'subject to the normal planning and consultation stages'.

At this stage, an uneasy course was being charted by both mayor and cabinet, with the desire to secure the new health facilities seen as a major objective, while recognising that the public opposition to the link road could jeopardise the scheme. The mayor and councillors were very aware of the need to respond to public opinion. The mayor commented in interview that she would 'do the right thing' for the town, a view expressed by most elected mayors and of course a view taken by all elected representatives – the problem is, who decides what is best for whom and on what basis do they make that type of political judgement?

Mayor and councillors were both the recipients of public pressure opposing the construction of the link road from the M1. Yet it is fair to say in this case that, as the project had a clear authority-wide impact, it was the mayor rather than individual councillors who was identified very early as the appropriate point of protest.

The mayor's carefully cultivated neutral and investigative public position enabled her to act as a broker on the issue, politically within the council and externally with the SHA and local campaigners. The mayor was thus a central figure in the way the issue developed. Such brokerage in these circumstances is a difficult task, requiring some political skill, but the office of elected mayor, as the mayor admitted, made the process manageable and conducive to the employment of the required political skills because of the high-profile and direct mandate her office held. The office of mayor carried a weight when it came to providing political leadership on the issue and a legitimate governing position which protestors, and agencies supporting the project, recognised and to which they responded. Yet it was the mayor alone who had to consider whether the right course of action would be to abandon her long-standing opposition to the road in order to secure the promise of improved health care and the economic benefits that were also promised to flow from the development: politics here is the art not only of the possible, but also of the most desirable.

The Liberal Democrat mayor of Watford had originally opposed the introduction of an elected mayor to the borough and announced before her election (as mayor) that she wished to see it replaced. She freely admitted in interview to having changed her mind on the matter and saw elected mayors as a powerful and positive system of local governance and as enhancing local political accountability.

Conclusions

The three case studies set out in this chapter display a number of themes common to the experiences of English directly elected mayors. The elected mayor is clearly seen by citizens as having a legitimate governing role in the locality; that is, the mayor can make decisions and make things happen, or can use the office for political and moral leverage to influence decisions made by others. The elected mayor, however, does not escape the tension between governing an area and representation of, and response to, the views of citizens and their reactions to local events. Rather, the mayor experiences, much the same as councillors, a tension between making or influencing governing decisions and responding to public engagement in local issues.

By acting as a lightning-rod for public engagement the office of directly elected mayor has fulfilled one of the objectives of its introduction into English local government: to provide high-profile and visible political leadership. In interviews with mayors a common theme which emerged was the high level of public awareness of them as individuals and of the office of elected mayor within the locality.[15] One mayor reported on the near impossibility of 'going to the shops in the town without spending hours and hours just talking to people about one thing or another'. He admitted to being 'on duty 24 hours a day, 365 days of the year'.

Closely linked to experiencing the governing–representing tension also experienced by councillors was the mayoral response of 'doing the right thing' when faced with a difficult political decision that had stimu-lated public engagement and public concern or outright opposition. There are two dimensions to this tension: stimulated public engagement directed at a decision the mayor or council has taken; and public engage-ment and political activity stimulated by a decision or action (or inaction) from another public or private agency or body, but where citizens expect the mayor to act on their behalf to solve or resolve the issue. Mayors are clearly seen as 'leaders' with regard to the pursuance of local concerns.

'Doing the right thing' can be seen as mayoral code for taking a broad governing decision for the benefit of all, but one which attracts high levels of public protest and which might adversely affect the quality of life of a small number of citizens within the council's area. In other words, 'doing the right thing' is exactly what councillors do when taking broad governing decisions for the benefit of the whole, but which attract public protest. The only difference for councillors is that the ward-based nature of local representation in English local government results in local citizens having a high expectation that their councillor will 'do the right thing' by his or her patch, not necessarily the whole council area.[16] English mayors are no different to any politician in this regard and, despite the fact that they are the only politicians directly elected to a governing office, the public expect that governing will be tempered by responding to and representing local views.

In two of the case studies, the mayor and council were not the final decision-makers for resolving the issue. Rather, the mayor and council were part of a complex network of political interaction and governance. The mayor's role was to provide a broad governing response, while the council had the added responsibility of being the planning authority – which, rather than strengthening its hand to respond to public engagement, prevented it from developing a policy response. The political leadership role of the mayor in these cases was about developing and sustaining a high public profile and levels of public engagement in the matter. The mayor also had the role of a broker at the centre of a political, administrative and judicial network.

Whatever the preference of any mayor for focusing on the internal running and leadership of the council, or on broader political governance beyond the confines of the council, mayors, as well as making things happen, must respond to the decisions and actions of others. The case studies show not only that English mayors must navigate a complex set of interrelationships when governing but also that they cannot rely on being able to make a decision at the end of such negotiation. Rather, they may see that decision lifted out of the remit of local government altogether and placed with central government or the courts. Here, elected mayors are no different to any other local council leader.

Despite the deliberate and widely inaccurate inflation of mayoral power by those opposed to this form of local government, the reality is very different: the power of the English mayors is simply inadequate to enable them to govern and to take governing decisions locally that would extend into the political environment beyond the role of the council and its responsibilities. Mayors cannot compel other agencies to act, nor can they prevent them from doing so, but, as mayors are directly chosen by the entire electorate, there is a case for giving them more direct power to act beyond the confines of running a council. To inform debate about the political and governing powers English directly elected mayors could (or should) have, we need to look at how some systems overseas have configured the political role and power of the office of elected mayor, and this is done in the next chapter.

Notes

1 Svara, J., 1990. *Official Leadership in the City: Patterns of Conflict and Co-operation*, Oxford University Press; Svara, J. (ed.), 1994. *Facilitative Leadership in Local Government: Lessons from Successful Mayors and Chairpersons*, San Francisco, CA, Jossey-Bass; Clarke, M., H. Davis, D. Hall and J. Stewart, 1996. *Executive Mayors for Britain? New Forms of Political Leadership Reviewed*, London, Capita; Leach, S. and D. Wilson, 2000. *Local Political Leadership*, Bristol, Policy Press.
2 Hobbes, T. (R. Luck, ed.), 1992, first published 1651. *Leviathan*, Cambridge Texts in the History of Political Thought, Cambridge University Press, p. 62.
3 *Hartlepool Evening Gazette*, 5 September 2003.
4 *Ibid.*, 28 July 2003.
5 *Ibid.*, 7 January 2004.
6 Cars, G., P. Healey, A. Madanipour and C. de Magalhaes, 2002. *Urban Governance, Institutional Capacity and Social Milieux*, Aldershot, Ashgate.
7 *Hartlepool Evening Gazette*, 11 November 2003.
8 *Ibid.*, 4 November 2003.
9 *Ibid.*, 12 November 2003.
10 *Evening Chronicle*, 8 December 2003.
11 *The [North Tyneside] Journal*, 11 March 2004.
12 *Watford Observer*, 27 October 2004.
13 www.watfordhealthcampus.info/pages/home/intro.php.
14 Watford Borough Council, cabinet minutes, 8 November 2004.
15 See also Randle, A., 2004. *Mayors Mid-Term: Lessons from the First Eighteen Months of Directly Elected Mayors*, London, New Local Government Network; Stoker, G., 2004. *How Are Mayors Measuring Up? Preliminary Findings – ELG Team*, London, ODPM.
16 Young, K. and N. Rao, 1995. 'Faith in Local Democracy', in J. Curtice, R. Jowell, L. Brook and A. Park (eds), *British Social Attitudes: The Twelfth Report*, Aldershot, Dartmouth, pp. 91–117.

7

The elected mayor:
lessons from overseas

Introduction

English directly elected mayors have been parachuted into the existing landscape of local government with little in the way of new powers, roles and responsibilities to enable them to govern in a uniquely mayoral fashion, and with little thought given to the way mayoral councils should be changed to reflect the new arrangements – other than through internal restructuring. The government may have wished for elected mayors to act in different ways to council leaders and for them to provide a more legitimate platform for local political leadership, but it did not provide a distinctly mayoral council organisation or powers from which a new form of local politics could be delivered.

In this chapter the English elected mayor is placed in a comparative context. The chapter looks at mayoral systems in five countries and explores the powers and roles of the mayor, as well as the structural and political relationships mayors have with councils and citizens. To see what lessons can be learnt from overseas for the development of the English approach to mayoral local government, the chapter takes an overall system approach, as such an approach avoids losing such lessons in the detailed consideration of mayoral arrangements in specific cities and the character of particular mayors; at this stage in the English experiment, more can be learnt from overall systems comparisons than from city-by-city detail. When considering mayoral government in the United States, however, New York City is used as an example of a 'strong' mayor to distinguish this model from the US 'weak' mayor – most of whom are selected by the council. In looking at New York, it is the mayoral system and not the incumbent that is the focus of interest.

The countries considered in this chapter have been selected because the approach taken to mayoral local government has some clear lessons for the way in which England could adapt its system of elected mayors. Moreover, the mayoral arrangements within the countries selected highlight a range of issues which have been ignored or misjudged in the development of the English approach. Thus, the chapter considers those mayoral models from overseas that are particularly pertinent to the debate about the development of the English experiment with directly elected mayors in areas such as: the power, responsibility and roles of the elected mayor; the balance of power and checks and balances between mayor and council; the prominence, or otherwise, of the elected mayor within the wider governance network; and how citizens can act as a check and balance within local politics.

The Italian mayor: the search for a new style of political leadership

The direct election of an executive mayor was introduced in Italy in 1993, by Law 81. There are two systems of election to mayor, and these apply to the *communi* (of which there are around 8,000) and the *provincie* (of which there are ninety-seven, at the second tier of sub-national government, below the twenty *regioni*). In both systems, although mayoral candidates are associated with a party list, the principle of direct election of the mayor is maintained: in the smaller authorities voters may cast a preference vote for a council candidate separately from that of the mayor; and in the larger authorities, the mayoral candidate can be linked with several party lists and voters may choose to vote for a mayoral candidate and associated list, or a mayoral candidate without choosing an associated list, or for a mayoral candidate and a list not associated with him or her.

Where no mayoral candidate secures an absolute majority, a second ballot is held between the two front-runners from the first vote. Thus, elected mayors do not head a party list in a way that requires voters simply to choose a list in the knowledge that the first named candidate would become mayor if that list secured a majority of seats or became the largest party, as with the French system. Rather, Italian voters can cast votes for mayor, council candidate and different lists – depending on the size of the authority in which they live.[1] To avoid political instability, the successful mayoral candidate's list is given a winning supplement in the distribution of council seats – a political bonus for winning the election, to provide the mayor with a governing majority.

The political factors behind the Italian adoption of the elected mayor (and for that matter the direct election of the Presidents of the *provincie*) have parallels with the English experience. Caulfield and Larsen have summarised the move towards a directly elected political executive as having the following objectives: to enhance the national prominence of local government; to strengthen local democracy and encourage greater citizen involvement in politics and elections; to provide a focus for community leadership; to strengthen the organisational leadership of local authorities; and to reduce the impact of party politics.[2] In the Italian context, the activities of political parties, the scandals associated with the Italian party system and its near collapse saw the development of a distinctly 'anti-party' mood, which sought a system of local political decision-making which was 'decollectivised' and which reflected a desire to create a system based on high levels of individual responsibility and accountability for decisions and policy. Indeed, Magnier concluded that the reforms were aimed at introducing 'a modern anti-party style of decision-making'.[3] In Italy, much as in England, local decision-makers had hidden behind the smokescreen of the political party to obscure political responsibility and hinder the process of political accountability.[4] Moreover, party discipline had served to rob the public space of genuine political discourse, again, much as it has done in England, and party loyalty was rewarded with mayoral office.[5]

While the Blair government's modernisation agenda shared the values identified by Caulfield and Larsen, its reasoning for the introduction of directly elected mayors into England was not driven by the 'anti-party' mood that had developed in Italy. Indeed, the reaction from party politicians in England to the election of a number of independents as mayors, and the fear that a mayor from the world of celebrity or the political periphery may secure office, are used as reasons why the experiment should be abandoned. Indeed, Deputy Prime Minister John Prescott poured scorn on the mayoral model because a candidate in a monkey suit (in Hartlepool) had been elected to office. He failed to realise that this successful candidate, and the voters in Hartlepool, had made bigger monkeys out of the political parties by rejecting them in favour of an independent mayor.

While some of the political factors which led to the adoption of elected mayors in Italy echo those that saw their arrival in England, it is in the powers of the mayoral office and in the nature of the checks and balances on it that we see real differences (as well as some similarities) in the approach to local political leadership. It is the mayor who appoints the executive body (*la giunta*) and the mayor can choose non-councillors to be part of this body (*assessori*); the mayor can dismiss its members but must inform the council of the reasons for dismissal. Indeed, the *assessori* are often clearly identified during election campaigns as the mayor's future executive members. The regulations around the *assessori* vary, depending on the size of the municipality and local governing statutes. In smaller areas they can be ordinary citizens not elected to the council or councillors; in larger areas they cannot hold the office of councillor at the same time – thus mayors must look beyond the council for their governing body. The mayor is a member of the council and both mayor and *assessori* can serve only two consecutive terms.

Legislation (article 23 of the 1993 Law) limits the number of *assessori* to no more than two in areas with up to 3,000 inhabitants; between 3,001 and 10,000 the mayor can appoint four; in areas with between 10,0001 and 100,000 six; and in areas with more than 100,000 inhabitants and large metropolitan areas eight *assessori* are permitted. Here we see a much more refined series of controls over mayoral cabinet patronage than that of the English system, where the mayor's cabinet cannot exceed nine other members, regardless of the size of the council or of the population governed. In addition to the *assessori*, the Italian mayor can appoint and dismiss the council's representatives to agencies, enterprises and other bodies, the heads of council offices and services, along with managers and a wide range of representatives on external bodies that work in partnership with the council.

The Italian mayoral system, introduced in the 1990s, has shifted the balance of local political power in favour of the mayor over the council, as it has given the mayor wide executive powers. The council will discuss the executive's programme and can suggest changes, but the results of such debate are not binding on the mayor and there is no fixed deadline for council approval of the mayoral programme. Where agreement cannot be found, the executive carries on without council approval, or the council tables a motion of no confidence in the mayor. The Italian no-confidence motion, if carried, is a weapon of mutually assured destruction: if a no-confidence motion in the mayor is passed by the council, not only does the mayor resign but so too must the council, and new elections for both are called. Such a refinement is used because the mayor's inflated majority of seats in council would mean that a new mayor elected would not have a governing majority. Moreover, dissolving the council tempers the use of the no-confidence motion by councillors, who, if not fearing for the loss of their own seat, may be tempted to use a wide range of inappropriate personal and party political reasons to remove the mayor – who, after all, serves by virtue of the direct public vote.

The two tiers of Italian sub-national government which have a directly elected political head are responsible between them for a wide range of vital public services. The *provincie* cover areas such as: roads, secondary education, environmental protection (shared with the region), public order, social services and social security; the *communi* are responsible for environmental health, housing, social security (shared with the *provincie*), planning, public works, police, transport, local roads, recreation and markets. Yet the array of service responsibilities masks the real political power and influence that rests with the Italian elected mayor, who acts as a powerful focal point of political decision-making and is able to speak in all tiers of Italian government as a legitimate political leader and ambassador for the area. Indeed, mayors are often important players in the distribution of national resources to the localities.[6]

Unlike in England, the Italian system has embraced, rather more readily, the notion of a separation of powers, with majority parties on the council often seeing themselves as the counterpoint to mayoral authority. Yet the anti-party impetus behind the introduction of an elected mayor has been somewhat thwarted. Whereas the first elections to mayoral office saw the mayoral candidate take public precedence over the parties and party system, more recent elections have seen parties re-establish themselves as the prime mechanism by which mayoral candidates are selected and governing programmes developed and implemented.[7]

The US elected mayor: a strong or a weak political leader

In the United States, local government is a state and not a federal area of responsibility, and within and between the America states a wide variety of mayoral arrangements exist. Local government systems depend on a range of local factors, state constitutions and state laws,[8] and many US mayors are indirectly elected by the council. Depending on state legislation, the local government system may be open to change by citizen petition and referendum. The discussion of the US mayoral system here is not intended to be a detailed overview of the entire range of mayoral arrangements available, as that is beyond the scope of this book.[9] Indeed, Morgan and Watson commented that: 'every US city has a mayor; there the similarity ends'.[10] The section sets out, however, the main distinctions in the approach to elected mayors in the United States and focuses on the strong mayoral model, elaborating the discussion with the example of New York. It does this to provide an indication of the enhanced powers required by English mayors if they are to be able to offer a distinctive local political leadership to their localities.

Broadly speaking, the US mayor is normally categorised as either 'strong' or 'weak' and these terms relate to the balance of power in the institutional arrangements of local government. Most strong mayors are found in the mayor–council form of government and are directly elected by local voters. Most weak mayors are mayors in a council–manager form and are elected by the council of which they are a member. Table 7.1 distinguishes between the two models.

A 'strong' directly elected mayor has his or her political and executive authority legally established and has a veto over the ordinances passed by the council; the mayor is responsible for the budget and for a range of local services and activities. With the weak mayor model, by contrast, it is the council which largely has both legislative and executive functions. The council appoints council officers, develops policy and produces the budget. The mayor is 'weak' because the office lacks executive powers and a veto over council action.[11] Broadly speaking, the 'strong' mayor predominates in the larger cities and the 'weak' mayor in medium-sized and smaller towns.[12]

Table 7.1 Some distinctions between the US 'weak' mayor and the US 'strong' mayor

The 'weak' mayor	The 'strong' mayor
The council is powerful, with legislative and executive authority	The mayor is the chief executive officer, with centralised executive power
The mayor is not a chief executive and has limited power and/or no veto	While the council has legislative power, the mayor has a veto
The council can prevent the mayor from effectively supervising the city administration	The mayor directs the administrative structure of the city, appointing and removing departmental heads
There may be many administrative boards that operate independently from the city government	The council does not control the day-to-day running of the city

Source: National League of Cities, www.nlc.org.

As well as the mayor and council arrangement, a mayor and council manager system is also available to the US town. Here the local executive consists of a directly elected mayor and an appointed council manager; the legislative and executive functions of the council are separated, but the balance of executive power is tipped in favour of the appointed manager rather than the elected mayor. Indeed, in some such council areas, the mayor has only a ceremonial or ambassadorial role (in contrast, in other councils, even the institutionally 'weak' mayor has been able, by force of personality, to enhance the status and power of the office). The mayor and manager model arose from the demands of municipal reformers of the late nineteenth century for action to be taken against machine party politics and the power that political parties wielded over sections of the local community; that is, the mayor and manager system was largely a reaction to the problems associated with party politics.

The strong US mayor has very real executive political authority. He or she is the head of the local administration and is able to appoint and dismiss a wide range of departmental heads, in many cases without the approval of the council, and this alone gives the mayor a tremendous ability to direct and coordinate the policy of local authority departments and to ensure the quality of their work and services. In New York, the mayor was at the centre of the response by a wide range of local, state and national bodies to the terrorist atrocity of 11 September 2001 and the mayor was the focus of activities designed to maintain the running of city government as the consequences of the attack became apparent.[13] The strong mayor: sets the policy agenda for the city; determines the details of the city budget; and has a veto over council decisions, although this may be subject to an overriding vote passed by two-thirds of the council. In some cases a strong mayor presides over the council.

As well as being institutionally strong in relation to the council, the mayor is also clearly identified as the source of local political power. The mayor is a symbolic leader of the city and the individual holding the office of a strong mayor can accrue more political resources by dint of personality. The council does have approval powers over the mayor's budget and acts as a scrutiny mechanism over mayoral policy and activity. The council will often have its own chair, speaker or 'leader'. The political interaction between mayor and council is, however, primarily one of debate, negotiation and the seeking of compromise and alliances and, while mayors may use informal influence to strengthen their position, so too can the council.[14] In many US municipalities where politics exists on a legally non-partisan basis and where the party allegiance of the candidate is not declared on the ballot paper, the power of personality and the ability to be able to project a public persona and to raise one's political profile are often at a premium for both mayors and councillors, which in turn enhances the US local politician's ability to accrue informal political resources.[15]

New York

The directly elected mayor of New York is elected to serve a four-year term and any one mayor is limited to serving a maximum of two terms in office. The mayor has a wide range of executive powers under the city charter, which was granted by the New York state legislature; he or she also oversees the general activity of New York City. The city was created in 1898, when its five constituent boroughs were brought together, and the system of government has remained virtually unaltered since that time.

New York itself, of course, was founded as New Amsterdam in 1625 and in 1653 was incorporated as a city; a council of legislators sat as the local law-making authority. The present council was created in 1938, under a new city charter, with a twenty-six-member council elected by proportional representation, the members of which could serve only two terms; this was extended to four terms in 1945 and these terms were to coincide with the term of office of the mayor. Proportional representation was abolished in 1949 and replaced by the election of one councillor for each state senate district and two members at large from each of the five boroughs. In 1983 the existence of these ten at-large members was deemed, by a federal court, to violate the US constitution's one-person one-vote principle. In 1989, after a Supreme Court ruling, a new charter provided for the redrawing of the council's district boundaries to increase minority representation; it also increased the number of councillors from thirty-five to its present fifty-one. The council's power, however, is limited in nature and it acts mainly as a check and balance on the mayoral executive. The mayor's budget can be overturned by a two-thirds majority and the council must vote on legislation proposed by the mayor. The city council acts as a deliberative and investigative body, calling witness, debating issues and issuing reports. The council also monitors the performance of city agencies and departments, makes decisions on land use and can pass local legislation governing the city, a recent example being the banning of smoking in public places.

While the city council claims it is an equal partner with the mayor in governing the city, in reality New York has a distinctly 'strong' mayoral system and the mayor is the highly visible and recognisable political leader of the city. Moreover, while New York City council has long been controlled by the Democratic Party, it has had to work, for the two-terms of mayor Rudolph Giuliani's administration and for the current mayoral incumbent Michael Bloomberg's administration, with a Republican executive; and the powers of the city council prevented neither of these Republicans from governing.[16] The powers and responsibilities of the mayor are considerable. He or she oversees all city departments, including police, fire, office of emergency management, hospitals, social services, refuse collection, planning and the bridges and tunnels of New York. The mayor is also responsible for appointing city judges, proposing new legislation and approving or vetoing legislation from the council.

The mayor has powers of appointment to city departments, deputy mayors and the members of special commissions, although such nominations do require the approval of the city council. The Municipal Arts Commission, the Board of Health, the Board of Standards and Appeals, and the City Planning Commission are all appointed by the mayor, again, with council approval. The mayor oversees the activities and policies of the Office of Immigrant Affairs and Language Service, the Office of Management and the budget, the Office of Operation and the Office of Medical Examiner, as well as the departments of consumer affairs, correction, cultural affairs, environment, finance, law, record and transportation – to name but a few. Moreover, the existence of a powerful mayor's office, which coordinates and oversees policy implementation, provides a political resource that further strengthens the hand of the mayor in city government.

Together these appointment powers to city departments and to various city commissions display mayoral power and the ability to coordinate city activity in a way that is beyond the dreams of an English mayor. Yet they also raise the stakes for the mayor when it comes to public political accountability. The success or failure of departmental initiatives are seen to be the responsibility of the mayor; the average New Yorker knows that the mayor is responsible for the police and fire departments; the response to the terrorist attacks on 11 September 2001 clearly rested with the mayor and, in normal political circumstances, the buck stops at the mayor's desk!

The experiences of the New York mayoralty, and the other strong US mayors, indicate two key lessons for the English experience. First, to govern locally, the mayor must have the power to do so and to take the necessary action to initiate, develop, implement and coordinate policy across a wide range of local and sub-national governing departments and agencies. Taking this lead, some responsibilities currently resting with central or regional authorities in England could safely be passed to the English directly elected mayor. Second, as in all politics, the qualities, skills and abilities of holder of the office matter to political success, even where the office-holder is granted institutional strength and political resources; strong mayors, and for than matter any politician, are effective only if the holder of the office is up to the job – and the choice about the qualities required and the candidates who display them should rest with the voter.

Japan and the directly elected political leader

Japanese local government has a position that is clearly recognised within the country's constitution, adopted in 1946, which contains an article in chapter 8 that declares 'respect' for the notion of local autonomy and its principles. The constitution sets out the requirement for the legislative and executive branches of local government to be directly elected. The organisational and management arrangements of local government are defined in the Local Autonomy Law of 1947, and are based on the prefectures and municipalities that existed before 1947. The Act set out the responsibilities of both prefectures and municipalities in a clear fashion but, over time, both tiers of local government have come to share responsibility for functions in the same field. The legal relationship between prefectures and municipalities is not one of superior and subordinate: prefectures, as regional authorities, can provide municipalities with guidance and advice based on a regional perspective, but they do not control municipal activity. Indeed, prefectures and municipalities were described by Muramatsu *et al.* as 'completely self-governing bodies'.[17]

Prefectural areas are based on local administrative units dating back as far as the eighth century and are well established features of the political landscape; the scale of municipalities has developed since 1947 and from 1953 to 1961 there was a trend for towns and villages to merge to improve the fiscal basis of the local political unit and to promote local autonomy. Thus, local government in Japan has developed to reflect the pressures of modern social, economic and political factors, and these factors have steadily resulted in larger units of local government at the level of the municipality.[18]

Despite the wide range of service responsibilities that rest with the Japanese local authority, Muramatsu *et al.* argued that it was not until the 1970s that local government became a major force in the democratisation of Japan, when it became a major forum for politically contentious activity and policy innovation and assisted in the process of strengthening civil society.[19] The 1999 Law Concerning the Provision of Related Laws for the Promotion of Decentralisation of Power (the Omnibus Decentralisation Act) clarified the division of responsibilities between central and local government and gave local government a very broad range of responsibilities: a clear focus of responsibilities for the centre and localities are defined aspects of Japan as a nation.

Political parties have a powerful tendency to reunite that which a constitution and statute have set apart and this is the case in Japanese politics. Political parties, mayors, governors and Diet members must and do cooperate in the political process to win power at various levels of Japanese government. It is also true of Japanese politics that elected representatives come from a wide range of bodies and interests, not just political parties. Moreover, a clear rural–urban difference is evident in the nature of local politics, with urban areas being far more party politicised and rural areas clinging to the notion of a representative as representing an area, not a party.

Japanese local government consists of a legislative and an executive branch. The legislature (the council) determines the local budget, enacts local legislation or by-laws and determines its own policy. The executive body – governors at prefecture level and mayors at municipal level – implement the policy decided by the council. Governors and mayors are directly elected separately from the council and the relationship between council and executive is one of a separation of powers and a system of local political checks and balances. One major check on the governor and mayor is that the executive itself is divided and includes a number of administrative committees independent of the governor and mayor, such as boards of education, public safety and election committees, which are responsible for the running of their respective service areas. Governors and mayors are elected for a four-year term and they cannot serve in these offices at the same time as being a member of the national Diet or a local councillor.

Japanese elected mayors are responsible for the quality and consistency of the services provided by the authority and for the conduct of all affairs of the local authority, excluding those of the council and the administrative committees; the governor and mayor do, however, have a wide power of appointment to these administrative committees. Prefectures and municipalities have their own boards of education, the members of which hold office for four years and are appointed by the governor or mayor, but members of these bodies must secure council approval of their appointment. The governor appoints the members of the public safety committee (not created in municipalities) and the members of this body serve for a three-year term. A number of other administrative committees at prefecture and municipal levels are appointed by the governor or mayor. Election committees are appointed by the council in both prefectures and municipalities. The governor and mayor are recognised in law as the representatives of their areas and have a powerful ambassadorial role to play in integrating their own authorities into governance networks.

The Japanese system rests, then, on a separation of powers and one which reflects elements of the US system, arising as it does from the post-war reconstruction period. In Japan governors and mayors can act independently of their prefecture or municipal council and each element of the local separation of powers has its own area of responsibilities. It is in how the executive and legislative branches of the local separation act with and on each other that lessons emerge for the English experience. In any separated system of political decision-making, a certain amount of negotiation, discussion and compromise is required of all participants; when this process breaks down or fails to deliver acceptable policies or outcomes, the checks and balances within the system will point to where the balance of power lies.

If the governor or the mayor cannot reach agreement with the council, or after any other sort political impasse, the council can vote on a confidence motion in the mayor. To have effect, a quorum of two-thirds of the membership is required for the meeting called to consider the motion and three-quarters of those present must vote in favour of it. The governor and mayor, however, have at their disposal the dissolution of the council and the calling of new elections to resolve the crisis that led to the no-confidence motion. If no such dissolution is passed within ten days of the confidence motion, the governor or mayor must resign. If, however, new elections are called and the council at its first meeting passes yet another motion of no confidence in the mayor or governor, then the council cannot be dissolved and the governor or mayor must resign. The system here, like the Italian system, has an element of mutually assured destruction, in that no-confidence motions in the mayor can result in the calling of new council elections, thus the power of the council to remove a mayor is tempered, but still exists.

On the other hand, governors and mayors have the power of veto over council decisions and to demand that particular decisions, policies or actions are reconsidered. Moreover, in certain circumstances, the governor or mayor is able to make decisions on behalf of the council in order to construct some compromise or to improve public services. The governor or mayor is able to take such 'extraordinary executive action' even if the council disagrees, but responsibility for the matter that prompted such action rests with the governor or mayor.

In normal political circumstances, it is the body of elected councillors that decides the policies of the local authority and is able to approve, abolish or amend local by-laws and has the right to determine council budgets. Moreover, the council can insist that the governor or mayor, or any of the administrative committees which are part of the executive arrangements, submits reports to the council. While it is the governor or mayor who has the power to call council meetings, the council can call an extraordinary meeting itself if one-quarter of the membership so demand. Councillors, as well as governors and mayors, have the right to introduce local bills, although certain types of local bill have to be introduced specifically by either the executive or legislature; budget bills, for example, are the responsibility of the governor or mayor to introduce.

Not only do the executive and legislature of the locality in Japan act as a check and balance on the other, but the citizenry are also able to check the activity of either element. If one-third of local electors sign a petition for the council to be dissolved then a referendum is held and if the majority vote in favour of dissolution the entire council must stand for re-election. Similarly, if one-third of local electors call for the dismissal of the governor or mayor and a local referendum provides a majority for that call, the governor or mayor is thereby dismissed from office. Further, such powers rest with the citizenry also with regard to vice-governor, deputy mayors, treasurers and members of the election, audit and public safety committees. The Japanese citizen has a powerful accountability mechanism and check against those who govern them locally, should that be required. In addition, under the Japanese constitution, by-laws specific to an individual authority require ratification by a majority of voters in a referendum before they become law.

The Japanese system is a carefully balanced separation of powers which rests on a powerful directly elected governor or mayor. The council is able to remove a mayor from office but may in turn first face re-election itself. The clear distinction between the areas of responsibility of elements of the executive and the local legislature, and the division of the executive into independent, administrative committees, also acts as an intelligently designed balance in the system. In Japan, however, the ultimate check and balance on political activity rests with the voters, as they hold the ultimate authority for the removal of the mayor and the council.

Germany: a locally 'elected monarch'

There are three levels of political authority within the German system: the federal government or *Bund*; the state government or *Land*; and local government units within the various *Länder* – the *Kreis* or county, and the *Gemeinde* or county city or municipality. The legal position of German local government is set out in article 28 of the federal constitution of 1949, which states that the *Gemeinden* and *Kreise* have the 'right to deal with all matters of the local community in their own responsibility in the framework of existing law'. The constitution guarantees local self-government and grants local authorities a degree of political autonomy, a broad range of functions and a form of general competence over local affairs.

The powers and functions of the counties and municipalities are set in law. The *Kreise* are responsible for areas such as: road construction, education and further education, economic development, financial borrowing, the expansion and acquisition of public companies, maintenance of the countryside and the police and security services. The *Gemeinde* are responsible for areas such as economy and trade, electricity and water supply, sewage, environmental protection, fire services, health and social care, waste collection, protection of historic monuments, leisure facilities and cultural development. In addition to these functions, German local authorities carry out such tasks and functions as are delegated to them by the *Länder* and as a result the political arrangements and functions of German local government vary across *Länder*. Many of these *Länder* delegations can fall directly on the elected mayor and, as a result, the mayor becomes an agent of the *Land* government.

As Wollmann shows, the German political system reflects the different influences and political structures favoured by the Allies after the war and are displayed in the local governmental systems of those parts of Germany that were under British, American or French control.[20] It was in the southern German *Länder*, controlled by the Americans, where the directly elected German mayor arose and where most directly elected German mayors can be found (not all German mayors are directly elected). Since the 1990s, however, the direct election of the mayor has spread quickly across German *Länder*, along with the direct election of the head of the county councils; directly elected mayors can now be found across Germany. As well as the powers and functions of the mayor varying across the *Länder*, so too does the term of office of the mayor, which ranges from five years in some to eight in others. Indeed, eleven of the thirteen *Länder* have mayoral terms of office that extend beyond the term of office of the council, with most councillors elected for a five-year term. Thus, a German mayor of one party can quite often find himself or herself faced with a council controlled by another party – much as is the case for the English mayor.

The mayoral model favoured in the southern German *Länder* rests on a politically and institutionally strong mayor, a system which has been in existence for some fifty years. Indeed, Wehling went as far as to liken the German mayor to an 'elected monarch'.[21] Yet, because of the federal structure of Germany, elected mayors will vary, between *Länder*, in the power they are granted and the position they hold within the structure of local government; they can have strong formal powers in some areas while in others the balance of power is tipped in favour of the council.

The broad German system rests on a sharing of power between the elected mayor and the rest of the council, with the council as the supreme decision-making political power of the locality. Yet it is the task of the elected mayor to ensure that the decisions taken by the council are implemented and pursued effectively by the council machinery. In other words, the German mayoral system comes close to an interpretation of the term political 'executive' as one that does not make decisions but rather implements or executes those decisions taken elsewhere. In addition, however, the mayor also carries out those tasks and responsibilities delegated by the *Land* government, and the council has no influence over the activities of the mayor in this regard; rather, it is the *Land* government which oversees the conduct of those matters delegated to the mayor. Mayors are also able to undertake any matters of routine local self-government and, thus, have a form of general competence all of their own.[22]

A further indication of the balance of power being tipped towards the council rather than the mayor in the German model is in the appointment of deputy mayors. It is the council that elects the deputy mayors and these are normally appointed in proportion to the political party composition of the council. Thus, a mayor from one party will be working with deputy mayors from other parties; together, mayor and deputy mayors form the local political administration. Yet, even though these deputies will form part of the executive appointed by the council and head individual departments of the council, they are responsible and subordinate to the elected mayor. A careful balance of power is constructed by this system of appointment between the mayor and council and the parties within the council, a balance which ensures that parties outside of the majority or largest party are guaranteed a place in government. Such a method of appointing the deputy mayors is logical in the context of the use of the party list system for the election of local councillors.

The German elected mayor can be faced with the strongest of all checks on the power of political office: the right to recall. In three eastern *Länder* if between 15 and 33.3 per cent of citizens (depending on the *Land*) petition to recall the mayor, a new election must be held; in Brandenburg between 1993 and 1998 10 per cent of mayors lost office as a result of local recall referendums. In other *Länder*, the council, on majority votes of 50 per cent, 75 per cent or 67 per cent (depending on the council), can trigger a recall election of the mayor.

As would be expected in a federal state, there is a diversity in the mayoral system that reflects local concerns, traditions and political histories. Yet within that diversity a basic approach to mayoral government exists and a careful balancing act occurs between the powers of the mayor and the council. The German system also demonstrates that where the mayor may not be all powerful the political skills and ability of the individual office-holder are at a premium, as these can ensure that the mayor is able to provide effective political leadership and policy direction. Indeed, political leadership is as much about mayors accruing additional power and influence by the employment of political skill as it is about institutional power and structure; but informal power is no substitute for formal political power.

Canada: a diverse system

In the Canadian federal system the sub-national tiers of provincial or territorial governments lie immediately below the central government. While the federal and provincial arrangements are structurally uniform across the country, the local municipal level is governed by an array of school boards, other boards, agencies and commissions, and there are also separate governing arrangements for cities, towns, villages, town-ships, counties, improvement districts and special service areas. It is this diverse municipal level that is responsible for roads, tax collection, policing, by-laws, refuse collection, parks, sewers, water services and, in some areas, health and welfare services.

All local governments, or municipalities, are the creation of the provincial, not the federal government. A clause in the Canadian consti-tution enables provinces to delegate certain responsibilities to another, lower-tier, governing body. It is the size of any local area that determines whether it will be known as a city, town or township and, where there is a county or a region involved in the provision of services, each of these three localities are then referred to as 'lower tier'. The Municipal Govern-ment Act 1999 gave Canadian citizens the right to directly elect the mayor of a town or a regional municipality; in rural areas, referred to in the Act as county or district municipalities, the head of the council may, if the council chooses, be elected directly and is known as a mayor; if the council chooses to elect the head of the council itself, the office is known as a 'warden'. The political head of the lower tiers of local government are known as 'reeves' or 'mayors'. Depending on the locality, councillors are elected either from wards or at large.

Under the 1999 Act, if a county or district council wishes to change from having a warden, selected by the council, to a mayor, elected directly by the citizens, it must make a determination to do so nine months before the next following regular council election. Thus, the decision to change the governing arrangements in these authorities rests with the council rather than the citizenry.

For the directly elected mayors in Canada, the separation of powers mirrors that of the English directly elected mayor rather than that of the US one. The legislation does not set out any distinct powers and responsibilities that rest only with an elected mayor; rather, the mayor's role and powers are comparable to those of the indirectly elected counterpart in Canadian local government: the warden. Mayor and warden may both: monitor the administration and government of the council; and suggest to the council changes and improvements to policy, finance, administration and governance of the area.

The political power of the Canadian elected mayor rests on a recognition of the legitimacy provided to the office-holder by the public vote. The elected mayor is seen as a political leader, ambassador and spokesperson for the entire area, in a way which his or her indirectly elected counterparts cannot hope to emulate. The system rests on the strength of the mayoral mandate and on the sanctioning of the mayor's leadership that direct election provides. The successful mayor will therefore need to rely not on institutional arrangements but on his or her political skills to ensure that the council follows his or her lead. To pursue policy preferences and initiatives, the directly elected Canadian mayor must rely on deliberation, negotiation, compromise and the forging of political alliances – much like his or her English counterpart. He or she also relies on the council responding positively to the direct mandate granted to the mayor by the voters – not something which can be taken for granted in either Canada or England!

How the mayor hones and displays his or her political skills and how he or she develops a unique public profile are key elements for successful local politics in Canada. In October 2004, for example, the well respected and popular mayor of Halifax, Nova Scotia's largest city, with a population of 360,000, was re-elected with an increased majority. The mayor had been a focal point of the city's recovery from the effects of hurricane Juan, which had hit the area in 2003. The mayor, Peter Kelly, was known to have been, almost Giuliani like, at the centre of the city's activities during and after the hurricane and particularly during the vital clear-up period. He had himself manned overnight the phones at the emergency centre set up during the crisis. Moreover, Kelly had been a high-profile and vocal advocate of his city and its communities, and had led the city in several battles with the province over taxation issues and for extra funding to improve the environment of the heavily polluted harbour area of Halifax. Kelly had led initiatives to regenerate the economy of the area and to encourage business to locate and invest in the community. The political skills of the individual mayor can be sufficient to overcome the inadequacies of power in the office, but such skills mixed with adequate political power and resources enable directly elected political leaders to operate far more effectively.

Important to the success of the mayor in Canadian local government is the almost complete absence of party politics – certainly in the way that we understand it to organise and function in England. Thus, the mayor's own political skills are again at a premium in the Canadian system. The need for the mayor to forge governing and single-issue alliances and to drive a policy agenda from a relatively weak political position *vis-à-vis* the council and other bodies of governance has distinct parallels in the English arrangements. Moreover, the multilayered governing structure of Canada, from federal through provincial to two- or single-tiered local government, also sets the elected mayor in a complex network of governing arrangements, which must be carefully navigated if he or she is to be successful locally and to secure re-election.

A number of factors make political life difficult for the Canadian mayor, in much the same way as they do for the English directly elected mayor. The control of local government by a superior tier of government, in the Canadian case the provinces, means that local government is subject to potential change at the behest of another layer of government, rather than at its own initiative. Moreover, the allocation of service responsibilities results in some councils having very few such responsibilities and others rather more.

In addition, the role of the province in service areas which are of considerable interest to municipal areas, such as education, health and policing, results in mayors and their indirectly elected counterparts, and councils, having to negotiate with a superior governing institution or local provider of services (board or agency). Yet, despite these structural and political problems, Canadian elected mayors are seen as legitimate local political leaders and the more successful ones have been able to drive policy agendas beyond what might be expected given the restraints against which they operate. As with their English counterparts, Canadian directly elected mayors have equivalent indirectly elected counterparts, who are able to undertake broadly similar activities but without the legitimacy that comes from direct election.

Conclusions

A directly elected mayor as a local political leader and part of a governing executive or administration has been a long-standing feature of many local government systems across the globe. It is also a model which is being adopted, in one form or another, by many nations seeking to enhance local democratic accountability, and to bring electors and local politicians closer together, in turn making the latter more responsive to the former, and seeking to create a system of legitimised, highly visible local political leadership.

Some important general lessons emerge for the English experiment from the five national approaches to mayoral government considered in this chapter and from the similarities and distinctions that exist across and within the systems. The main lesson is about the nature of mayoral power and political responsibility, and the balance between the legislatively defined and granted power and the accrued power that rests with the mayor's own political skills. Some legislative source (even if it is a city charter or council constitution) can clearly set out whether the mayor is powerful or not, but all politicians can accrue additional power through their own acumen. In the United States, Germany, Italy and Japan, mayors are given very clear powers in relation to both their day-to-day activities and the council with which they work. Canadian mayors, on the other hand, much like their English equivalents, are less well placed in relation to the council and must rely more on personal rather than on institutional resources to influence events.

Mayors who are seen to be 'running' the city and responsible not only for the day-to-day provision of services but also for the broader policy framework in which council departments operate are institutionally powerful local leaders and that power is reflected in the control they have over the administrative machinery of the council. While mayors in different countries will have different relationships to the council machinery, the case studies show that appointment to a range of offices is a key institutional power and one which can enhance the mayoral office. Mayors who appoint departmental heads (civil servants), or heads of other boards, commissions or organisations independent from the city council, not only can stamp their policy mark on those bodies but also can exert a powerful influence over the policies and activities of those bodies.

While some might worry that giving English mayors such day-to-day power would be a dangerous move, other nations have dealt with that concern, not by refusing to grant citizens the power to decide how they wish to be governed but rather by building two distinct elements into the system of checks and balances that are designed to hold elected mayors to account. The first element is in the relationship the mayor has with the council. In the countries considered in this chapter, a common theme of the mayoral system is the careful design of the balance of power between mayor and council, and while one will have the balance of power tipped in its favour, checks remain to hold the use of that power to some form of public accountability.

Such accountability and checks on power come through the existence of either council and mayoral vetoes or through removal powers; it is how the different nations deal with this common theme that varies. In some systems a form of mutually assured destruction exists, where the council can remove the mayor but may find itself dissolved and facing new elections as a consequence; or the mayor can dissolve the council but may end up losing office or reinforcing the position of those opposing mayoral policy. Less extreme checks exist in the sharing of appointment powers to various bodies between executive and council, the size of mayoral cabinets (see the Italian approach) and the sharing of legislative power between executive and council.

As well as the institutional arrangements between executive and council, the citizen can also act as a check and balance on either of the local governing arrangements: executive mayor and council. In the United States, Germany and Japan the local citizen can either petition to recall the mayor and hold new mayoral elections, or petition and vote on whether the entire council should be dissolved to face new elections. Granting citizens the power over their local mayors and councillors to be able to remove them from office is the most effective check and balance on any local politician, and one sadly lacking in England.

The nature of party political power and dynamics and the role of party politics in the localities influence the mayoral office. In those countries that have seen the development of an 'anti-party' mood, such as Italy, or where party politics is largely absent, as in Canada, or where elections are non-partisan, as in the United States, the mayor operates in a different context to those in countries, such as Germany or England, where parties play an important local role. Parties can serve to damage public accountability if they place party loyalty before mayoral accountability, or they can make the mayor's task of governing easier if a council majority can be guaranteed – which is always the case for the Italian mayor with his or her mayoral seat supplement. In many cases, parties can interfere with the public mechanism of political accountability that exists in a separation of powers.

Part of the answer to the role of the political party can be found in whether the terms of office of mayor and council (i.e. the elections to these offices) are co-terminous. Mayors elected at a different time to the council are more likely to find themselves facing a council controlled by another party or none than when the council and mayor are elected on the same day. The mayoral supplement granted to Italian mayors guarantees that they can form an administration and thus removes the notion of an election as a check and balance mechanism. When elections are held to mayoralty and councils at separate times, there is more of a desire evident for the system to act as a check and balance mechanism.

An overlapping period of office, with either the mayor's or councillors' terms exceeding the other, provides the voters with an opportunity to cast a judgement on the mayor – by rewarding his or her party or grouping at an election – or a judgement on the council, by rewarding or punishing, at the polls, the governing party or coalition. In addition, such arrangements draw the voters' attention much more clearly to what has been happening locally, rather than allowing them to focus on national political events. The issue here of course is which political institution – mayor or council – should have the longer term of office and for what reason. Short terms for any politician focus political attention on the voter; long terms distance the politician from the voter but provide a period of time for the effectiveness of policy to become apparent. Alternatively, terms of office could be for the same period for mayor and council but with staggered elections, so that a council election follows on two years after a mayoral election.

Elected mayors, wherever they are based and whatever the term of office or distribution of power between mayor and council, are clearly local political leaders in their own right. They are a focus for public, community, media and governmental attention and negotiation in a way that a collective decision-making body such as a council cannot be. If structural arrangements do not provide for a powerful mayor, then the political skills and acumen of the mayoral office-holder are at a premium when it comes to developing local political leadership and community advocacy. Yet much time and energy can be wasted in the pursuit of an informal power base; it is better to provide mayors with an institutionally strong position and clearly identified and publicly accountable political resources, and let them get on with the job for which they were elected.

Held against the mayoral models from overseas, the English approach is sadly lacking as an attempt to forge a new form of local politics and to reconfigure the workings of local political leadership. Moreover, it fails to grant mayors any real powers by which they can govern an area, rather than run a council, or even use the council machinery as a governing resource – unlike some of the mayors we have seen in this chapter. Reforms are clearly needed to make the English directly elected mayor a stronger and genuine local political leader. The final chapter explores those reforms in more detail.

Mayors of course do not govern alone: they share that task with councillors. To explore the English experience with (and version of) directly elected mayors further, it is necessary to explore the relationship they have with councillors and how councillors have reacted to their arrival on the local political landscape.

Notes

1 Fabbrini, S., 2000. 'Presidentialisation of Italian Local Government? The Nature and the Effects of Semiparliamentarism', paper presented to a workshop on Presidentialisation of Parliamentary Democracies, ECPR, Copenhagen, Denmark, 14–19 April; Magnier, A., 2004. 'Between Institutional Learning and Re-legitimisation: Italian Mayors in the Unending Reform', *International Journal of Urban and Regional Research*, Vol. 28, No. 1, March, pp. 166–182.

2 Caulfield, J. and H. Larsen (eds), 2002. *Local Government at the Millennium*, Opladen, Leske and Budrich, p. 111–133.

3 Magnier, 'Between Institutional Learning and Re-legitimisation', p. 167.

4 Yanez, C.J., 2004. 'Participatory Democracy and Political Opportunism: Municipal Experience in Italy and Spain (1960–93), *International Journal of Urban and Regional Research*, Vol. 29, No. 4, pp. 819–838.

5 Fabbrini, 'Presidentialisation of Italian Local Government?'; Heinelt, H. and A. Magnier, 2002. 'Structures of Local Government and Types of Mayors in Europe', paper presented to the conference on Political Leaders in European Cities, Madrid, May; Magnier, 'Between Institutional Learning and Re-legitimisation'.

6 Limosani, M. and P. Navarra, 2001. 'Local Pork-Barrel Politics in National Pre-Election Dates: The Case of Italy', *Public Choice*, Vol. 106, Nos 3–4, pp. 317–326.

7 Vandelli, L., 1997. *Sindaci e mito, sisifo, Tantalo e Damocle nell amministrazione local*, Bologna, Il Mulino (cited by Magnier, 'Between Institutional Learning and Re-legitimisation').

8 Frederickson, H.G., C. Wood and B. Logan, 2001. 'How American City Governments Have Changed: The Evolution of the Model City Charter', *National Civic Review*, Vol. 90, No. 1, pp. 3–18.

9 For such an overview, see DeSantis, V.S. and T. Renner, 2002. 'City Government Structures: An Attempt at Classification', *State and Local Government Review*, Vol. 34, No. 2, Spring, pp. 95–104.

10 Morgan, D. and S. Watson, 1996. 'Mayors of American Cities: An Analysis of Powers and Responsibilities', *American Review of Public Administration*, Vol. 26, No. 1, March, pp. 113–125.

11 Bowers, J. and W. Rich, 2000. *Governing Middle-Sized Cities: Studies in Mayoral Leadership*, Boulder, CO, Lynne Rienner Publishers, p. 11.

12 Clarke, M., H. Davis, D. Hall and J. Stewart, 1996. *Executive Mayors for Britain? New Forms of Political Leadership Reviewed*, London, Capita.

13 Giuliani, R., 2002. *Leadership*, New York, Little, Brown.

14 Pressman, J., 1972. 'Preconditions of Mayoral Leadership', *American Political Science Review*, Vol. 66, No. 2, June pp. 511–524; P. Peterson, 2000. 'The American Mayor: Elections and Institutions', *Parliamentary Affairs*, Vol. 53, No. 4, pp. 667–677.

15 Stoker, G. and H. Wolman, 1991. *A Different Way of Doing Business: The Example of the U.S. Mayor*, Belgrave Papers No. 2, London, Local Government Management Board.

16 Although Bloomberg had long been a Democrat before standing as the Republican candidate in the mayoral election.

17 Muramatsu, M., F. Iqbal and I Kume, 2001. *Local Government Development in Post-war Japan*, Oxford University Press, p. 4.

18 Nagata, N., 1998. 'The Development of Japanese Local Government and Its Reform Towards the Globalised Age', *International Review of Administrative Sciences*, Vol. 64, No. 2, pp. 219–233.

19 Muramatsu *et al.*, *Local Government Development in Post-war Japan*.

20 Wollmann, H., 2004. 'Urban Leadership in German Local Politics: The Rise, Role and Performance of the Directly Elected (Chief Executive) Mayor',

International Journal of Urban and Regional Research, Vol. 28, No. 1, pp. 150–165.

21 Wehling, H.G., 1999. 'Besonderheiten der auf Gemeindeebene', in H.H. Arnim (ed.), *Demokratie von neuen Herausforderungen*, Berlin, Druker and Humblot, pp. 91–102.

22 Lehmann, G. and J. Dieckmann, 2001. 'The Administration of German Cities', in K. Konig and H. Siedentopf (eds), *Public Administration in Germany*, Baden-Baden, Nomos, pp. 183–196; Wollmann, 'Urban Leadership in German Local Politics'.

8

Councillors: a new and developing role or a diminished responsibility?

Introduction

The arrival of mayoral politics in England changes the structure and dynamics of political decision-making and strikes at the very nature of what it means to be a councillor on an English local authority. It demands a new approach from councillors to representation and governing locally, and a new set of relationships with citizens and the party. It also demands that councillors now become a vital element of the processes of political accountability, rather than retaining the power of manipulation of local politics to undermine political accountability, including their own.[1]

Mayoral politics demand a new form of discursive and inquisitorial politics, and require councillors and their parties to share political space with a broad range of political associations. These associations may have either single-issue concerns or a broad set of objectives; they may be short-lived or a permanent feature of the political landscape. Equally, all such organisations must accommodate mayoral politics. Councillors under mayoral government are faced with rethinking and recasting what it is to be a councillor, to meet a new set of political circumstances, and to conduct politics within a more participatory framework.[2]

This chapter explores councillors' experiences of conducting political business alongside an elected mayor. The next section briefly reminds us how councillors have managed the tensions that exist between governing in the interests of the entire council locality and representing the views and interests of the wards or divisions, or communities of interest, that make up that locality.

In the following section the results of a survey of councillors on all mayoral authorities, conducted as part of the research for this book, are reported and explored. The survey examined councillors' experiences of:

- aspects of the role of the elected mayor;
- mayoral leadership;
- political decision-making;

164

- local representation;
- the role of the councillor on mayoral authorities.

The section assesses the councillors' responses in the light of their political affiliation, to see whether that is a powerful discriminator of councillor attitudes, as it has been in past surveys.

The following section explores how one mayoral council – the London Borough of Newham – set out to redefine the role of the councillor.

The chapter concludes with a consideration of the wider lessons that can be drawn from councillors' experiences of mayoral government for our understanding of local democracy and representation and the political role of the citizen and party.

Councillors: governing or representing in a mayoral authority

The tension at the heart of English local democracy between the councillor's role in governing an area and representing and articulating the views that emanate from the ward or division has been explored in detail elsewhere.[3] That tension displays itself when local communities are spurred into political action to exert pressure on the council to change a decision. Here, as Boaden *et al.* argued:

> people are less willing than they were to accept authoritarian styles of leadership. Action groups and public protest have become a regular feature of policy development. The receding tide leaves pools of interest where new initiatives are taken.[4]

The governing role of the English councillor is an assumed one (as is the governing mandate arising from the local election), assumed as a result of one party or another securing a majority of council seats. Yet, when voting, the elector is not only choosing a local administration to act in a governing fashion: he or she is also electing a local representative, one who will be required to promote the general interests of the local community and to act in its specific interests against the whole, should the need arise.

The *crisis of representation* that occurs when the councillor faces the competing demands of a local community seeking his or her support as a representative and the party group demanding the councillor's loyalty as a governor has been described in detail elsewhere.[5] Suffice to say here that such a crisis, when it occurs, exemplifies the governing/representing tension at the heart of English local politics. That tension is generated by the demand of loyalty and discipline made on the councillor by his or her party group – demands to which, by and large, most councillors are willing to respond positively.

Nonetheless, the councillor who places the interests of the ward above those of the whole council area, the true parochial, exists on many councils and among all parties.[6] The parochial judges all issues and decisions and reacts to them by the effect they have on the patch represented. Such councillors will face intense pressure from party colleagues to act in a governing fashion in all but the most exceptional of circumstances.[7] Indeed, the term 'parochial' is often used in a pejorative sense by councillors, rather than to indicate a local representative with an overwhelming concern for those who elected him or her. It stands alongside the term NIMBY ('not in my back yard') in the lexicon of councillor abuse levelled at those who reject the idea of being governed locally as one which overrides the existence of very local concerns arising from identifiable communities. Yet the ODPM, in a discussion paper entitled *Vibrant Local Leadership*, continues to pursue the idea that councillors can both govern an area and represent the needs of a patch, without recognising the tensions that exist in this process.[8]

The classic defence of the councillor as governor was summed up by one Labour London borough leader, who commented in interview:

> The group is the supreme policy-making body of the council and will remain so. We [the group] have a political mandate from the election to implement our manifesto and we will do that. If people protest at some of our decisions, that is their right – but we, not they, have been elected and we [the group] will make the decisions that will be for the benefit of the whole council. You cannot let a few people override what will be best for everyone.

These views resonated across the political spectrum, with a Conservative district councillor commenting thus:

> I believe Edmund Burke was right: you elect your representatives to make decisions and you judge them on those decisions at election time. I believe I have the right to make decisions and that they are properly made with my colleagues in a group meeting and then in council … if the voters do not agree with those decisions they have the right to vote for another party – that is the best form of accountability.

A Liberal Democrat district council leader argued in a similar vein:

> People really are too parochial sometimes. I know that might sound odd for a Liberal Democrat, but someone has to balance out all the conflicting views – that person should be the elected councillor. We discuss things in the group, make our decisions and I expect everyone to stick to those decisions. We run a pretty tight group here, I can tell you.

Thus, a governing role for councillors can conflict with the representation of very local concerns, and in such circumstances the councillor is largely expected, by colleagues, to place the government of the area above the interests of the very local. Yet, in the vast majority of English local government, there is no clearly identifiable source of governmental authority that has been granted, in an unambiguous fashion, the right to govern. The absence of clear governmental authority allows political parties, with their demands for group loyalty, to fill the vacuum that exists. When such a clear political authority with a specific mandate to govern exists – in the shape of the elected mayor – what happens to the role of the councillor?

Councillors: governing and representing in a mayoral system

The arrival of the English version of the directly elected mayor eases the tension between governing and representation as it is experienced by the councillor. It does this in a number of ways. First, the direct election of the head of the executive – the mayor – provides that individual with a clear and distinct mandate to govern an area, a mandate that is not assumed by virtue of being the majority (or at least largest) party. Second, the formation of a cabinet by the mayor (or the appointment of a council manager in the mayor and manager model) clearly distinguishes that group of representatives as the political executive and as a governing administration with a general policy capacity as well as specific policy portfolio responsibilities. Third, the mayor can be held directly to account for his or her political action or inaction by the electorate, and indirectly to account by the councillors outside the executive. As councillors bear no direct responsibility for the mayor's tenure in office, the ties between mayor and majority group, while not broken, are loosened somewhat and this serves to ease the governing/representing tension for councillors.

Yet the ability of the mayor and cabinet to act as the point of political responsibility for governing does not exclude councillors outside the executive entirely from a governing role. Rather, it relocates the relationship councillors have with governing, from specific involvement in the making of a decision to becoming the point of accountability for that decision.

The relocated governing role that is now open to councillors is a strengthening of the office of councillor and at the same time opens up that office itself to greater accountability. By holding up mayoral policy, decisions and initiatives for public scrutiny, by exploring that policy and activity, by challenging and questioning the mayor and members of the cabinet, by seeking justification and explanation for mayoral decisions and initiatives and by pursuing change in mayoral proposals and direction by negotiation and compromise, councillors are employing a more complex, sophisticated and powerful set of tools for governing than those involved in the old committee system. Moreover, the separation of powers enables councillors to maintain loyalty to the party manifesto on which they as a group were elected, and to pursue those policies from a broad governing orientation, while at the same time being able to challenge and explore mayoral policy and initiatives. The separate mandates of the mayor and the councillor reinforce the separation of powers in the council and provide a psychological, as well as a real, distinction for the councillor between his or her role in governing and the mayor's role in the same process.

Governing for the councillor in a mayoral authority, then, is related to the robustness of the mechanism for mayoral accountability that councillors create and develop. Yet robust accountability of the political head of the council and his or her cabinet will emerge only if councillors are able to see themselves as members of a body charged with a vital accountability function and role in acting as a check and balance on executive action first, and as a party representative charged with party loyalty and the pursuit of party interests second.

As well as holding the mayor to account, the councillor's governing role is displayed in policy initiation, review and development, through the overview and scrutiny process. Again, the councillor's role is not about the taking of a decision: rather, it is about the much more complex and discursive process of collecting evidence, sifting the views of different sources of opinion, seeking discussion and negotiating a compromise or course of action, by building alliances and coalitions of interest both inside the council (and across the party groups) and outside the council, and by relying on the political skills of the councillor. This contrasts with the force of the party group acting in public to secure its own way. The dynamic of the policy role in governing for the councillor is very different under an elected mayor to that in the leader and cabinet executive; the leverage of unseating the leader (if in the majority party) does not exist as a form of covert influence for the councillor. But direct election of an executive mayor does not exclude councillors from any input into the governing processes. It simply reconfigures the relationship councillors have with that process and the responsibilities they have within it.

Councillors and representation under a mayoral system

With the repositioning of the councillor's relationship with the governing of the locality comes greater freedom for the councillor to develop the role of community champion or advocate, as foreseen by the government.[9] Moreover, representation of the interests of a geographical patch or of a community of interest becomes integral, rather than peripheral, to the governing role of the councillor and the other facets of the councillor's role.[10] The processes of political negotiation are no longer between the councillor (as a representative of the group) and the council (here acting at variance with the expressed wishes of a particular section of the public), in a 'crisis of representation'; rather, the councillor acts far more distinctly as a conduit bringing a range of political views and pressures into the policy-making process and for bringing those views, as they emerge more clearly, to mayoral attention.

Relieved of the need to justify all the actions of the administration to the public, or to oppose them all simply because the mayoralty is held by another party, the councillor, even if sharing the political affiliation of the mayor, is in a position to challenge mayoral policy or initiatives for their effect on a specific ward. Moreover, as the mayor is elected to govern the authority with an authority-wide mandate, the councillor can use his or her specific and very local mandate to defend or promote a local interest or concern. Thus, mayoral government has the potential to strengthen the links the councillor has with the ward he or she represents.

It is the councillor who speaks for and on behalf of the very local community and it is the councillor who acts as a conduit of local opinion to the council and the mayor. Thus, councillors retain the position of the arbitrator of very local affairs and are required to balance the often competing opinions to which they may be subject from the citizenry, competing that is with each other, or with what the council – or the mayor – wishes to do. In this process the danger Hirst foresaw, of rule by unrepresentative minorities, and of issues being dislocated from a broader policy perspective, is avoided in the mayoral model because both the very local interest and strategic concerns are championed by two different facets of the political processes – mayor and councillor.[11]

While the government made it clear that it wished to see councillors develop their role of a powerful community champion and advocate, the Local Government Act 2000 did not provide any new architecture within which this role could develop. However, the government has more recently extolled the virtues of rethinking the settings within which politics takes place, beyond notions of a political executive and the council; for example, local area arrangements are experiencing renewed interest from government.[12] How councillors respond to the challenges of developing new settings and approaches to the conduct of local politics and council affairs will depend on how they respond to the new political decision-making processes of mayoral government. What councillors think of those new structures and processes is explored in the next section.

Councillors and the elected mayor

While surveys of the public indicate a groundswell of support for the concept of a directly elected mayor, councillors have generally demonstrated a long-standing hostility to the idea that the public and not councillors

should select the political head of the council.[13] In those English authorities with directly elected mayors, many councillors, and in some the
overwhelming majority of councillors, were opposed to the new system
and campaigned actively against it. What, then, do those councillors
working alongside the mayor think about the way in which that system is
working and the impact it has had on their role as a councillor?

As part of the research for the book, a survey was conducted in
mayoral authorities in March 2004, after some eighteen to twenty-four
months of experience of the mayoral arrangements. Councillors were
asked to indicate whether they agreed or disagreed with the propositions
that the directly elected mayor, as a new form of executive, allowed for
political decision-making to be:

- efficient;
- transparent;
- accountable;
- open.

They were also asked to express how much they agreed that the new
political arrangements provided for:

- the involvement of all councillors in decision-making;
- a powerful role for all councillors;
- strong civic leadership;
- strong political leadership;
- strong corporate leadership.

Each of the terms used in the statements were defined and respondents
were given a specific meaning to the terms to employ when completing
the questionnaire. Table 8.1 presents the responses to these statements
by councillors' political affiliation.

When responding to the statements, councillors were asked to think
about the office of the directly elected mayor, rather than the current
holder of that office. Care must be taken in interpreting the results, for
a number of reasons. First, it is difficult for councillors to distinguish
between the office and an individual. Second, where the councillor and
mayor are from the same party, responses may be more positive than
where political affiliations vary (this was borne out somewhat when
looking at the responses from separate authorities). Third, some of the
statements solicited a relatively high neutral response, which could
simply be a result of councillors needing more experience of some
aspects of mayoral government before they could come to a conclusion
about how those aspects were working. In addition, antipathy towards
the mayoral model may have generated reluctance among some to give

Table 8.1 Percentage of councillors agreeing and disagreeing with statements regarding executive arrangements for the elected mayor, by party affiliation

Statements and party affiliation	Agree/ strongly agree	Neither agree nor disagree	Disagree/ strongly disagree
Conservative			
Efficient decision-making	57	14	29
Transparent decision-making	43	21	36
Accountable decision-making	50	21	29
Open decision-making	43	14	43
Involvement of all councillors in decision-making	14	0	86
A powerful role for all councillors	0	7	93
Strong civic leadership	50	7	43
Strong political leadership	64	0	36
Strong corporate leadership of the council	57	0	43
Labour			
Efficient decision-making	69	17	14
Transparent decision-making	44	24	32
Accountable decision-making	62	7	31
Open decision-making	36	26	37
Involvement of all councillors in decision-making	18	12	69
A powerful role for all councillors	17	10	73
Strong civic leadership	64	21	15
Strong political leadership	59	19	23
Strong corporate leadership of the council	63	18	19
Liberal Democrat			
Efficient decision-making	44	25	31
Transparent decision-making	34	31	34
Accountable decision-making	50	12	37
Open decision-making	39	10	52
Involvement of all councillors in decision-making	0	19	78
A powerful role for all councillors	0	25	72
Strong civic leadership	41	25	34
Strong political leadership	37	22	41
Strong corporate leadership of the council	47	19	34
Independent			
Efficient decision-making	76	0	23
Transparent decision-making	47	12	41
Accountable decision-making	56	6	37
Open decision-making	35	12	53
Involvement of all councillors in decision-making	18	23	59
A powerful role for all councillors	18	23	59
Strong civic leadership	53	18	29
Strong political leadership	35	18	47
Strong corporate leadership of the council	65	0	35

any indication as to how the new system was working – let alone agree
that it was working well.

Despite these areas of caution, some clear patterns emerge from councillors' experiences of, and attitudes towards, the working of mayoral
government. When it comes to questions about the efficiency, transparency, accountability and openness of political decision-making on mayoral
authorities, independent councillors gave a surprisingly positive set of
responses (though not overwhelming so and less so with the issue of openness) to the notion that mayoral government has improved these aspects
of the political processes and particularly when it comes to the efficiency of
political decision-making, an area of improvement recognised across the
political spectrum (with the exception of the Liberal Democrats). Councillors also saw that accountability of decision-making was achieved but,
again, the responses were not overwhelming in that direction.

The responses here are not wildly dissimilar to those found by Rao,
who tested broadly similar though not identical aspects of mayoral
government.[14] The differences between Rao's survey and the survey conducted for this book can be accounted for by the different emphases given
to aspects of the mayoral role and the wording of the questions. Rao concluded that the positive views she uncovered may be a result both of the
newness of the mayoral system and of negative feelings about the regime
it replaced. While the mayoral experiment was also new to councillors
when the research for this book was conducted, the research found that
councillors had quickly adjusted to the system and their place within
it; the results here suggest that councillors are responding to aspects of
mayoral government in a way that reflects experience, tempered by their
feelings about mayoral government.

When it comes to concerns about the transparency and openness of
the mayoral experience among councillors, the responses do show that
very real distinctions are made by these politicians about the nature and
effect that mayoral government has on aspects of the political decision-
making process. Accountability can be enhanced at the same time that
openness and transparency recede and this is so because the mayor is the
focal point of council politics and his or her responsibility for decisions
is clear and known. Yet the responses also indicate that greater openness
and transparency are needed in mayoral government, at least for the way
in which councillors see the system as enabling them to conduct the role
of an elected representative.

The responses are unambiguous about the role of the councillor, both
in terms of their involvement in decisions and in a more general, broader
sense as a local politician and member of the council. The introduction
of an elected mayor was seen, across all parties and independents –
including those sharing the mayor's party affiliation – as having greatly
reduced both the specific and general role and standing of the councillor

in terms of council business and local politics. Thus, one objective of the modernising agenda, securing a powerful role for all councillors, had not been achieved in mayoral authorities, at least as these councillors were experiencing mayoral leadership.

The way in which the mayoral system provides leadership was a source of some uncertainty among councillors. Leadership, for the purpose of the survey, was presented in three distinct facets – civic, political and corporate – and councillors were asked to consider how such elements of leadership were facilitated by mayoral government. It is clear from the responses that the councillors did distinguish between these facets, and in some instances quite remarkably so. Liberal Democrats were the most reluctant to admit that any area of leadership was enhanced by mayoral government, with responses from this source fairly evenly divided on the matter. Labour and Conservative councillors displayed a greater degree of certainty that leadership, across the three facets, is secured as a result of mayoral government.

Intriguingly, independent respondents saw mayoral government providing for strong civic and corporate leadership but not political leadership. Questioning of independent councillors on authorities with independent and party political mayors revealed what was behind these responses. Independent councillors viewed the notion of political leadership very differently from their counterparts in the political parties. They viewed political leadership as something which offends against the principle of 'political independence' and thus saw it, more so than party councillors, as a process which drives or encourages councillors to share a particular view or course of action. Independents were less likely than their party colleagues to view political leadership as the processes by which the community is governed. Independents also argued that leadership should reflect, not set, the political trends of an authority. Yet civic leadership and the mayor acting as an advocate or ambassador for the area, and corporate leadership, in the running of the authority, did not provoke such antipathy from independent councillors.

Liberal Democrat councillors responded in a similar vein to their independent counterparts when it came to political leadership and for similar reasons. Liberal Democrats have the most politically fissiparous tendencies of the three main parties and this is reflected in their views of political leadership. They too reflect the notion that political leadership is not about, as one councillor put it, 'telling me what to do; I make my own mind up'. Liberal Democrats do not take too kindly to being led, at least in local government. They also have a view of leadership as a reflective and responsive process and one which involves community engagement and empowerment, which conflicts with notions of strong leadership.[15]

In fact, the responses to the statements reflect more the independents' and Liberal Democrats' attitudes towards political leadership *per se* than their attitudes to the mayoral office facilitating strong leadership. As one independent said, 'The mayor certainly has a clear direction and view, and works hard to take us with him. Once he's made his mind up that's it; if that's strong leadership then we have it.' A Liberal Democrat summed up the view of many of her colleagues when she said 'I have a natural objection to being told what to do, but in some circumstances that is what is needed; someone has to make a decision and get on with it. The elected mayor can and does do just that.'

Labour and Conservative councillors, on the other hand, tended to be much more amenable to ideas of leadership of any kind (and for the Conservatives notions of political leadership in particular). They viewed politics much more as about making decisions and doing things – or not. If decision-making is easier and quicker within a framework that allows for strong and firm leadership, then so much the better – and the mayoral model, whatever else they thought of it, gave them just that.

The survey also asked councillors to think about certain facets of the mayoral role and to respond to statements regarding whether it was important that the mayor:

- implement his or her party-based local manifesto;
- represent his or her party (if not independent);
- represent the views of the electorate.

The responses indicate that on mayoral authorities councillors made important distinctions about the importance of mayoral activity in each of these areas. Table 8.2 sets out the responses from councillors, by party, to the statements.

There is little doubt that the councillors saw the mayor as having an important role in ensuring that the manifesto on which he or she was elected was implemented. Labour councillors attached more importance to this role than other councillors and this reflects the greater resonance of 'manifestoism' among Labour members than among their

Table 8.2 Percentage of councillors agreeing or strongly agreeing that particular mayoral roles were important, by party affiliation

Statement	Conservative	Labour	Liberal Democrat	Independent
Implement his or her party manifesto	64	71	59	63
Represent his or her party	46	53	28	37
Represent the views of the electorate	71	77	91	88

counterparts; they maintained this view despite manifestoism being described by Wolman and Goldsmith as a 'fiction at all levels of British politics, and particularly so at the local level'.[16]

The positive response received from independent councillors to the importance of a manifesto is not as surprising as it might initially seem. The independent views a manifesto not in party political but in personal terms; the manifesto is a powerful compact between the independent and the electorate. Manifestoism is as prominent today for councillors as it has been for some time and the responses reflect what we already know about the power and importance of a political manifesto for councillors.[17]

Labour councillors saw a greater importance for the mayor in representing his or her party than Conservative, Liberal Democrat and (not surprisingly) independent councillors. More independent councillors attached an importance to this role than Liberal Democrat councillors, but only marginally so. It would appear from these responses that party ties are beginning to be fractured as a result of mayoral politics and this becomes even clearer when the responses to the importance of the mayor in representing the views of the electorate are taken into account. Here, councillors across the political spectrum shared a positive view of the importance of the mayor in this regard. Indeed, party councillors were distinguishing between the facets of the mayoral role and responding in ways that indicate the emergence of new attitudinal patterns within mayoral authorities. Whether those attitudes result in new patterns of behaviour remains to be seen.

Interviews for the book indicate that there is some way to go before such new patterns of behaviour begin to emerge. Liberal Democrats, despite the opposition they displayed towards mayoral government, did see it as a way of negating the impact of party politics on local government. As one said:

> If we are going to have these mayors then they must act in the best interest of the whole people and not play party politics. You can get away with some of these party shenanigans as a councillor, but mayors can't do that sort of thing. The mayor we have here seems to have risen above it quite well.... Mayors must do what is best and any Liberal Democrat mayor that put the Liberal Democrats above doing what was best, even if we suffered as a result, would be irresponsible.

Conservative and Labour councillors were less prone to this type of political self-denial than Liberal Democrats, with a Labour councillor saying quite categorically, 'A Labour mayor is just that, a Labour mayor and does what's best for the party'. A Conservative councillor commented, 'A Conservative mayor must act as a good Conservative and I would expect him to adhere to Conservative principles and to the party's interests'.

Yet, at the same time, councillors of all affiliations overwhelmingly saw the mayor as having a powerful and important role in representing the views of the electorate (though with Liberal Democrats' and independents' responses in this regard more emphatic than those of Labour and Conservative councillors). Yet, for party councillors, representing the party and the views of the electorate merge; thus, when the mayor is pursing the party's views, he or she is at one and the same time representing the views of the electorate. The position is slightly more complicated, however, where mayor and councillors come from different parties or none. It is here that councillors still maintain an expectation that the mayor will pursue party concerns and interests, and that the councillor's job is to defend the interest of the electorate by pursing, where possible, the policies of his or her own party. As one Labour councillor said, 'I intend to do whatever I can to stand up for Labour policy; that's why they voted for me in my ward'.

For the party councillor, the interests of the electorate are best served by the implementation of his or her party's platform; that the mayor has a distinct and different mandate does not prevent the councillor from pursuing an alternative vision. In this way, councillors are still assuming a governing mandate even though it is the mayor who has been granted such a governing legitimacy by the electorate. When looking at aspects of mayoral power and decision-making we see similar trends emerging from responses to the following three survey statements:

- The mayor does not have enough power to enable him/her to do a good job.
- There is adequate consultation with the public by the mayor on mayoral decisions.
- Council officials have too much influence on mayoral decisions.

Table 8.3 presents the responses to these statements, by political party.

Labour, Conservative and Liberal Democrat councillors clearly indicated that they felt the mayor had sufficient power to be able to conduct the role of the office. Councillors here were reflecting the often expressed view that elected mayors represent an over-concentration of power in the hands of one individual – despite the fact that all voters have an input into the election of the mayor.

Labour councillors expressed the greatest degree of satisfaction with the level of consultation between mayor and public, although at only 45 per cent of respondents, and only around a quarter of Conservative, Liberal Democrats and independents agreed with the proposition that there was adequate consultation. Some of these responses reflect the greater preponderance of Labour councillors serving alongside a Labour mayor and so they were much more likely to have a different view about

Table 8.3 Percentage of councillors agreeing and disagreeing with statements regarding aspects of mayoral decision-making, by party affiliation

Statement and party affiliation	Agree/ strongly agree	Neither agree nor disagree	Disagree/ strongly disagree
Conservative			
The mayor does not have enough power to enable him/her to do a good job	14	14	71
There is adequate consultation with the public by the mayor on mayoral decisions	21	14	64
Council officials have too much influence on mayoral decisions	43	29	29
Labour			
The mayor does not have enough power to enable him/her to do a good job	13	11	76
There is adequate consultation with the public by the mayor on mayoral decisions	45	20	35
Council officials have too much influence on mayoral decisions	37	24	39
Liberal Democrat			
The mayor does not have enough power to enable him/her to do a good job	7	17	77
There is adequate consultation with the public by the mayor on mayoral decisions	27	17	57
Council officials have too much influence on mayoral decisions	47	17	37
Independent			
The mayor does not have enough power to enable him/her to do a good job	35	6	59
There is adequate consultation with the public by the mayor on mayoral decisions	23	35	41
Council officials have too much influence on mayoral decisions	76	12	12

mayoral consultation than councillors confronted by a mayor of a different political persuasion.

The responses additionally indicate, however, that mayors not only need to consult with the public but also need to be seen doing so by the councillors on their authorities. In addition of course there is the political reality that no matter how much a mayor consults, he or she, like all politicians, is not bound to accede to the results of that consultation.

Table 8.4 Percentage of councillors agreeing and disagreeing with statements regarding mayoral authority, by party affiliation

Statement and party affiliation	Agree/ strongly agree	Neither agree nor disagree	Disagree/ strongly disagree
Conservative			
My role as a councillor is to defend the mayor's policies in public	7	7	86
My role as a councillor is to hold the mayor to account	93	7	0
I see my role in overview and scrutiny meetings as defending mayoral policy	0	33	67
I see my role in overview and scrutiny meetings as challenging and trying to change mayoral policy	9	64	27
My role as a councillor is to speak against the mayor's policies in public	7	50	43
My role as a councillor is to vote against the mayor's policies in public	0	50	50
Labour			
My role as a councillor is to defend the mayor's policies in public	41	14	45
My role as a councillor is to hold the mayor to account	75	9	16
I see my role in overview and scrutiny meetings as defending mayoral policy	7	20	73
I see my role in overview and scrutiny meetings as challenging and trying to change mayoral policy	28	42	30
My role as a councillor is to speak against the mayor's policies in public	4	17	79
My role as a councillor is to vote against the mayor's policies in public	5	19	76

Where a mayor is not seen to be accepting the results of consultation and pursues an alternative line, then, for the councillor, this is inadequate consultation. It is of course a response to consultation that is not unique to elected mayors. Rather, all politicians will respond positively to views with which they agree, or find acceptable, and will counter those views with which they disagree.

The responses received from party councillors concerning the influence that council officers have over the decisions made by an elected mayor reflect the findings of a similar question asked by the Widdicombe committee in

Table 8.4 *Continued*

Statement and party affiliation	Agree/ strongly agree	Neither agree nor disagree	Disagree/ strongly disagree
Liberal Democrat			
My role as a councillor is to defend the mayor's policies in public	25	16	59
My role as a councillor is to hold the mayor to account	75	9	14
I see my role in overview and scrutiny meetings as defending mayoral policy	10	17	73
I see my role in overview and scrutiny meetings as challenging and trying to change mayoral policy	31	41	28
My role as a councillor is to speak against the mayor's policies in public	6	44	50
My role as a councillor is to vote against the mayor's policies in public	0	43	57
Independent			
My role as a councillor is to defend the mayor's policies in public	37	6	56
My role as a councillor is to hold the mayor to account	88	6	6
I see my role in overview and scrutiny meetings as defending mayoral policy	25	0	75
I see my role in overview and scrutiny meetings as challenging and trying to change mayoral policy	50	8	42
My role as a councillor is to speak against the mayor's policies in public	27	13	60
My role as a councillor is to vote against the mayor's policies in public	13	20	67

the 1980s.[18] In the present survey independent councillors were even more persuaded of officer influence than their party counterparts. Yet there is confusion around what we know about how councillors view officer influence and it is a confusion generated by councillors themselves.

Councillors are reluctant in questionnaire surveys to accede to the notion that officers have a powerful influence in the decision-making processes. Yet, in interviews for this book (and more widely) councillors were very willing to express disquiet at the role that officers play and comments like 'officers run this council' and 'officers have all the power' abounded. Councillors across the political spectrum made similar comments about officer influence: 'The mayor listens more to officers than to councillors', 'They [officers] only have to suggest something and it happens', 'You have to have an officer on your side if you want to do something' and 'The officers have day-to-day access to the mayor; we have to make an appointment.' Yet an alternative side emerged, with statements such as 'It's different now; the officers know who is in charge', 'It really shook them up having this mayor' and, thoughtfully:

> The mayor acts as an elected counterbalance to the power that officers have; I wasn't in favour of a mayor at first and voted against in the referendum, but you can feel the difference in the way things work. Although officers can still run rings around most councillors, it's different with the mayor – they respect that office more than they ever did councillors before.

Councillors on mayoral authorities are likely, as are their counterparts elsewhere, to maintain an ambiguous relationship with the notion of officer power, but the introduction of executive arrangements does reconfigure the relationships officers have, at least with a group of senior councillors sitting on the executive – with or without an elected mayor.[19]

Despite this ambiguity at the heart of council politics, councillors were far less reticent in the responses they gave to statements designed to uncover the relationship they saw between the mayor and councillors when it came to political power. Councillors were asked to express levels of agreement with the following statements:

- My role as a councillor is to defend the mayor's policies in public.
- My role as a councillor is to hold the mayor to account.
- I see my role in overview and scrutiny meetings as defending mayoral policy.
- I see my role in overview and scrutiny meetings as challenging and trying to change mayoral policy.
- My role as a councillor is to speak against the mayor's policies in public.
- My role as a councillor is to vote against the mayor's policies in public.

Table 8.4 presents the responses, by political party. It is worth repeating the note of caution here that responses received will no doubt reflect whether the councillor finds himself or herself faced with a mayor of the same party or a different one, or no party. Nonetheless, it is clear that on the question of the councillor's role in holding the mayor to account there are strong levels of agreement, across parties.

Clearly, a vital role for all councillors is that of being the vehicle through which mayoral accountability is secured. When it comes to defending or challenging the mayor's policies in overview and scrutiny committees, and to speaking and voting against the mayor's policies in public, councillors are more subtle than the usual dictates of party interaction would have demanded of them in the traditional committees. Rather than seeing themselves play an opposition or governmental role, that is, always challenging or always supporting an administration, councillors saw their relationship to mayoral government, at least in overview and scrutiny, as contingent on issues and policy. The separation of powers and the new scrutiny role in mayoral authorities are having some success in diluting notions of strict party loyalty overriding all other political concerns.

The picture is not as clear cut as the above suggests, however, as some councillors, notably those from minority parties, complained in interview that councillors sharing the mayor's political affiliation were not as assiduous as they could be in holding the mayor to account. As one Conservative councillor commented: 'Labour councillors just support the mayor – it's all sorted out in their group meeting'. A Labour councillor said: 'Despite all their complaints about us working as a strong group, all they do [Conservative councillors] is back the mayor'. Another Conservative councillor complained: 'I don't think they've [Labour councillors] raised a single thing [in overview and scrutiny] that poses any real challenge to the mayor – a few minor points just to look good'.

While the councillor–mayor relationship will always be a shifting one, moved by who holds the mayoralty and the political composition of the council, councillors' attitudes to the changes mayoral government has brought to the role of the councillor have also yet to settle into a clear pattern. Councillors were asked how much they agreed with the following statements concerning the changes in their role as a councillor under mayoral government:

- I am less able to influence council policy than before.
- I am better placed to represent my constituents.
- I feel my role has been downgraded.
- I am more aware of what is happening at the council.
- I am more able to make things happen than before.
- Being a councillor is less important than before.

Table 8.5 sets out the responses received.

When considering the impact of mayoral local government on the broad activities of the councillor, a mixed pattern of responses emerged: councillors within and across parties responded differently to the circumstances in which they found themselves. Around 50 per cent of councillors, across parties, felt less able to influence policy under an elected mayor than previously. Similar levels of agreement were received to the notion that the role of the councillor had been downgraded under mayoral government. Labour councillors were far more evenly divided in their responses than their counterparts on whether or not mayoral government placed them in a better position to represent their constituents.

Table 8.5 Percentage of councillors agreeing and disagreeing with statements regarding their changed role, by party affiliation

Statements and party affiliation	Agree/ strongly agree	Neither agree nor disagree	Disagree/ strongly disagree
Conservative			
I am less able to influence council policy than before	55	0	45
I am better placed to represent my constituents	27	18	55
I feel my role has been downgraded	55	9	36
I am more aware of what is happening at the council	45	9	45
I am more able to make things happen than before	27	0	73
Being a councillor is less important than before	36	27	36
Labour			
I am less able to influence council policy than before	48	9	42
I am better placed to represent my constituents	45	20	35
I feel my role has been downgraded	43	13	44
I am more aware of what is happening at the council	36	19	44
I am more able to make things happen than before	36	15	49
Being a councillor is less important than before	32	13	56
Liberal Democrat			
I am less able to influence council policy than before	53	27	20
I am better placed to represent my constituents	29	29	42
I feel my role has been downgraded	50	20	30
I am more aware of what is happening at the council	26	29	45
I am more able to make things happen than before	23	37	40
Being a councillor is less important than before	32	23	45
Independent			
I am less able to influence council policy than before	50	14	36
I am better placed to represent my constituents	40	13	47
I feel my role has been downgraded	47	13	40
I am more aware of what is happening at the council	53	7	40
I am more able to make things happen than before	44	6	50
Being a councillor is less important than before	40	0	60

Table 8.6 The preferences of councillors on mayoral authorities for constitutional arrangements, by party affiliation

Governing arrangements	Conservative	Labour	Liberal Democrat	Independent
A directly elected mayor	42	41	37	53
Return to the committee system	33	26	37	20
A council leader and cabinet elected by the council	25	32	27	27

Rao found that 36 per cent of her respondents on mayoral authorities felt it was 'easier to find out about council policy';[20] in the present survey, 45 per cent of Conservative councillors, 36 per cent of Labour, 26 per cent of Liberal Democrats and 53 per cent of independents felt 'more aware of what is happening at the council'. While testing a similar area of concern, the party breakdown of councillor affiliation indicates that councillors were responding differently to notions of how in touch they were with council affairs and that much of this was down to whether the councillor was from the same party as the mayor.

Councillors generally did feel somewhat dislocated from power, and the perception of a weakening and diminution of their role is reflected in the 32–40 per cent of respondents who felt that being a councillor was less important under an elected mayor. Councillors also indicated that they did not feel any more able to 'make things happen' while working alongside an elected mayor than previously had been the case; Conservative and Liberal Democrat recorded higher levels of agreement with this proposition than independents and Labour councillors.

Taking the responses to the impact of elected mayors on the role of the councillor into account, it is surprising that, when councillors were asked which form of constitutional arrangements they would prefer, their responses were as set out in Table 8.6.

While these responses are not a ringing endorsement of mayoral government, they do not reflect the rejection that might have been expected, particularly taking into account the opposition (expressed in the interviews) among councillors on some mayoral authorities to the adoption of this system. Whether or not councillors adapt to mayoral government or not and whether past opposition to the approach is dissipated will depend on how the role of the councillor develops on mayoral authorities. Moreover, the nature of the working relationship between councillors and mayors that emerges in these authorities will depend on how the separation of powers works in practice. It will also depend on how mayors and councillors develop their respective roles within that separation. What follows is how the London Borough of Newham has addressed the changing role of the councillor on a mayoral authority.

A new role for councillors: case study of the London Borough of Newham

Any radical change to established political structures, processes and behaviour requires a conscious rethinking of what particular political institutions or offices are for and how those roles are to be undertaken. One mayoral authority, the London Borough of Newham, has set out to redevelop and reinforce the role of the councillor within a mayoral system through its 'influential councillor' policy.

At the time of the case study, the London Borough of Newham had a Labour directly elected mayor, Sir Robin Wales, alongside whom there were fifty-nine Labour councillors and a lone Christian People's Alliance councillor. Labour in Newham has, on more than one occasion, and for a full council term, held all sixty council seats. As one of the most deprived boroughs in the country Newham has long required a local political system that can provide strong leadership to an ethnically diverse community and a leadership that can pursue the policies of political change needed to improve the quality of life in this east London outpost. It got just that with the election of Robin Wales as mayor in May 2002.

Wales recognised immediately on his election that the new mayors, while able to drive a policy agenda and pursue particular mayoral initiatives, also need to work alongside a strong body of councillors, firmly linked to their local communities and acting as the voice of those communities. Thus, ironically, it was he as the mayor, rather than the council as a collective body of councillors, who launched the 'influential councillor' initiative – developed to reformulate the role of the councillor as a community representative.

The 'influential councillor' policy seeks to strengthen the role of councillors but by placing them in an enhanced participatory framework. It does not, however, seek to cede power – away from councillors – to communities. In fact, to the contrary, the programme recognises councillors as: 'representatives of their diverse communities in a way that those who tend to voice opinions at meetings are rarely likely to be'.[21] While this ignores the fact that councillors will voice opinions only from the community they find party politically acceptable and will filter out of political discourse those views they find unacceptable, it does promote the role of the councillor as a legitimate and authoritative community representative. Moreover, the programme is linked to the mayor's particular vision of community leadership, localism and the role of the councillor as an integral part of the processes of local governance.

The 'influential councillor' policy not only recognises communities of place within the councillor's ward, but it also aims to enhance the councillor's position in representing a range of communities of interest, which extend beyond geographical boundaries. It further recognises the need for councillors to influence strategy decisions; the focus of the programme is, then, to enhance the role of the councillor both in the very local context and in the development of policy and strategy.

The policy rests on supporting councillors in their collection and assessment of intelligence gathered by them and the council to influence, negotiate, construct coalitions of interest, seek compromise and conduct an inclusive form of local politics. Indeed, 'influential councillors' will 'collect the aspirations and concerns of the local community and bring them to the attention of the council.'[22] Political decentralisation of this sort is not unique in English local government; it is, however, unique when placed in the setting of a directly elected mayor and a mayor with a very specific and clear vision of the role councillors can play in the governance of the locality.

Mayor Wales' vision for the development of the role of the councillor is a long-term one, with full implementation of the changes he foresees not expected until 2010; the 'influential councillor' is no quick fix or party political expedient (Labour doesn't need the latter in Newham!). Rather, it rests on a series of practical, cultural, administrative and political developments that are aimed at placing the local councillor at the centre of local politics. Moreover, the notion of an influential councillor is recognised as possible within a mayoral model only if there are strong links existing between councillors in their wards and the mayor, and only if the mayor consults and negotiates with councillors individually and collectively concerning ward-based issues and strategy.

The guiding principle of Newham's 'influential councillor' policy is defined in the bold statement that 'all councillors should be able to influence local decisions on behalf of the local community that elected them'. This includes 'decisions delegated to officers and those taken by local partners.'[23] If Newham achieves this, it will be one of the first councils, let alone mayoral council, do to so!

The 'influential councillor' programme integrates the elected member role with the existing community forums across the borough so that ward-level interests can be addressed through groups of councillors working in these forums. Each forum has a councillor, appointed by the mayor, to act as its lead member to coordinate the work of the forum and to report to the mayor. The lead member is expected to seek community opinion and views, assisted by other councillors who are forum members, by making links with a wide range of local organisations: tenants' associations, school governing bodies, local faith groups and special interest groups, for example.

Yet the programme recognises that, while the community forum structure is vital, the role of the councillor is not based primarily on that structure. Rather, councillors, working with the lead member, will link to all aspects of political and community life within the area of the forum; thus, the forum acts as a form of mini-council, designed to reach out to all communities of place and interest within its boundary. In such a scheme, the profile, standing and status of councillors are enhanced, as they are clearly seen as the people who can get things done within that specific locality. Furthermore, at the time of writing, consideration was being given to removing from the mayor the power of appointment of the forum lead member, replacing it with the election of a form of mini-mayor by the forums, elected to pursue local issues and concerns and to negotiate with the borough mayor.

The influential councillor as developed in Newham is represented diagrammatically in Figure 8.1.

Newham's 'influential councillor' initiative will rest for its success on three distinct elements: the information and support available to councillors; communication networks with the mayor and into the broader governance system; and a radical scheme of delegation to the forum, instigated by the mayor. If councillors are to have a powerful input into

Figure 8.1 The influential councillor. Source: London Borough of Newham, 2004. *The Influential Councillor: Community Leadership in Newham*, Report to the Mayor in Consultation with the Cabinet, London, London Borough of Newham Council.

a range of decisions made by the council and other bodies and agencies, they will require independent and robust sources of information and advice, perhaps even forum advisers to match the mayoral advisers already existing, and linking overview and scrutiny to the forums.

At the heart of the issue of enhancing the role of the councillor is raising the status of the councillor among senior officers. If councillors are to effect change, they must be recognised as a source of authoritative decision-making and as a point of contact for senior officers. Newham is addressing improvements in councillors' ability to influence decisions by developing a scheme of delegation to councillors, to be used in consultation with the mayor. Here we see just the opposite of what the opponents of elected mayors fear. Rather than a highly centralised system with decision-making power resting with the mayor, this mayor will use the power of delegation to enhance rather than to diminish the role of the local councillor.

What remains to be seen in Newham's approach to enhancing the role of the councillor is how successful it is in moving beyond concerns with council services and into a much broader political and representative role. It is clear that the Newham approach rests very heavily on councillors as an electorally legitimised voice of the people and, as such, must be careful not to alienate those voices that wish to articulate a view without seeking elected office. If there is open access to political space for public discourse, then all opinions can be heard and there is no need to delegitimise views that are deemed politically unacceptable, simply because they have not been elected to a representative office.[24] With these caveats to one side, Newham's policy of raising the profile, standing and effectiveness of the councillor could enhance councillor influence above that found in other mayoral and non-mayoral councils.

Newham stands alone among mayoral authorities in England as the only council to fundamentally review and revise the role and standing of the councillor to meet the new political realities of the mayoral system. Yet, ironically, it was the mayor who offered councillors greater influence, rather than councillors seeking it. Councillors in mayoral authorities can enhance their role, depending on their – and the mayor's – willingness to experiment with democratic innovations, new forms of politics, new approaches to democracy and representation and new ways of interacting with the communities of place and interest that they represent.[25]

Not all elected mayors are in the favourable position of Newham's Mayor Wales – if one's party holding all but one of the council seats is a favourable condition. Other mayors do not have the strong grip on the council through the party group as Wales does in Newham. Thus, much of the political risk in enhancing the role of the councillor is removed from the Newham experiment, as Labour councillors will have party loyalty, discipline and the desire to avoid acrimonious public division at the back of their mind. Other mayors who seek to strengthen the role of the councillor may be handing themselves a politically poisoned chalice and thus decide to do nothing to reassess and reconfigure the politically representative role of the councillor. In such circumstances it is up to councillors to rise to that challenge.

Conclusions

Councillors elected to mayoral authorities are not excluded from political power; neither are they automatically marginalised by the new office of mayor. Rather, the office of mayor makes it easier for councillors to manage the tension that has always existed between their political focus on governing an authority area and their specific (ward-based) community responsibility to act as a very local representative. It does this because the governing mandate is clearly given to the mayor, not to councillors. Yet councillors can take part in the governing processes by holding the mayor to account and through policy development and initiation in overview and scrutiny. Indeed, on all councils, if the separation of powers is to work, the executive requires a 'strong counterbalance in the form of effective political accountability'.[26]

Councillors on mayoral authorities have recognised their role in relation to mayoral accountability, but perceive that their role has been diminished as a result of the direct election, by the public, of the political head of the council. Yet that diminution is neither a condition of mayoral government nor caused by it. It is clear that councillors retain a vital role as local elected representatives, but it is a role which needs to change to meet the specific political dynamics of mayoral government in the English context. Certain conditions are necessary for councillors' roles and influence to develop within mayoral authorities:

- recognition that a new set of political skills is required of councillors – influencing, questioning, negotiation, compromise, coalition and alliance building – and that these need to be developed in a mayoral context;
- provision of robust information systems covering the activities of the council and other agencies of governance;
- ward-based information and data;
- research and policy support for councillors;
- strong communication linkages, both formal and informal, into the mayor's office and direct to the mayor;
- delegation of powers to councillors from the mayor;
- raising of the status of the councillor among senior officers and recognition of councillors' responsibilities;

- raising of the status of the councillor within his or her ward and the delegation of appropriate local decision-making to the councillor;
- support for the councillor's representative role within his or her ward.

Councillors in mayoral authorities do not face any greater hurdles than those sitting on leader and cabinet authorities when it comes to revising the role and responsibilities they have as representatives. It is for councillors, not just the mayor, to take the initiative and to review and change the nature of local politics and the way in which the office of councillor relates to both governing an area and representing communities of place and interest. As yet, this is a challenge to which councillors, on mayoral councils, are still to rise.

Notes

1 Phillips, A., 1996. 'Why Does Local Democracy Matter?', in L. Pratchet and D. Wilson (eds), *Local Democracy and Local Government*, London, Macmillan, pp. 20–37.
2 DETR, 1998. *Modern Local Government: In Touch with the People*, London, DETR.
3 Copus, C., 2004. *Party Politics and Local Government*, Manchester University Press.
4 Boaden, N., M. Goldsmith, W. Hampton, and P. Stringer, 1982. *Public Participation in Local Services*, Harlow, Longman.
5 Copus, C., 2000. 'Community, Party and the Crisis of Representation', in N. Rao (ed.), *Representation and Community in Western Democracies*, London, Macmillan, pp. 93–113; Copus, *Party Politics and Local Government*.
6 Glassberg, A., 1981. *Representation and Urban Community*, London, Macmillan.
7 Muchnick, D., 1970. *Urban Renewal in Liverpool*, Occasional Papers on Social Administration, the Social Administration Research Trust, London, Bell and Sons; Elkin, S., 1974. *Politics and Land Use Planning: The London Experience*, Cambridge University Press; Colenutt, B., 1979. 'Community Action Over Local Planning Issues', in G. Craig, M. Mayo and N. Sharman (eds), *Jobs and Community Action*, London, Routledge and Kegan Paul, pp. 243–252.
8 ODPM, 2005. *Vibrant Local Leadership*, London, ODPM.
9 DETR, *Modern Local Government*; DETR, 1999. *Local Leadership: Local Choice*, London, DETR.
10 Heclo, H., 1969. 'The Councillor's Job', *Public Administration*, Vol. 47, No. 2, pp. 185–202; Corina, L., 1974. 'Elected Representatives in a Party System', *Policy and Politics*, Vol. 3, No. 1, September, pp. 69–87; Jones, G.W., 1973. 'The Functions and Organisation of Councillors', *Public Administration*, Vol. 51, No. 2, Summer, pp. 135–146, at p. 142; Newton, K., 1976. *Second City Politics: Democratic Processes and Decision-Making in Birmingham*, Oxford,

Clarendon Press; Rao, N., 1994. *The Making and Unmaking of Local Self-Government*, Aldershot, Dartmouth.

11 Hirst, P., 1994. *Associative Democracy: New Forms of Economic and Social Governance*, Cambridge, Polity Press, p. 29 and p. 30.

12 ODPM, *Vibrant Local Leadership*.

13 DoE, 1991. *Local Government Review. The Structure of Local Government in England: A Consultation Paper*, London, DoE; Working Party on the Internal Management of Local Authorities in England, 1993. *Community Leadership and Representation: Unlocking the Potential*, London, HMSO; DETR, 2001. *Public Attitudes to Directly Elected Mayors*, London, DETR.

14 Rao, N., 2005. *Councillors and the New Council Constitutions*, London, ODPM, table 8, p. 14.

15 Pinkney, R., 1983. 'Nationalizing Local Politics and Localizing a National Party: The Liberal Role in Local Government', *Government and Opposition*, Vol. 18, pp. 347–358; Pinkney, R., 1984. 'An Alternative Political Strategy? Liberals in Power in English Local Government', *Local Government Studies*, Vol. 10, No. 3, May/June, pp. 69–84; Meadowcroft, J., 2000. 'Community Politics: Ideals, Myths and Realities', in N. Rao (ed.), *Representation and Community in Western Democracies*, London, Macmillan, pp. 114–137.

16 Wolman, H. and M. Goldsmith, 1992. *Urban Politics and Policy: A Comparative Approach*, Oxford, Basil Blackwell, p. 140.

17 Committee of Inquiry into the Conduct of Local Authority Business (henceforth Widdicombe committee), 1986. *Research, Vol. II: The Local Government Councillor*, London, HMSO; Copus, C., 1999. 'The Attitudes of Councillors Since Widdicombe: A Focus on Democratic Engagement', *Public Policy and Administration*, Vol. 14, No. 4, pp. 87–100.

18 Widdicombe committee, *Research, Vol. II*, table 7.1, p. 65.

19 Fox, P. and S. Leach, 1999. *Officers and Members in the New Democratic Structures*, London, Local Government Information Unit.

20 Rao, *Councillors and the New Council Constitutions*, p. 14, table 8.

21 London Borough of Newham, 2004. *The Influential Councillor: Community Leadership in Newham*, Report to the Mayor in Consultation with the Cabinet, London, London Borough of Newham Council.

22 *Ibid.*

23 *Ibid.*

24 Copus, *Party Politics and Local Government*.

25 Stewart, J., 1996. *Further Innovation in Democratic Practice*, Occasional Paper No. 3, Birmingham, Institute of Local Government Studies; Stewart, J., 1997. *More Innovation in Democratic Practice*, Occasional Paper No. 9, Birmingham, Institute of Local Government Studies; Stewart, J., 1999. *From Innovation in Democratic Practice Towards a Deliberative Democracy*, Occasional Paper No. 27, Birmingham, Institute of Local Government Studies.

26 John, P. and F. Gains, 2005. *Political Leadership Under New Political Management Structures*, London, ODPM, p. 18.

9

Conclusion

Introduction

England's experiment with elected mayors is an attempt to solve the perceived problems of a disconnection between communities and councils, decreasing turnout in local elections, slow and inefficient political decision-making structures and processes, lack of visible and clearly identifiable local political leadership, poor mechanisms and procedures for political accountability, and the low salience that local government generally has for the public.[1] In this regard, the mayoral experiment was one that was set up to fail and this chapter explores why that was so. It also sets out an alternative vision of the development of mayoral government, and how direct election to local political executive office could have a powerful role in overcoming the problems outlined above.

The first years of the mayoral experiment have produced evidence of a number of successes for individual mayors dealing with specific issues within their own councils and evidence of public satisfaction with mayoral government.[2] Yet the results of the various referendums held on introducing elected mayors and the turnout at mayoral elections indicate the experiment has a long way to go to stimulate the public. More importantly, elected mayors themselves have struggled to rise above their own local setting and become players on a regional or even national political stage. On the other hand, mayors have developed a high public profile in their own areas and have a high recognition factor among their own local voters.[3] Moreover, many of the English mayors have very quickly immersed themselves in reconfiguring both the political relationships of their councils and the bureaucratic structure to suit their mayoral priorities and policy agenda. Others have striven to look beyond the council, towards a broad interpretation of community governance and local political leadership.

Yet this book (and indeed the mayoral experiment itself) is not about the success or failure of individual mayors. Rather, it has been an exploration of what the mayoral experiment can tell us about the nature of

191

English local politics and democracy and how local government could be made more accessible and open to public engagement. It also about what the mayoral experience can tell us, to enable a fundamental reassessment of the role of local government and politics in England. It is about these factors that the mayoral experiment has much to say.

Mayors: separating English politics

Much has been made in the book of the notion that elected mayors are an essential part of any local separation of powers and we saw in Chapter 5 how the English approach to this has thus far been of a very limited nature. It is of no surprise that we should find a very blurred separation existing locally, as this mirrors the practices and traditions of the approach to the separation of powers in central government. Yet, despite its limitations, any notion of separation is a radical change from the previous practices of local political decision-making, a change which, as we saw in Chapter 8, has caused many councillors to perceive that their position and status had been downgraded.[4]

Yet the directly elected mayors have also expressed their frustrations with the configuration of political power within their councils. The mayors of North Tyneside, Bedford and Mansfield had run up against the power of the council when it came to aspects of mayoral governance. Indeed, one mayor commented in an interview:

> Full council has frustrated much of what I want to do and has prevented the executive from using any flexibility in virement between budgets, for example. The council has reduced my scope for moving funds around to meet new priorities and I can be defeated in council; I have had very real problems in getting a budget agreed.

Such defiance of a mayor and the ability of the council to frustrate mayoral policy fly in the face of the often anecdotal evidence provided by councillors about the downgrading of their role under an elected mayor. It also indicates that councillors and councils need to become more attuned to the idea of a separation of powers and to be more aware of the respective roles that an elected executive and an elected council can play. There is little evidence from mayoral councils that the council has developed its role as a body with the task of ensuring mayoral accountability; one mayor described council meetings as 'pretty run of the mill'.

However, in one regard, the advent of directly elected mayors has certainly generated a separation of the executive from the council and that is displayed in whether the mayor focuses inwards, towards managing the council, or outwards, towards broader notions of community governance and political leadership. The ability to act as a political figurehead, to negotiate with different types of communities and to speak to a range of institutions and agencies detaches the mayor from the council far more effectively than any notional institutional and structural separation of powers. A common theme emerging from mayoral experience is that the mayor, either by political style or by force of circumstance, is seen as the public face of the council and is expected to work directly with individuals and organisations outside the council. As one mayor simply put it in interview: 'you have to be out there, not in the town hall'.

A very distinct separation of powers can be problematic for local government, in that it makes governing a more difficult task and removes the certainty of outcome from political discourse and decision-making that strict party boundaries and a collective decision-making structure ensure. Among the real and most powerful conceptual challenges the advent of elected mayors provides to local government is perhaps the notion that government should be difficult for the politician, not convenient and easy! But this requires a further conceptual leap on the part of English politicians, to recognise that there are, indeed, distinct and separate roles to be played by different types of politician within the same local political institution – the council.

Yet, as we have seen, the idea of a form of separation of powers and direct election to local executive office in English local politics has a long history – one that stretches back to the Middle Ages.[5] We have also seen (in Chapter 5) that Jeremy Bentham in his 'Constitutional Code' set out an entirely new system of local government for England and proposed that at the lowest level of local government would stand the 'local headman', an executive post elected by the majority of the electors.[6] While Bentham's proposals were not enacted and a separation of local powers has, until the 2000 Act, been absent from English local government, the idea that direct election to executive office is some recent foreign import is far from accurate.

Local politics and the politics of the council

When it comes to the conduct of day-to-day politics within mayoral authorities, both inside and outside the council, no clear pattern of change in political behaviour has emerged. Rather, the party composition of the council, the stability or changeability of party control and the traditions of political behaviour, dynamics and party relationships all remain powerful factors in dictating the nature and quality of local political activity; the party allegiance or non-party allegiance of the mayor is a powerful but not overriding factor when it comes to how local politicians choose to conduct local politics.

Local politics has three dimensions. First, there is the politics of the council – that series of interactions and processes within and between the parties represented on the council. Second, there is the political space outside the council within which political interactions and activity occur, between a host of organisations and groupings and individual citizens – which may or may not be targeted at the council. Such local politics crosses the boundary between political action and civil society in a fairly fluid fashion, as groups are confronted with issues and events that may draw them into political activity, which was not necessarily the primary purpose of their existence.[7] Third, there is the politics that occur when councillors interact with the politics of the locality. But have England's elected mayors have had a demonstrable impact on these three political dimensions?

The impact of the English elected mayors on local politics can be assessed by considering the way in which they understand and approach political action and how they see the role of the mayor within it. Here, English directly elected mayors fall into three broad types, constructed as a result of the research for the book: the *visionary* (a term also employed by Randle[8]), the *insider* and the *gradualist*. As this book has carefully avoided making any judgements about individual mayors being more or less able and more or less effective than others (and has certainly avoided the production of a league table of mayors), the discussion that follows is anonymised.

The *visionary* is the mayor who is determined to make a difference to the conduct of politics on the council and to the broader local political environment; he or she has a clearly articulated view of how politics should change and envisions a more inclusive and participatory set of political process. Furthermore, the visionary is not afraid to see the political party dislodged from its dominant position locally. Three English mayors (excluding the London mayor) fell into this category, one of whom was from a political party. Based on evidence collected from the mayors concerned and from councillors sitting on the three councils, the texture of political interaction had changed since the arrival of the mayor and the quality and level of political engagement of citizens and council had developed a sharper edge. As one councillor commented in interview: 'Since he [the mayor] was elected things feel very different and we are much more aware of what people think about what the council is proposing; he leads from the front this one'. A councillor from another authority commented:

> I was opposed to elected mayors and still am, but this mayor acts like a lightning-rod for trouble and argument, but seems to thrive on it. I've seen him go out of his way to find out what people think and then dis-agree with it to get a reaction. But all the while he is building up a stock of

knowledge and getting people to contribute – he never misses a trick in that respect – the council is moving much more to the centre of people's attention in the area.

The visionary may prompt argument and disagreement and may even court controversy, but it is done with a clear view that such action stimulates and helps maintain public engagement and interest in the political process. What marks out the visionary is the action he or she takes to stimulate an all-encompassing political climate locally. What drives the mayor is the desire to create a new style of local politics and a belief that the office of directly elected mayor is the most powerful tool by which to achieve this aim. As well as changing how the politics of the council are conducted and how the council relates to the citizenry, the visionary also seeks to create a more active local political community, independent of the council. As such the visionary is never satisfied with politics as they are, but rather seeks politics as they can be: open, dynamic and effective. The politics of deliberation and debate are what the visionary seeks. The mayors that fell into this category did not claim they were anywhere near achieving that objective, but they did claim to be constantly working towards a new form of local politics.

The *insider*, as the name implies, is at home with the conduct of politics, both on and off the council, as they were before the advent of the office of elected mayor. Such a mayor sees no great advantage or disadvantage from the creation of a different style of politics and understands, and is able to work within, a political system dominated by political parties and a largely disengaged citizenry. The insider is not necessarily a party member, as some independent mayors also displayed a deep understanding of and appreciation for the rules of the political game. The insider sees the office of mayor as ideally suited to enabling him or her to negotiate the deals and support required to pursue political initiatives and policy preferences, as well as to dealing with the day-to-day running of the council.

The insider sets out not to radically change the conduct of local politics but rather to ensure that the existing processes are developed to accommodate the new office and to recognise the role and position that go with that office. Moreover, the insider is concerned to ensure that the office of mayor accrues as much political power as possible to play the existing political game, while respecting the existing status quo of organisation and structure and wishing, as far as possible, to avoid political controversy.

The insider also adheres to the same interpretations of concepts such as politics, democracy, representation and government as those held by the overwhelming majority of councillors and for that matter of party activists. Where insider mayors were found, interviews with councillors often uncovered the view that council politics had maintained their existing pattern and that the mayor was seen much as a council leader was seen in the past. Indeed, in one council a councillor commented in interview that: 'the mayor was leader before he became mayor and all that's changed is what we call him'. Two of the five insider mayors were particularly dismissive of their visionary counterparts, seeing them as fixed on a wider political theatre than the council, as courting controversy for the sake of it and as disturbing the settled pattern of politics of their council.

The *gradualist* welcomes the opportunity for a new style of politics that the office of elected mayor potentially provides, but does not see the sole purpose of the mayoral office as that of ushering in a new dawn of local political activity. Rather, the gradualist opts for business as usual, unless specific areas of the political decision-making processes within the council require change and development. Moreover, the gradualist views the interaction between council and citizenry from a very pragmatic point of view – what works stays, and what does not work stays until it becomes necessary to change it.

The gradualist sees politics – much like the insider – as the politics of the council and the council acting with the citizenry. He or she makes little attempt to engage with local politics for its own sake or to extend the meaning of local politics to encompass activity by groups and individuals that crosses the boundary with civil society. Transient organisations and groupings are tolerated and engaged with insofar as they affect council affairs; the gradualist has no long-term agenda to change politics in any way other than incrementally. Yet the gradualist is willing to engage public controversy and debate, unlike the insider, who generally wishes to dampen down public controversy and debate and is more inclined towards the private processes of political decision-making. Three mayors were categorised as gradualist on the basis of the research conducted for this book.

Whether the mayor is a visionary, insider or gradualist and whether the mayor sees his or her role as ushering in change, avoiding change, or embracing it where it is needed, the political circumstances and the locations in which the electorate chooses to have an elected mayor are an important part of the way the office develops and what it can achieve. Visionary mayors, for example, were found in very different parts of the country and, as a consequence of these location differences (and personal and political differences), the visions held by each mayor were different and how far they could move towards those visions varied. As one councillor commented in an interview: 'When [named mayor] was elected we all knew it was going to be different; say what you like about him, and people do, he knows what he wants, but what I want to see is if he knows how to get it'. Interviewed again after two years the same councillor, when reminded of this comment, said: 'He [named mayor] knows the area, he understands the people and he understands the area; he knows how to get what he wants alright, but only because he knows the area.' He added somewhat reluctantly:

> I thought it was a disaster when he won the election, but he's turned out a better politician than many I know. It's a different sort of politician though: he likes a public fight and all that goes with it and you have to understand that otherwise you'll never be able to work with him.

A councillor working alongside an insider mayor commented:

> None of us wanted an elected mayor and we feel it has been forced on us as a result of a clever campaign. But [named mayor] knows what he's doing, he's one of us, he understand the council (he's been a member long enough) and he understands the group and what it wants and what it won't put up with. So, if we've got to have a mayor, then it might as well be one of us. He hasn't pushed anything we [the ruling group] don't like and what he has done he has got our support for – not everyone agrees with everything of course – but that's politics!

One gradualist mayor in interview summed things up thus:

> I came into politics to make a difference and to change things, but you can't throw the baby out with the bath water; we have to have a sense of perspective on what's right and wrong in the system rather than change everything for the sake of it. Being mayor helps to give me that perspective, but it's a political perspective which I've tempered with my own beliefs. I don't think I'm much different to when I was leader – but I know I can act differently and I do, but when it's needed.

When interviewing mayors what came over strongly was the sense of location that they had, with the word 'unique' often applied to their area and council. One mayor commented: 'I was not going to stand for election, but during the referendum campaign everyone assumed I would, including the political parties; it's unique this area for the way things get round.' Another mayor stated: 'We have a unique set of problems in the borough and I've tried to address them in a new way and to put people before politics'. A third said: '[named council] has a unique position and problems unique to our multicultural and deprived community, which is recognised by ministers'. Mayors, and for that matter councillors and citizens, see their areas as unique and as requiring solutions to problems that recognise the traditions, cultures and very uniqueness of the areas concerned.

Yet the mayor's mandate, willingness and ability to change the texture of local politics, within and outside the council, rest not only on whether he or she adopts a visionary, insider or gradualist approach, but also on the personality and qualities of the mayor as an individual. It is here that we see an absolutely fundamental change in the nature and conduct of local politics brought about by the office of elected mayor: the elevation of the personality of the individual candidate for mayoral office and individual mayor above what passes for the norm or even decency in local politics of the more traditional kind.

Personality matters

One thing has become crystal clear from England's experience with directly elected mayors: holding local executive political office is not the sole property of the political party. Incumbent independent mayors have shown not only that can those outside a political party win office but also that they are just as able as any party-based candidate to come to terms with the complex issues of governance, to hold to account an unelected bureaucratic machine and to balance governing and representation. Indeed, those who have had experiences outside of party politics may make as good politicians, if not better, as those who have served a long party political apprenticeship.

Political skills can be developed in a number of settings and honed from a wide range of experiences – not just those to be had within a political party. Indeed, it is a commonplace experience in North America (though not exclusively there) for mayoral candidates to have had only a passing interest in party politics or a casual association with a party and to concentrate on developing a career before moving into politics.[9] Other North American mayors have been prime examples of the consummate party insider and machine politician.[10] It is the norm in English local politics for candidates for local office from political parties to have a record of party activity and membership of a reasonable, if not considerable, period. While it is true that some parties, in some areas, will experience a dearth of willing candidates, particularly in the less urban locations, the safe seats are often occupied by well entrenched and long-standing party members, or see hard-fought selection battles between party members.

It is not unheard of for the Liberal Democrats to recruit council candidates from outside the party while conducting local campaigning work; the Conservative Party has, in some areas, advertised for candidates to stand for the council under the party banner; Labour on the other hand is the most reluctant to look outside the party for candidates, preferring to encourage members who do not wish to be a councillor to stand as 'paper candidates' in unwinnable seats. Yet the office of elected mayor is different and, in the fullness of time, may require political parties in England to take a very different view of candidate selection and to go as far as supporting mayoral candidates from outside the party – rather than standing a party candidate in the race. Such a move would signal a seismic shift in political attitudes among English political parties.

There is no getting away from the fact that the personal characteristics of the individual mayoral candidate and mayor matter, and that the personality of the individual counts when it comes to success in the mayoral office and in winning that office in the first place. Indeed, the personal qualities of the candidate can enhance a party's appeal and transcend its national standing, as candidates display their qualities, policies, virtues, strengths and weaknesses to all the voters. Compare this with the selection of a council leader by councillors and the superiority of direct over indirect election becomes very apparent. In selecting a council leader, councillors in the ruling group employ criteria such as: political ideology, party factionalism, personal likes and dislikes, their own political ambitions and career aspirations, the malleability or pliancy of leadership candidates to group pressure, and simple 'any candidate but X' choices. Moreover, it is a truism of local politics that the best person for the leadership is not the one most likely to get it. Rather, the successful candidate is the one who ensures that more of his or her supporters attend the group meeting held to decide on the position of leader than attend from among supporters of his or her opponents.

Many opponents of elected mayors appear to be fearful of the personalisation of local politics, believing that it some how eases consideration of important local issues out of local election campaigns and focuses on the qualities, rather than policies, of individual candidates.[11] Yet such a view is fundamentally wrongheaded and reflects the notion that, in electing local political leaders, the voters need know nothing about those leaders as individuals. In reality the contrary is true: when voters are electing their local political leaders they need to know of the personal qualities and foibles of the individual, as these will reflect on that individual's ability to pursue and implement the policies on which he or she is seeking election. Moreover, if anything eases the consideration of local issues out of local political space it is the domination of local politics in England by political parties, aided and abetted in this by the anonymity and collective hiding place provided to councillors by the party group. It is these factors that are responsible for the de-localisation of local politics and for preventing an inclusive and deliberative local democracy from emerging, not the arrival of directly elected mayors.

To argue that the personality of the political leader – however he or she is chosen – should be downplayed or, worse, should have no role to play at all in selection to political leadership imposes an enormous deceit on the electorate. When voting for a party candidate, voters have little if any idea what hides behind that label, where on the party spectrum that candidate rests, whether he or she is trustworthy, assiduous, hardworking, dedicated, a skilled politician and a competent negotiator. Nor do they know what that candidate believes and what interpretations he or she has of political representation, democracy and politics, and how amenable the candidate is to citizen engagement.

When confronted with a candidate that all one knows of is his or her party label, one can be more or less certain of one thing: that, when faced with the demands of party loyalty and discipline, that candidate will follow the party line. A reliance on party label makes parties, their candidates and the electorate lazy, for without a party label the individual candidate's profile and local knowledge would be at a premium, for to vote other than for a party an 'elector must know something of the personal characteristics of the candidates'.[12] Indeed, the 'relatively disinterested [*sic*] elector' may rely on party labels to make local elections 'more readily comprehensible'.[13]

Direct election to executive political office is the best way of ensuring not only that the issues of importance to the voters are confronted and policy options are debated, but also that the personal quality of the candidate seeking office is held up to scrutiny, as it should be. Knowledge of a candidate's personal qualities and preferences indicates their own political priorities and provides the voter with as clear an indication as is possible in local politics of the way in which a potential mayor will react to political circumstances.[14]

Thus, elected mayors add something that is sadly lacking in English politics – a bit of knowledge about the individual who wishes to govern us locally. Such knowledge clearly had a part to play in the election of some of England's first executive mayors, particularly for independent candidates such as Ray Mallon in Middlesbrough, Stuart Drummond in Hartlepool, Frank Branston in Bedford, Tony Egginton in Mansfield and Mike Wolfe in Stoke-on-Trent, all of whom emphasised the importance to their successful election of the local profile they had developed and the knowledge that local voters had of them as individuals. Some of these mayors of course were better known locally than others; some had to work harder to develop a local profile during the campaign and, as Mayor Drummond freely admitted, had to work hard to change the image the electorate had.

Yet, in the crop of party mayors studied, personal skill and quality were not the sole preserve of the independents. It was just that the independents were more prepared than was the political party to trumpet personal qualities. A focus on the candidate rather than the party can distance the mayor from the party and make the political territory less secure for party domination. One message from the first elections to mayoral office in England was quite clear: personality and individual quality and skills matter in local politics. The political parties will find this an uncomfortable message, but it is one they must heed. The electorate, who have the task of electing the mayor, need much more to go on than simple party label if they are to make a judgement about the best candidate for the position. It is wholly right that the public know as much as possible about those who seek to govern locally.

Nonetheless, the personal qualities, skills and abilities of the individual mayor can only go so far in providing effective political leadership and government to local communities. The mayor also needs the power to do the job for which he or she was elected.

Political power and the elected mayor: a legitimate governing role

The question of what and how much political and administrative power will be granted to any sub-national elected official or body will always be a vexed one, but nowhere more so than in a unitary system such as that in Britain, where a supreme Parliament decides the powers and responsibilities that other political institutions shall hold. It is not surprising that no serious consideration was given to the question of the power that would rest with the mayor's office, or whether those councils introducing directly elected mayors should be granted greater powers over their own activities and communities as governing bodies than other, non-mayoral authorities – a carrot which may have tempted more recalcitrant councils to experiment with an elected mayor. Rather, the assumption was made that the powers of the mayor would be those that already existed within local government and that the powers and responsibilities of the mayor would in reality be only a reconfiguring and repositioning of existing powers of the council within the mayor's office. Moreover, the powers and responsibilities of the mayoral council would be the same as those of any other council and reflect the council's existing role and responsibilities, at whatever tier of local government it was located.

The mayoral experiment has suffered from government reluctance to empower local government and from the constitutional inertia of the British unitary system of government. It has also suffered from the structure of the 2000 Act itself, which failed to distinguish adequately between the political and administrative roles of local government or to differentiate significantly between mayors and council leaders in any way other than the mode of election and the relationship they have with the cabinet. What was required was separate enabling legislation that clearly granted elected mayors specific and wide roles, powers and responsibilities beyond those of council leaders. Indeed, granting elected mayors and mayoral authorities general competence within their areas would set them apart from other councils, which would be left with the more restricted 'well-being powers' of Part I of the 2000 Act.[15] While mayors have a clear mandate to govern, granted by the electorate, they lack the power granted by Parliament to do so.

Mayoral power and responsibility rest currently on the type of council the mayor inhabits: district, county, unitary or London borough. For example, Bedford, Mansfield and Watford are second-tier authorities and the relationship they have with their respective county authorities did not change as a result of the arrival of an elected mayor. The distinct mayoral political power as it currently stands quite simply boils down to the ability of the mayor, enshrined within the Act, to select a cabinet and to allocate portfolios to cabinet members, a power also open to council leaders if the council so decides.

English mayors, if they are to make a difference, need political power. Moreover, mayors should be granted a role that extends beyond the council, because of the direct mandate received; the power of the council leader, by contrast, should be reduced in comparison with that held by a mayor, as with no direct mandate there is no justification for a council leader to have the same power to act as should a directly elected mayor. That way, citizens voting in a mayoral referendum will know that, when the mayor is elected, his or her mandate will make a difference to the governance of the area and that there will be a real purpose to mayoral office. The mayor is elected to govern and should be able to do so; the council leader is not and should not!

The English mayor cannot govern in the way in which many mayors overseas can, where mayors often have a far wider range of powers and responsibilities when it comes to the governance of their communities and to the provision of public services. We have seen that the Italian mayor appoints the executive body and can choose non-councillors to be part of this body; he or she chooses and dismisses all members of the executive board. The mayor also appoints senior council officials and directly oversees the running of various departments. In those US cities with 'strong' mayors, the mayor has almost total authority. He or she can: appoint and dismiss departmental heads without council approval; veto council proposals; and prepare and administer the budget (but it must be passed by council). Moreover, many elected mayors of smaller US towns are fiercely proud of the fire and police departments (however small) their communities sustain.

The Bulgarian mayor performs a far wider range of executive functions than his or her English counterpart, directly managing the municipal administration as well as ensuring the implementation of the municipal budget or budgetary policy and that the decisions of the council are implemented. The Greek mayor is responsible for a range of activities directly delegated from ministers in central government. And many other examples exist of powerful local political leaders chosen by and respon-sible to the voters. In Japan elected mayors and governors are responsible for ensuring overall consistency in the local authority's services and functions. They represent the authority externally and have control over administrative committees. They have rights to enact regulations, draft budgets, introduce bills and appoint members of administrative committees. The mayor or governor implements the policies decided by the elected council.

The book has deliberately avoided too much of a focus on overseas directly elected mayors because it is the English experience which is of interest here. Moreover, considerable caution is needed in drawing out the lessons from overseas, where different cultural, political and governmental systems are at work. But one very telling general lesson can be drawn from what often happens overseas: direct election to local executive political office grants far deeper and far wider-reaching powers to govern locally and to take and implement governing decisions than is the case for the English mayor.

Yet it is also true that in some countries, such as New Zealand, Canada and Norway, and in some US towns, the mayoral office is politically weak, sometimes merely a figurehead, and real power lies with the council; when it comes to mayoral power you pays your money and you takes your choice! The latter point is the key issue for the development of the English mayor and can be summed up by asking just how much power do we want local government to have and what do we want it to be able to do? If it is to provide political leadership and govern local communities, then the existing legislative power of the directly elected mayor is simply insufficient to raise local government above its currently low levels of salience or relevance to local communities.

As usual in English politics, greater power has to be earned, not granted as of right, and elected mayors must prove a case for more power, for both their office and their council. To do that elected mayors must be able to display the effectiveness of their own governing role and of their own councils, but this must be an effectiveness that stands apart from measures imposed or calculated by one government inspectorate or another and from the administratively and bureaucratically driven CPAs conducted by the Audit Commission. How might we then assess the effectiveness of directly elected mayors as political leaders with oversight of important local services and what indicators can be used to assess mayoral effectiveness when it comes to governing local communities?

Indicators of mayoral political and governmental effectiveness

In judging the effectiveness of elected mayors in governing their communities, we need to take cognisance of the fact that in a complex, dynamic, often turbulent political environment no one agency or individual governs by themselves and in isolation from any external factors.

Those who govern operate in a political space that is shared by a range of agencies concerned with elements of the governing process.[16] Yet political action must be judged by different criteria to managerial concerns and evaluating governmental activity from what might be described as a technocratic standpoint.

It is both dangerous and wrong to reduce politics to a set of quantifiable targets and figures as though political interaction and deliberation can somehow be counted rather than experienced. Is a decision ineffective because some people do not like it politically, or disagree with its aim and intention? Is a politician to be judged ineffective because he or she was unable to overcome a certain political problem? If they are ineffective, will voters refrain from supporting them? Such questions have no technocratic or measurable answer and indicate that the political process must be separated from the quality of local public services; political effectiveness requires a value judgement rather than an evaluation or auditing system.

Judging the effectives of politicians is fraught with difficulty because voters are often prone to vote for those they agree with or prefer politically, irrespective of performance. So, what follows is a set of criteria against which elected mayors can be judged for their political effectiveness; or at least a series of questions that can be asked about the mayor and his or her policies and actions. Political accountability is enhanced if the voter has some form of criteria against which to judge the actions or inactions of the mayor – or any politician for that matter. Such a set of criteria for mayoral effectiveness should include the following points:

- high public profile;
- voter name recognition;
- stakeholder name recognition;
- public awareness of mayoral action;
- high-profile and innovative policy schemes;
- generating and sustaining political discourse;
- public engagement in local political discourse;
- ambassadorial role;
- working relationship with the council;
- working relationship with officers;
- dealing with authority-wide problems;
- dealing with sub-authority-wide problems;
- pursuing a clear political vision;
- communicating a clear political vision;
- relationships with other governance bodies;
- profile beyond the authority;
- providing political leadership to the community;
- a positive impact on election results.

It is against the criteria set out above that we can start to make a judgement about the overall political effectiveness of any individual elected mayor, as distinct from any technocratic measurement of the effectiveness of the council in providing public services. Thus, the criteria are deliberately open to a value-laden interpretation and a value-laden conclusion – scientific objectivity is not the purpose of judging mayoral political effectiveness; rather, what is sought here is some way of ordering how to make a political judgement about the way in which the mayor conducts his or her role in office.

Any such judgement on a mayor's political effectiveness will always be open to the political preferences and affiliation of the individual making it. Political activists and party members will never admit that their opponents are 'effective' in any sense, and this sort of party knee-jerk reaction can be removed from consideration of mayoral effectiveness. The voter, on the other hand, and the community group, stakeholder organisation, business group or other organisations from the political and civil world may of course have their political party preferences, but may be more willing to judge a mayor, and therefore vote for or against such a mayor, based on some assessment of his or her performance as a politician and governor, rather than a party candidate. Such an assessment, if undertaken by the voter, is one more nail in the coffin of political party dominance of local politics.

Finally, it is necessary to consider why the criteria set out above are applicable only to elected mayors and not to council leaders or council majority groups. First, the act of direct election to executive office requires a judgement to be made on a political leader, not a local councillor, who may or may not hold any executive position and who has a representational relationship with a ward or division, rather than a direct governing role to play; the corollary of this point is that the electorate cannot cast a judgement on the leadership qualities of the leader and so a more indirect method of assessment is needed in these cases. Second, a majority party, or for that matter a minority party, acts as a cohesive bloc of members with an assumed governing mandate, but the voter cannot cast a judgement on the group as a whole, only on his or her councillor. Third, it is more appropriate to use such criteria to assess the actions of an individual who, in many cases, can act alone, without the need for party support on the council, unlike the council leader.

Effects of individual mayors on election results

Even if we set aside mayoral re-election or defeat as a criterion for effectiveness, as voters may dismiss notions of effectiveness anyway and vote for party preference, we can still look at the results of local elections

Table 9.1 Council composition, 2002 (when mayors were first elected) and 2004 (last full year of mayoral office in four councils)

Council	Conservative	Labour	Liberal Democrat	Other	Mayor
Bedford					
2002	25	14	11	4	Independent
2004	16	15	13	10	
Doncaster					
2002	7	42	9	5	Labour
2004	9	27	13	14	
Hackney					
2002	9	45	3	0	Labour
2004	9	45	3	0	
Hartlepool					
2002	8	23	12	4	Independent
2004	4	25	9	9	
Lewisham					
2002	2	45	4	3	Labour
2004	2	41	7	4	
Mansfield					
2002	5	39	2	0	Independent
2004	2	15	4	25	
Middlesbrough					
2002	4	41	7	1	Independent
2004	7	32	5	4	
Newham					
2002	0	59	0	1	Labour
2004	0	59	0	1	
North Tyneside					
2002	19	34	7	0	Conservative
2004	27	26	7	0	(Labour 2005)
Stoke-on-Trent					
2002	6	24	8	22	Independent
2004	5	35	5	15	(Labour 2005)
Watford					
2002	7	15	13	1	Lib. Dem.
2004	4	4	26	2	

Source: Figures provided by the Local Government Chronicle Elections Centre at the University of Plymouth.

to see if any mayoral impact is evident. That is, have individual mayors acted as a boost to their party or association's local electoral standing, or has their tenure in office damaged their party's or association's electoral fortunes? Table 9.1 sets out the results of the elections for councillors held in the mayoral authorities (up to the time of writing) since the advent of the elected mayor.

Great care must be taken in looking at any set of local election results in isolation; such results can be fully understood only when set against the national set of local election results and when a wide range of local and very local factors are taken into account. That said, a casual glance at Table 9.1 indicates a remarkable feature of the local elections for council-lors in mayoral authorities: that is, since the election of the first mayors in 2002, the party composition of some mayoral authorities has changed markedly. The election of a Conservative mayor in North Tyneside saw a subsequent change in party control of the council from a Labour majority to the Conservatives becoming the largest party; the election of a Liberal Democrat mayor in Watford saw the subsequent capture of the council by the Liberal Democrats; the election of an independent mayor in Mansfield was followed by a remarkable shift in control of the council from Labour to independent. These results indicate some form of swing in favour of council candidates sharing the political affiliation of the mayoral incumbent. On the other hand, Doncaster council saw its Labour majority overturned, despite having a Labour mayor, and Stoke-on-Trent's independent mayor saw the fortunes of the independent group decline. Here we see local election results indicating a swing away from the incumbent mayor's political affiliation. (The Postscript to the book provides a review of the 2005 mayoral election results.)

Despite the caveats above, it can be concluded that the advent of elected mayors may be a powerful contributing factor to reversing the trend of local elections being seen as a judgement on the government of the day, a trend which has already begun to fracture in local election results. The existence of powerful local politicians, directly elected by the voters, gives the electorate all the more reason to pay attention to local issues and factors when voting in local elections – if mayors can help achieve that, then this is another compelling reason for their adoption across England.

Developing mayoral local government: an agenda for reform

Set, as elected mayors are, within the structure of the traditional English council, their effectiveness or otherwise, as judged by the criteria set out above, is contingent not only on mayoral skill but also on a range of institutional and political arrangements which act as potential barriers to mayoral effectiveness. One early conclusion it is possible to draw from England's experiment with elected mayors is that, rather than seeing an incumbent to a new form of local political office with new powers and responsibilities located in the mayoral office, England, in reality, has simply introduced a system that gives us a directly elected council leader. It is for that reason the opening paragraph of this chapter identified the mayoral experiment as one that had been set up to fail. To achieve anything like the degree of political and governmental effectiveness that would be attained if the criteria set out above were met, and to have any chance of promoting local political leadership and powerful, relevant local government, radical reforms are needed to the office of directly elected mayor.

The problem associated with locating a new political office within a traditional English council arrangement and expecting it to achieve great things is that the new office will simply lack the power, structure and resources needed. Such is the case with the English version of a directly elected mayor and it is clear that while overseas experience may have influenced the desire of some to see elected mayors arrive on the shores of England, there was little real intention that mayors should be able to do any more than existing local political structures were already charged with doing, or that the mayor should be a powerful local political player in his or her own right. Hence the conclusion is that the English version of the mayor is little more than a directly elected council leader.

Two key sets of changes are required to create a mayoral office for English local government that will enable the mayor to wield effective political power, to provide clear, visible and effective political leadership, to control a large public service bureaucracy, to influence and direct the activities of a range of agencies and to negotiate on behalf of the communities governed: first, to the broad nature of local government that the mayor inhabits; and second, to the power and responsibilities of the elected mayor. These conclusions are based on the assertion that if the electorate selects, in a referendum, a mayoral system of government, then that system should be able to offer more in the way of dealing with local problems and issues than just a titular and electoral change to the office of the political head of the council.

Mayoral local government

It should be made clear to voters at the time of the referendum on intro-ducing an elected mayor that a 'yes' vote will not only result in the arrival of an elected mayor: it will also introduce a new constitutional settle-ment between the locality and central government, as well as with other sub-national bodies of governance.[17] That settlement would include the transference of the local authority to unitary status on its existing geographical boundaries (if the council does not already have that status). Such a move would come only for existing district rather than county councils, as counties moving to unitary status would be too large and remote to be *local* government. Districts moving to unitary status maintain a small and cohesive community far more easily than a county. Also, the purpose of the referendum, namely to decide on whether to have a directly elected mayor, should not be detracted from by arguments about unitary status and boundaries; therefore existing districts should simply move to unitary status on existing boundaries. The government has set a precedent for such dual referendums with its insistence that elected regional assemblies should be linked to unitary reorganisation.

The settlement would also require a second constitutional change: a 'yes' vote in a referendum should also mean that the mayor and council are granted a general competence to act – relieving them of the need to identify precise legal authority for their actions and so giving them the ability take any action deemed necessary in governing a community, save that specifically prohibited in legislation. Indeed, the granting of general competence to mayor and council should be coupled to an extension of the power of the council and mayor to allow both to devise and pass council ordinances (local legislation) controlling a range of activities within their areas – in line with national legislation, which of course could not be negated or overturned locally. Indeed, mayoral councils should not need Private Bill procedures; rather they should pass their own local legislation. Finally, mayoral councils should be free from government inspection regimes; the only inspection and judgement required on them are those performed by the electorate!

The power of general competence could be drawn very widely and set out in a single general enabling Act of Parliament that would come into force with the arrival of an elected mayor. The Act would allow mayoral authorities, among other things, to govern in areas hitherto the responsibility of central government; it would devolve powers from central government and from a range of regionally organised bodies to the mayoral council. Moreover, with the power to legislate locally, the mayoral council could pass local legislation on issues as diverse as bans on fox hunting, smoking in public places, or a change in the local voting system. A local referendum could be required to give final public agreement to mayoral and council legislation.

A third aspect of the constitutional settlement would involve a change in local tax-raising powers with the introduction of a directly elected mayor. Mayoral councils should not be council-tax capped and should have available to them a range of additional tax powers, such as sales or tourist taxes, and have the freedom to shift the basis of their tax regime from property to a local income tax.

With such a constitutional framework in place, elected mayors could make a real difference to the quality of democracy and the quality of life within local communities. Moreover, when voting in a referendum called to introduce an elected mayor, voters would know that with the mayor would come greatly enhanced local self-government. The choice for the electors about how they wish to be governed locally would have real purpose, power and significance.

A new form of elected mayor

As well as a new constitutional settlement between localities and central government, the new English directly elected mayor requires an enhanced set of powers and responsibilities. Such powers are required to enable the office-holder to make a difference to the quality of democracy and life locally, to take quick, decisive action, and to pursue a clearly articulated long-term policy vision for the area. Therefore, hand in hand with existing mayoral responsibility, the following changes to mayoral power are required:

• the power to appoint and dismiss all senior officers, from the chief executive and directors/heads of department to heads of service;
• unlimited ability to form boards and commissions to advise on mayoral policy, or take action delegated by the mayor, with membership to be drawn from inside or outside the council;
• the mayoral cabinet to comprise wholly or in part members appointed by the mayor from inside or outside the council;
• adequately resourced mayoral offices and advisory staff – with no legislative restrictions on size or budget;
• a mayoral veto over council decisions;
• appointment of mayoral representatives to outside bodies and organisations, distinct from representatives appointed by the council.

Coupled to these changes would be the municipalisation, under mayoral councils only, of a range of public services or responsibilities, such as police, hospitals, health care, fire and rescue, and ports and docks. Indeed, those areas with an elected mayor would see a sweeping away of the powers of national and regional quangos, central government agencies and other bodies, and the transference of responsibility (though not delivery) into the mayoral authority. The chief executives and senior officers of these bodies would all be subject to appointment and dismissal by the mayor. Moreover, mayoral approval would need to be sought by any organisations taking action which would affect the mayoral authority.

Overview and scrutiny committees would be charged with the duty of holding to public account the policies and activities of all external bodies which affected the mayoral authority. Moreover, all public agencies would be required to redraw their boundaries to ensure they were co-terminous with the boundaries of the mayoral authority, so that the council area formed a distinct geographical sub-unit of the agencies. Such a move would be necessary to make a reality of mayoral appointment of the chief executive of the local health authority sub-unit, for example, or the borough police commander, or other agency head.

The above is by no means an exhaustive list of what should be mayoral responsibility. Rather, it represents the type of municipalisation that should occur on the arrival of an elected mayor – the devil is of course in the detail and that is beyond the remit of this book. These changes in the mayoral office, linked to general competence and a power to pass ordinances (sub-national legislation applicable within the council area), would provide for a very strong political leader. Such a strong set of political arrangements require very strong checks and balances, some of which should be in the hands of the council, others of which should rest with the electorate.

The full council and overview and scrutiny would hold the mayor to account and act as a check and balance on his or her authority. Such a public accountability role would have to transcend party allegiance, and councillors would have to be as robust in holding their party's mayor to account as they would a mayor of any other party or an independent mayor. With current political practices and loyalties this may seem a naïve hope, but it is required! To match the mayoral veto, full council would also require a veto over mayoral action, but a veto requiring a two-thirds majority of members voting; the council veto, however, should be a delaying and not a prohibiting mechanism, providing for negotiation and discussion time, not preventing the mayor from acting.

Overview and scrutiny should have the right to subpoena any witnesses, from within or without the council; the holders of any mayoral appointment inside or outside the council should be subject to overview and scrutiny subpoena and should report to overview and scrutiny on a regular basis. In addition, all mayoral appointments – political and administrative – should be subject to council confirmation hearings before the appointment becomes active; appeals against dismissals of administrative staff (not political appointments and dismissals, against which there should be no appeal) would be made to the council and strict time limits for dealing with such hearings would be firmly set.

As far as the electorate is concerned, a power of mayoral recall should be available, based on the collection of a petition by local citizens to force a recall election. Safeguards would be needed to prevent political parties simply petitioning to remove a mayor from another party; specific reasons and requirements for recall elections would need to be set down publicly. The term of office of the mayor should be reduced to three years, as should the term of office of councillors, which would make any revival of the government's suggestion to move to annual elections in all authorities more easily realisable.[18] Shorter terms for elected representatives keep the political eye focused on the reactions of the electorate to political policy and action, far more clearly than most other mechanisms of accountability.

What emerges here is a framework in which to set the development of the English directly elected mayor as a political leader and to form a powerful local political system with robust mechanisms for public engagement and accountability. It requires, however, a new constitutional settlement between the centre and the localities, with a new form of independent local government arising in the mayoral areas.

Conclusions

The term 'experiment' has been employed throughout the book when referring to the English experience with directly elected mayors; this is to indicate not only that much can be learnt from that experience, but also that, as with many experiments, much argument can be had about the results and outcomes. However, to understand those results it is necessary to separate out local government as a provider of public services from local government as a politically representative and governing institution and, further, to separate that from the dynamics of party and non-party politics outside the confines of the council. The quality of local democracy and politics is not dependent on the quality of local public services. Rather, it is dependent on: the levels of engagement in the political process; the effectiveness of the interactions between citizens and representatives; the salience of local public policy to local communities; the ease of access and egress to the political processes for the citizen or community group; and the responsiveness of mayors, councillors and councils to public concerns. Moreover, the health of local democracy is very much damaged by the dominance of political parties over local politics and how willing or reluctant they are to share political space with a range of political participants from outside the world of party politics.[19]

The issue of whether England should extend or abandon its experiment with elected mayors has little (if anything) to do with the quality of public services, with the bureaucratic and managerial priorities of LSPs, or with any another service-based managerialist concern. Rather, it is a political question which can be put very simply: should the public be able to elect for themselves the political head of the council, or should councillors have the power to make that decision for the public, using a range of criteria which may often have little bearing on the good governance and healthy politics of the area? The answer, however, is extremely complex and rests on the interpretations held by supporters and opponents of elected mayors about the nature and meaning of politics, democracy, representation, government, governing for the whole or the part, the role of political parties and the amount of trust the local political elite has in local citizens to do the right thing when it comes to electing their representatives. Local politicians and those active in party politics quite simply do not like the choice of political leadership being taken out of their own hands and placed in the hands of the voter.

Yet, despite the reluctance of the local government establishment to relinquish its control over the appointment of the local political leader to the voters, those voters, as a result of the referendum provisions of the 2000 Act, do have some control over the shape of local government and over the way in which they are governed locally. Moreover, politicians in many areas of the country have been forced during referendum campaigns to justify and explain the system they prefer and to secure support for it. Such public discourse and campaigning as have taken place during the referendums have left behind a pool of knowledge and interest among people that may yet pay dividends in generating a more inclusive and participatory set of local political processes.

Despite the small number of elected mayors across England, and despite three models of mayoral government being available in England (including the London mayoralty and Greater London Authority), there are lessons that can be drawn from that experiment for the future conduct of local politics and for local government. The mayoral experiment highlights the need for:

- new ways of enhancing the political legitimacy of local government to act as a community leader;
- a rethinking of the role and purpose of local government, linked to a devolution of power to localities;
- a clear distinction between local government's tasks in providing public services and its political representative and governing role;
- locally devised strategies for overcoming the low salience of local government and politics for the citizen and communities;
- local politicians to provide leadership to the community and to govern an area rather than being involved in the minutiae of running a council;
- the dominance of party politics within local government not to be taken as a given and recognition that candidates from outside the world of the political party can secure office and succeed in that office without the backing of a political party that has a national base;

- local political leaders to be responsive to citizen engagement in local political issues;
- a high-profile and visible political leadership as a powerful tool for ensuring public engagement with local government and developing a healthy local democracy;
- a more open and responsive political culture in local government and an outward-looking and energetic political system.

To make a real difference to governing locally and to local political leadership, the English mayor must be so much more than a directly elected council leader, which is the result of the current arrangements. The English mayor, compared with his or her indirectly elected counterpart, requires a different legislative framework, a different political and institutional set of arrangements, and considerably more political and governing power than currently is the case if the quality and effectiveness of local political leadership and governance are to be enhanced. Presenting local citizens with those choices when they vote in a referendum to adopt a directly elected mayor really would result in local leadership and local choice.

Notes

1 DETR, 1998. *Modern Local Government: In Touch with the People*, London, DETR, para. 1.2.
2 Randle, A., 2004. *Mayors Mid-Term: Lessons from the First Eighteen Months of Directly Elected Mayors*, London, New Local Government Network.
3 *Ibid.*
4 Snape, S., 2004. 'Liberated or Lost Souls? Is there a Role for Non-Executive Councillors?', in G. Stoker and D. Wilson (eds), *British Local Government into the 21st Century*, Basingstoke, Palgrave Macmillan, p. 75; Rao, N., 2003. 'Options for Change: Mayors, Cabinets or the Status Quo?', *Local Government Studies*, Vol. 29, No. 1, Spring, pp. 1–16.
5 Tait, J., 1936. *The Medieval English Borough: Studies on Its Origins and Constitutional History*, Manchester University Press; Jewell, H., 1972. *English Local Administration in the Middle Ages*, Newton Abbot, David and Charles.
6 See also Redlich, J. and F.W. Hirst, 1958. *The History of Local Government in England*, London, Macmillan, pp. 98–101.
7 Grant, W., 1989. *Pressure Groups, Politics and Democracy in Britain*, Deddington, Phillip Allen.
8 Randle, *Mayors Mid-Term*.
9 Abney, G. and T. Lauth, 1986. *The Politics of State and City Administration*, State University of New York Press.
10 Ostrogorski, M., 1902. *Democracy and the Organisation of Political Parties, Vol. II*, New York, Macmillan; Royko, M., 1971. *Boss: Richard. J. Daley of Chicago*, New York, Signet.

11 Bullman, H. and E. Page, 1994. 'Executive Leadership in German Local Government', in Joseph Rowntree Foundation, *Local Leadership and Decision-Making*, York, Joseph Rowntree Foundation.

12 Stanyer, J., 1970. 'Social and Rational Models of Man: Alternative Approaches to the Study of Local Elections', *Advancement of Science*, Vol. 26, pp. 399–407.

13 Grant, W.P., 1973. 'Non-partisanship in British Local Politics', *Policy and Politics*, Vol. 1, No. 3, pp. 241–254, at p. 245.

14 Stoker, G., 1996. *The Reform of the Institutions of Local Representative Democracy: Is There a Role for the Mayor–Council Model?*, London, Commission for Local Democracy, p. 14.

15 Part I of the Local Government Act 2000 gives councils the power to do anything which they consider is likely to achieve the promotion or improvement of the economic, social or environmental well-being of their area. While this is not a power of general competence, it does provide councils with a source of legitimacy for political experiments in the governance of the locality.

16 Atkinson, H. and S. Wilks-Hegg, 2000. *Local Government from Thatcher to Blair: The Politics of Creative Autonomy*, Cambridge, Polity Press; Goss, S., 2001. *Making Local Governance Work: Networks, Relationships and the Management of Change*, Basingstoke, Palgrave; Kooiman, J., 2003. *Governing as Governance*, London, Sage.

17 Gray, C., 1994. *Government Beyond the Centre: Sub-national Politics in Britain*, Basingstoke, Macmillan.

18 DETR, 1998. *Modernising Local Government: Local Democracy and Community Leadership*, London, DETR.

19 Copus, C., 2004. *Party Politics and Local Government*, Manchester University Press.

Postscript: the 2005 mayoral elections

May 2005 saw mayors Drummond in Hartlepool, Winter in Doncaster and Wolfe in Stoke-on-Trent face the voters as incumbents to seek re-election after three years in office. Mayor Arkley in North Tyneside had been elected in the first-ever mayoral by-election, which was held in June 2003 after Chris Morgan had resigned, so she faced the voters after only two years in office. The results for each election are set out in Table P1.

Thus, the 2005 results delivered: the re-election of one independent and one Labour incumbent; the defeat of one independent mayor (in Stoke-on-Trent), who did not even make it through to the second round; and the defeat of the Conservative mayor in North Tyneside; Labour candidates won the Stoke and North Tyneside battles, bringing Labour's total number of elected mayors to seven (including the mayor of London).

The former mayor of Stoke had, in his original election, stood as the 'Mayor 4 Stoke' candidate, but sought re-election under the label Supporting Green Shoots, a reference to development policies. Whether the change of affiliation had anything to do with his defeat is doubtful, but it is interesting to note that the sitting mayor secured only 106 first-round votes more than his British National Party opponent, and was nearly pushed into fourth place. Unfortunately, the timing of the election and the point at which this book was completed did not make research into the reasons for the mayor's defeat possible (there is clearly a fascinating case study in the making with the Stoke election result).

Also of note is the Doncaster result, with an independent candidate coming a very strong second after the counting of second preference votes. Indeed, although independents succeeded in seeing only one mayor re-elected, there were in these four contests twelve candidates who were independent, unaffiliated or from outside the established political parties, from a total of twenty-five candidates.

Stuart Drummond's re-election victory with a staggering final-count majority of over 10,000 indicates the depth of support for this independent politician – the result was particularly surprising given the local Labour Party's confidence at its chances of winning the mayoralty.

Table P1 Results of the English mayoral elections 2005

Candidate	Party/affiliation	First count	Second count	Result
Hartlepool				
S. Allison	Local Man, Local Issues, Hartlepool First	3,765		
I. Cameron	Independent	4,272		
S. Drummond (incumbent)	Independent	14,227	2,685	16,912 (elected)
S. Kaiser	Independent	2,701		
J. Lauderdale	Independent	1,821		
B. Pearson	Conservative	1,482		
C. Richardson	Labour	5,527	1,180	6,707
Doncaster				
R. Bartlett	Conservative	12,533		
M. Cooper	Independent	7,773		
J. Credland	Community Group	10,263		
M. Maye	Independent	27,304	10,004	37,308
D. Owen	British National Party	6,128		
R. Rolt	Green Party	4,930		
M. Winter (incumbent)	Labour Party	40,015	5,727	45,742 (elected)
North Tyneside				
L. Arkley (incumbent)	Conservative Party	35,467	3,991	39,458
N. Batten	National Front: Britain for the British	2,470		
J. Harrison	Labour Party	34,053	6,407	40,460 (elected)
J. Harvey	Liberal Democrat	12,761		
Stoke-on-Trent				
S. Batkin	British National Party	15,776		
G. Chevin	Unaffiliated	4,505		
G. Falconer	Unaffiliated	1,368		
J. Harvey	Unaffiliated	1,955		
R. Ibbs	Conservative Party	16,211	6,919	23,130
R. Meredith	Labour Party	27,253	9,708	36,961 (elected)
M. Wolfe (incumbent)	Supporting Green Shoots	15,882		

While, on the surface, the 2005 results indicate a resurgence on the part of the main political parties in taking mayoral offices, those elections can still present parties with an important challenge to their dominance of the local political scene. Moreover, the electorate can still replace a long-standing dominant political party with a mayoral candidate from another party, or with an independent, or a candidate from some small local political association or grouping.

Yet these results do not offend against the argument of the book that from mayoral local government emanates a more fluid and uncertain form (at least as far as party dominance goes) of local politics and local election campaign. A fluid system flows in more than one direction. At certain points in time, in individual localities, as issues, events and political circumstances emerge and develop, and as local campaigns and small local parties or political associations arise as a result of those issues and events, the mayoral office remains a far more tempting and realistic prospect for candidates wishing to change political power and control than does the office of councillor. As the issues, political circumstances or events that led to the emergence of a desire among those outside established parties to seek political office and leadership recede, so too will the support for candidates and incumbent mayors who rode to power on the backs of those issues. When the voter no longer needs the independent or political association mayor, he or she can and will revert to voting behaviour based on political parties.

What results from mayoral government is the prospect of a form of local politics that reflects the vision of Ostrogorski: a fluid politics where groups and associations enter and leave the political system as issues, circumstances and the voters demand or, as Ostrogorski would have exhorted, 'down with the party and up with the league'.[1]

The 2005 results, as far as winning candidates go, if not votes, indicate a shift back to what might be considered 'politics as usual'; future mayoral elections will no doubt provide some of the radical changes in local political leadership that the 2002 elections produced for some areas. Local politics in mayoral areas remains less certain than in other councils and certainly more exciting.

Note

1 Ostrogorski, M., 1902. *Democracy and the Organisation of Political Parties, Vols I and II*, New York, Macmillan.

Bibliography

Abney, G. and T. Lauth, 1986. *The Politics of State and City Administration*, State University of New York Press.

ALDC (Association of Liberal Democrat Councillors), 2000, updated 2001. *Model Standing Orders for Liberal Democrat Council Groups*, Hebden Bridge, ALDC.

Aristotle (S. Everson, ed.), 1992. *The Politics*, Cambridge Texts in the History of Political Thought, Cambridge University Press.

Atkinson, H. and S. Wilks-Hegg, 2000. *Local Government from Thatcher to Blair: The Politics of Creative Autonomy*, Cambridge, Polity Press.

Audit Commission, 2002. *The Comprehensive Performance Assessment Framework for Single Tier and County Councils*, London, Audit Commission.

Audit Commission, 2002. *Delivering Comprehensive Performance Assessments: Consultation Draft*, London, Audit Commission.

Audit Commission, 2002. *Guidance for Authorities on the Corporate Assessment Process: Consultation Draft*, London, Audit Commission.

Audit Commission, 2003. *Comprehensive Performance Assessment*, London, Audit Commission.

Audit Commission, 2004. *Mayoral Arrangements: Middlesbrough Council*, London, Audit Commission.

Back, H., 2005. 'Institutional Settings of Leadership and Community Involvement', in M. Haus, H. Heinelt and M. Stewart (eds), *Urban Governance and Democracy: Leadership and Community Involvement*, London, Routledge, pp. 65–101.

Batley, R. and A. Campbell (eds), 1992. *The Political Executive: Politicians and Management in European Local Government*, London, Frank Cass.

Beloff, M. (ed.), 1948. *The Federalist, or the New Constitution*, Oxford, Blackwell.

Birch, A.H., 1971. *Representation*, London, Pall Mall Press.

Birch, A.H., 1993. *The Concepts and Theories of Modern Democracy*, London, Routledge.

Blair, T., 1998. *Leading the Way: A New Vision for Local Government*, London, Institute of Public Policy Research.

Blunkett, D. and K. Jackson, 1987. *Democracy in Crisis: The Town Halls Respond*, London, Hogarth Press.

Boaden, N., M. Goldsmith, W. Hampton and P. Stringer, 1982. *Public Participation in Local Services*, Harlow, Longman.

Borough of Hartlepool, 2002. *Hartlepool Borough Council Constitution*, Hartlepool, Hartlepool Borough Council.

Borough of Middlesbrough, 2002. *Middlesbrough Council Constitution*, Middlesbrough, Middlesbrough Borough Council.

Bowers, J. and W. Rich, 2000. *Governing Middle-Sized Cities: Studies in Mayoral Leadership*, Boulder, CO, Lynne Rienner Publishers.

Bullman, H. and E. Page, 1994. 'Executive Leadership in German Local Government', in Joseph Rowntree Foundation, *Local Leadership and Decision-Making*, York, Joseph Rowntree Foundation.

Bulpitt, J., 1983. *Territory and Power in the United Kingdom*, Manchester University Press.

Cars, G., P. Healey, A. Madanipour and C. de Magalhaes, 2002. *Urban Governance, Institutional Capacity and Social Milieux*, Aldershot, Ashgate.

Caulfield, J. and H. Larsen (eds), 2002. *Local Government at the Millennium*, Opladen, Leske and Budrich.

Clarke, M., H. Davis, D. Hall and J. Stewart, 1996. *Executive Mayors for Britain? New Forms of Political Leadership Reviewed*, London, Capita.

CLD (Commission for Local Democracy), 1995. *Final Report. Taking Charge: The Rebirth Of Local Democracy*, London, Municipal Journal Books.

Cochrane, A., 1986. 'Community Politics and Democracy', in D. Held and C. Pollit (eds), *New Forms of Democracy*, London, Sage, pp. 51–77.

Colenutt, B., 1979. 'Community Action Over Local Planning Issues', in G. Craig, M. Mayo and N. Sharman (eds), *Jobs and Community Action*, London, Routledge and Kegan Paul, pp. 243–252.

Committee of Inquiry into the Conduct of Local Authority Business, 1986. *Report of the Committee*, London, HMSO.

Committee of Inquiry into the Conduct of Local Authority Business, 1986. *Research, Vol. I: The Political Organisation of Local Authorities*, London, HMSO.

Committee of Inquiry into the Conduct of Local Authority Business, 1986. *Research, Vol. II: The Local Government Councillor*, London, HMSO.

Committee of Inquiry into the Conduct of Local Authority Business, 1986. *Research, Vol. III: The Local Government Elector*, London, HMSO.

Committee of Inquiry into the System of Remuneration of Members of Local Authorities (Robinson committee), 1977. *Remuneration of Councillors, Vol. I: Report; Vol. II: The Surveys of Councillors and Local Authorities*, London, HMSO.

Committee on the Management of Local Government, 1967. *Report of the Committee*, London, HMSO.

Committee on the Management of Local Government, 1967. *Research, Vol. II: The Local Government Councillor*, London, HMSO.

Conservative Party, 1998, revised 2001. *Conservative Council Groups: Draft Model Rules*, London, Conservative Party.

Copus, C., 1998. 'The Councillor: Representing a Locality and the Party Group', *Local Governance*, Vol. 24, No. 3, Autumn, pp. 215–224.

Copus, C., 1999. 'The Attitudes of Councillors Since Widdicombe: A Focus on Democratic Engagement', *Public Policy and Administration*, Vol. 14, No. 4, pp. 87–100.

Copus, C., 1999. 'The Councillor and Party Group Loyalty', *Policy and Politics*, Vol. 27, No. 3, July, pp. 309–324.

Copus, C., 1999. 'The Party Group: A Barrier to Democratic Renewal', *Local Government Studies* (special edition), Vol. 25, No. 4, Winter, pp. 77–98.

Copus, C., 2000. 'Community, Party and the Crisis of Representation', in N. Rao (ed.), *Representation and Community in Western Democracies*, London, Macmillan, pp. 93–113.

Copus, C., 2000. 'Consulting the Public on New Political Management Arrangements: A Review and Observations', *Local Governance*, Vol. 26, No. 3, Autumn, pp. 177–186.

Copus, C., 2004. *Party Politics and Local Government*, Manchester University Press.

Corina, L., 1974. 'Elected Representatives in a Party System', *Policy and Politics*, Vol. 3, No. 1, September, pp. 69–87.

Crick, B., 1982. *In Defence of Politics*, Harmondsworth, Penguin Books.

Davis, J., 1989. 'The Progressive Council, 1889–1907', in A. Saint (ed.), *Politics and the People of London: The London County Council 1889–1965*, London, Hambledon Press, pp. 27–48.

De Tocqueville, A. (J.P. Mayer, ed.), 1994, first published 1835, 1840. *Democracy in America*, London, Fontana.

Dery, D., 1998. 'Elected Mayors and *De Facto* Decentralisation, Israeli Style', *Local Government Studies*, Vol. 24, No. 2, Summer, pp. 45–55.

DeSantis, V.S. and T. Renner, 2002. 'City Government Structures: An Attempt at Classification', *State and Local Government Review*, Vol. 34, No. 2, Spring, pp. 95–104.

DETR (Department of Environment, Transport and the Regions), 1997. *New Leadership for London: The Government's Proposals for a Greater London Authority*, London, DETR.

DETR, 1998. *A Mayor and Assembly for London*, London, DETR.

DETR, 1998. *Modern Local Government: In Touch with the People*, London, DETR.

DETR, 1998. *Modernising Local Government: Improving Services Through Best Value*, London, DETR.

DETR, 1998. *Modernising Local Government: Local Democracy and Community Leadership*, London, DETR.

DETR, 1998. *New Leadership for London: The Government's Proposals for a Greater London Authority*, London, DETR.

DETR, 1999. *Local Leadership: Local Choice*, London, DETR.

DETR, 2000. *New Council Constitutions: Modular Constitutions for English Local Authorities*, London, DETR.

DETR, 2000. *Petitioning for a Mayor: Information Pack*, London, DETR.

DETR, 2001. *Local Strategic Partnerships*, London, DETR.

DETR, 2001. *New Council Constitutions: Local Government Act 2000 Guidance to English Local Authorities*, London, DETR.

DETR, 2001. *Power to Improve Economic, Social and Environmental Well-Being*, London, DETR.

DETR, 2001. *Public Attitudes to Directly Elected Mayors*, London, DETR.

DoE (Department of the Environment), 1983. *Streamlining the Cities*, London, HMSO.

DoE, 1991. *Local Government Review. The Structure of Local Government in England: A Consultation Paper*, London, DoE.

Dowding. K., 1999. 'Regime Politics in London Local Government', *Urban Affairs Review*, Vol. 34, No. 4, pp. 515–545.

DTLR (Department for Transport, Local Government and the Regions), 2001. *Strong Local Leadership: Quality Public Services*, London, DTLR.

Dunleavy, P., K. Dowding and H. Margetts, 1995. 'Regime Politics in London Local Government', paper presented to the ESRC Local Governance Programme Conference, Exeter.

Elkin, S., 1974. *Politics and Land Use Planning: The London Experience*, Cambridge University Press.

Eulau, H. and J. Whalke, 1978. *The Politics of Representation*, Thousand Oaks, CA, Sage.

Eulau, H., J. Whalke, W. Buchanan and L. Ferguson, 1959. 'The Role of the Representative: Some Empirical Observations on the Theory of Edmund Burke', *American Political Science Review*, Vol. 53 No. 3, September, pp. 742–756.

Fabbrini, S., 2000. 'Presidentialisation of Italian Local Government? The Nature and the Effects of Semiparliamentarism', paper presented to a workshop on Presidentialisation of Parliamentary Democracies, ECPR, Copenhagen, Denmark, 14–19 April.

Fox, P. and S. Leach, 1999. *Officers and Members in the New Democratic Structures*, London, Local Government Information Unit.

Frederickson, H.G., G. Johnson and C. Wood, 2004. *The Adapted City: Institutional Dynamics and Structural Change*, New York, Sharpe.

Frederickson, H.G., C. Wood and B. Logan, 2001. 'How American City Governments Have Changed: The Evolution of the Model City Charter', *National Civic Review*, Vol. 90, No. 1, pp. 3–18.

Game, C., 2002. 'Elected Mayors: More Distraction than Attraction?', paper presented to the Eleventh One-Day Conference of the Political Studies Association Urban Politics Specialist Group, November.

Game, C. and K. Goymen, 2001. 'Directly Elected Wizards or Dragons: Some Reflections on Turkish Mayors' Contribution to Political Participation, Legitimacy and Accountability', paper presented to the Political Studies Association Annual Conference, Manchester, April.

Gillespie, J., 1989. 'Municipalism, Monopoly and Management: The Demise of Socialism in One County, 1918–1933', in A. Saint (ed.), *Politics and the People of London: The London County Council 1889–1965*, London, Hambleton Press, pp. 103–125 .

Giuliani, R., 2002. *Leadership*, New York, Little, Brown.

Glassberg, A., 1981. *Representation and Urban Community*, London, Macmillan.

Goss, S., 2001. *Making Local Governance Work: Networks, Relationships and the Management of Change*, Basingstoke, Palgrave.

Grant, W., 1989. *Pressure Groups, Politics and Democracy in Britain*, Deddington, Philip Allen.

Grant, W.P., 1973. 'Non-partisanship in British Local Politics', *Policy and Politics*, Vol. 1, No. 3, pp. 241–254.

Gray, C., 1994. *Government Beyond the Centre: Sub-national Politics in Britain*, Basingstoke, Macmillan.

Green, G., 1972. 'National, City and Ward Components of Local Voting', *Policy and Politics*, Vol. 1, No. 1, September, pp. 45–54.

Gyford, J., 1985. 'The Politicisation of Local Government', in M. Loughlin, M. Gelfand and K. Young (eds), *Half a Century of Municipal Decline*, London, Allen and Unwin, pp. 77–97.

Gyford, J., 1986. 'Diversity, Sectionalism and Local Democracy', in Committee of Inquiry into the Conduct of Local Authority Business, *Research, Vol. IV: Aspects of Local Democracy*, London, HMSO, pp. 106–130.

Hambleton, R., 2000. *Enhancing Political and Managerial Leadership: The Council Manager Model*, London, IDeA.

Hambleton, R. and D. Sweeting, 2004. 'U.S. Style Leadership for English Local Government', *Public Administration Review*, Vol. 64, No. 4, July/August, pp. 474–488.

Harding, A., 2000. 'Regime Formation in Manchester and Edinburgh', in G. Stoker (ed.), *The New Politics of British Local Governance*, Basingstoke, Macmillan, pp. 54–71.

Harrigan, J.J., 1991. *Politics and Policy in States and Communities*, London, Harper Collins.

Haus, M., H. Heinelt and M. Stewart (eds), 2005. *Urban Governance and Democracy: Leadership and Community Involvement*, London, Routledge.

Heclo, H., 1969. 'The Councillor's Job', *Public Administration*, Vol. 47, No. 2, pp. 185–202.

Hegedus, J., 1999. 'Hungarian Local Government', in E. Kirchner (ed.), *Decentralisation and Transition in the Visegrad*, London, Macmillan, pp. 132–159.

Heinelt, H. and A. Magnier, 2002. 'Structures of Local Government and Types of Mayors in Europe', paper presented to the conference on Political Leaders in European Cities, Madrid, May.

Held, D., 1993. *Models of Democracy*, Cambridge, Polity Press.

Hennock, E.P., 1973. *Fit and Proper Persons: Ideal and Reality in Nineteenth-Century Urban Government*, London, Edward Arnold.

Hill, D.M., 1974. *Democratic Theory and Local Government*, London, George Allen and Unwin.

Hirst, P., 1994. *Associative Democracy: New Forms of Economic and Social Governance*, Cambridge, Polity Press.

Hobbes, T. (R. Luck, ed.), 1992, first published 1651. *Leviathan*, Cambridge Texts in the History of Political Thought, Cambridge University Press.

House of Lords Select Committee on Relations Between Central and Local Government, 1996. *Report, Vol. I*, London, HMSO.

House of Lords Select Committee on Relations Between Central and Local Government, 1996. *Report, Vol. II: Oral Evidence and Associated Memoranda*, London, HMSO.

Jewell, H., 1972. *English Local Administration in the Middle Ages*, Newton Abbot, David and Charles.

John, P., 2001. *Local Governance in Western Europe*, London, Sage.

John, P. and A. Cole, 2000. 'When Do Institutions, Policy Sectors and Cities Matter? Comparing Networks of Local Policy-Makers in Britain and France', *Comparative Political Studies*, Vol. 33, No. 2, pp. 248–268.

John, P. and F. Gains, 2005. *Political Leadership Under New Political Management Structures*, London, ODPM.

Jones, G.W., 1969. *Borough Politics: A Study of Wolverhampton Borough Council 1888–1964*, London, Macmillan.

Jones, G.W., 1973. 'The Functions and Organisation of Councillors', *Public Administration*, Vol. 51, No. 2, Summer, pp. 135–146.

Jones, G.W., 1975. 'Varieties of Local Politics', *Local Government Studies*, Vol. 1, No. 2, pp. 17–32.

Jones, G.W. and J. Stewart, 1983. *The Case for Local Government*, London, Allen and Unwin.

Judge, D., 1999. *Representation: Theory and Practice in Britain*, London, Routledge.

Keith-Lucas, B., 1952. *The English Local Government Franchise*, Oxford, Basil Blackwell.

Kirchner, E. (ed.), 1999. *Decentralisation and Transition in the Visegrad*, London, Macmillan.

Kirtzman, A., 2000. *Rudy Giuliani, Emperor of the City*, New York, W. Morrow.

Kooiman, J., 2003. *Governing as Governance*, London, Sage.

Kotter, J.P. and P. Lawrence, 1974. *Mayors in Action: Five Approaches to Urban Governance*, London, John Wiley.

Labour Party, 1995. *Renewing Democracy, Rebuilding Communities*, London, Labour Party.

Labour Party, 2001, updated 2002. *Labour Group Model Standing Orders*, London, Labour Party.

Larsen, H., 2002. 'Directly Elected Mayors: Democratic Renewal or Constitutional Confusion?', in J. Caufield and H. O. Larsen (eds), *Local Government at the Millennium*, Opladen, Leske and Budrich, pp. 111–133.

Leach, S., 2001. *Making Overview and Scrutiny Work*, London, Local Government Association.

Leach, S. and C. Copus, 2004. 'Scrutiny and the Political Party Group in UK Local Government: New Models of Behaviour', *Public Administration*, Vol. 82, No. 2, pp. 331–354.

Leach, S. and D. Wilson, 2000. *Local Political Leadership*, Bristol, Policy Press.

Lehmann, G. and J. Dieckmann, 2001. 'The Administration of German Cities', in K. Konig and H. Siedentopf (eds), *Public Administration in Germany*, Baden-Baden, Nomos, pp. 183–196.

Limosani, M. and P. Navarra, 2001. 'Local Pork-Barrel Politics in National Pre-Election Dates: The Case of Italy', *Public Choice*, Vol. 106, Nos 3–4, pp. 317–326.

Local Government New Zealand, 2004. *The Council, Mayor and CEO: The New Zealand Way*. See www.lgnz.co.nz.

Locke, J. (P. Laslett, ed.), 1992, first published 1690. *Two Treatises of Government*, Cambridge Texts in the History of Political Thought, Cambridge University Press.

London Borough of Hackney, 2000. *The Constitution of the London Borough of Hackney*, London, London Borough of Hackney Council.

London Borough of Newham, 2004. *The Influential Councillor: Community Leadership in Newham*, Report to the Mayor in Consultation with the Cabinet, London, London Borough of Newham Council.

Loughlin, J., 2000. *Subnational Democracy in the European Union: Challenges and Opportunities*, Oxford University Press.

Lowndes, V. and S. Leach, 2004. 'Understanding Local Political Leadership: Constitutions, Contexts and Capabilities', *Local Government Studies*, Special Edition, Vol. 30, No. 4, pp. 557–575.

MacCormick, N., 1993. 'Constitutionalism and Democracy', in R. Bellamy (ed.), *Theories and Concepts of Politics*, Manchester University Press, pp. 124–147.

Madison, J. (M. Beloff, ed.), 1948, first published 1797. Paper No. XIV, in *The Federalist, or the New Constitution*, Oxford, Basil Blackwell, p. 62.

Madison, J. (M. Beloff, ed.), 1948, first published 1798. Paper No. XLVII, in *The Federalist, or the New Constitution*, Oxford, Basil Blackwell, pp. 245–252.

Magnier, A., 2004. 'Between Institutional Learning and Re-legitimisation: Italian Mayors in the Unending Reform', *International Journal of Urban and Regional Research*, Vol. 28, No. 1, March, pp. 166–182.

Meadowcroft, J., 2000. 'Community Politics: Ideals, Myths and Realities', in N. Rao (ed.), *Representation and Community in Western Democracies*, London, Macmillan, pp. 114–137.

Mill, J.S. (R.B. McCallum, ed.), 1948, first published 1861. *On Liberty and Considerations on Representative Government*, Oxford, Basil Blackwell.

Morgan, D. and S. Watson, 1996. 'Mayors of American Cities: An Analysis of Powers and Responsibilities', *American Review of Public Administration*, Vol. 26, No. 1, March, pp. 113–125.

Mouritzen, P.E. and J. Svara, 2002. *Leadership at the Apex: Politicians and Administrators in Western Local Government*, University of Pittsburgh Press.

Muchnick, D., 1970. *Urban Renewal in Liverpool*, Occasional Papers on Social Administration, the Social Administration Research Trust, London, Bell and Sons.

Muramatsu, M., F. Iqbal and I. Kume, 2001. *Local Government Development in Post-war Japan*, Oxford University Press.

Nagata, N., 1998. 'The Development of Japanese Local Government and Its Reform Towards the Globalised Age', *International Review of Administrative Sciences*, Vol. 64, No. 2, pp. 219–233.

Newton, K., 1976. *Second City Politics: Democratic Processes and Decision-Making in Birmingham*, Oxford, Clarendon Press.

Nickson, R., 1995. *Local Government in Latin America*, London, Lynne Rienner Publishers.

ODPM (Office of the Deputy Prime Minister), 2000 (updated 2001). *New Council Constitutions: Guidance to English Local Authorities*, London, ODPM.

ODPM, 2003. *Strengthening Local Democracy: Making the Most of the Constitution*, London, ODPM.

ODPM, 2005. *Vibrant Local Leadership*, London, ODPM.

Orr, K., 2004. 'If Mayors Are the Answer Then What Was the Question?', *Local Government Studies*, Vol. 30, No. 3, pp. 331–345.

Ostrogorski, M., 1902. *Democracy and the Organisation of Political Parties, Vols I and II*, New York, Macmillan.

Owen, D., 1982. *The Government of Victorian London 1855–1889: The Metropolitan Board of Works, the Vestries and the City Corporation*, Harvard University Press.

Page, E. and M. Goldsmith, 1987. *Central and Local Government Relations*, London, Sage.

Paine, T., 1985, first published 1791–92. *Rights of Man*, Harmondsworth, Penguin.

Parry, G., G. Moyser and N. Day, 1992. *Political Participation and Democracy in Britain*, Cambridge University Press.

Peterson, P., 2000. 'The American Mayor: Elections and Institutions', *Parliamentary Affairs*, Vol. 53, No. 4, pp. 667–677.

Phillips, A., 1996. 'Why Does Local Democracy Matter?', in L. Pratchet and D. Wilson (eds), *Local Democracy and Local Government*, London, Macmillan, pp. 20–37.

Pinkney, R., 1983. 'Nationalizing Local Politics and Localizing a National Party: The Liberal Role in Local Government', *Government and Opposition*, Vol. 18, pp. 347–358.

Pinkney, R., 1984. 'An Alternative Political Strategy? Liberals in Power in English Local Government', *Local Government Studies*, Vol. 10, No. 3, May/June, pp. 69–84.

Pressman, J., 1972. 'Preconditions of Mayoral Leadership', *American Political Science Review*, Vol. 66, No. 2, June, pp. 511–524.

Rallings, C. and M. Thrasher, 1997. *Local Elections in Britain*, London, Routledge.

Rallings, C., M. Thrasher and D. Cowling, 2002. 'Mayoral Referendums and Elections', *Local Government Studies*, Vol. 28, No. 4, Winter, pp. 67–90.

Randle, A., 2004. *Mayors Mid-Term: Lessons from the First Eighteen Months of Directly Elected Mayors*, London, New Local Government Network.

Rao, N., 1994. *The Making and Unmaking of Local Self-Government*, Aldershot, Dartmouth.

Rao, N., 2003. 'Options for Change: Mayors, Cabinets or the Status Quo?', *Local Government Studies*, Vol. 29, No. 1, Spring, pp. 1–16.

Rao, N., 2005. *Councillors and the New Council Constitutions*, London, ODPM.

Redlich, J. and F.W. Hirst, 1958. *The History of Local Government in England*, London, Macmillan.

Rhodes, R., 1997. *Understanding Governance: Policy Networks, Governance, Reflexivity and Accountability*, Open University Press.

Royko, M., 1971. *Boss: Richard J. Daley of Chicago*, New York, Signet.

Saint, A., 1989. *Politics and the People of London: The London County Council 1889–1965*, London, Hambledon Press.

Savitch, H. and P. Kantor, 2002. *Cities in the International Market Place*, Princeton University Press.

Schofield, M., 1977. 'The Nationalisation of Local Politics', *New Society*, 28 April, pp. 165–166.

Snape, S., 2004. 'Liberated or Lost Souls? Is There a Role for Non-Executive Councillors?', in G. Stoker and D. Wilson (eds), *British Local Government into the 21st Century*, Basingstoke, Palgrave Macmillan.

Snape, S., S. Leach and C. Copus, 2002. *The Development of Overview and Scrutiny in Local Government*, London, ODPM.

Soldon, N., 1974. '*Laissez-Faire* as Dogma: The Liberty and Property Defence League 1882–1914', in K. Brown (ed.), *Essays in Anti-Labour History: Responses to the Rise of Labour in Britain*, London, Macmillan, pp. 208–233.

Soos, G., G. Toka and G. Wright (eds), 2002. *The State of Local Democracy in Central Europe*, Budapest, Open Society Institute.

Stanyer, J., 1970. 'Social and Rational Models of Man: Alternative Approaches to the Study of Local Elections', *Advancement of Science*, Vol. 26, pp. 399–407.

Stewart, J., 1996. *Further Innovation in Democratic Practice*, Occasional Paper No. 3, Birmingham, Institute of Local Government Studies.

Stewart, J., 1997. *More Innovation in Democratic Practice*, Occasional Paper No. 9, Birmingham, Institute of Local Government Studies.

Stewart, J., 1999. *From Innovation in Democratic Practice Towards a Deliberative Democracy*, Occasional Paper No. 27, Birmingham, Institute of Local Government Studies.

Stewart, J., 2003. *Modernising British Local Government: An Assessment of Labour's Reform Programme*, Basingstoke, Palgrave Macmillan.

Stoke-on-Trent Borough Council, 2002. *The Constitution of Stoke-on-Trent Borough Council*, Stoke-on-Trent, Stoke-on-Trent Borough Council.

Stoker, G., 1996. *The Reform of the Institutions of Local Representative Democracy: Is There a Role for the Mayor–Council Model?*, London, Commission for Local Democracy.

Stoker, G., 2004. *How Are Mayors Measuring Up? Preliminary Findings – ELG Team*, London, ODPM.

Stoker, G. and D. Wilson, 2004. *British Local Government into the 21st Century*, Basingstoke, Palgrave Macmillan.

Stoker, G. and H. Wolman, 1991. *A Different Way of Doing Business: The Example of the U.S. Mayor*, Belgrave Papers No. 2, London, Local Government Management Board.

Stoker, G. and H. Wolman, 1992. 'Drawing Lessons from US Experience: An Elected Mayor for British Local Government', *Public Administration*, Vol. 70, Summer, pp. 241–267.

Stone, C., 1995. 'Political Leadership in Urban Politics', in D. Judge, G. Stoker and H. Wolman (eds), *Theories of Urban Politics*, London, Sage, pp. 96–116.

Streib, G., 1995. 'Strategic Capacity in Council–Manager Municipalities: Exploring Limits and Horizons', in H.G. Frederickson (ed.), *Ideal and Practice in Council–Manager Government*, Washington, DC, International City Management Association.

Sullivan, H. and C. Skelcher, 2002. *Working Across Boundaries: Partnerships in the Public Sector*, Basingstoke, Palgrave Macmillan.

Svara, J., 1990. *Official Leadership in the City: Patterns of Conflict and Co-operation*, Oxford University Press.

Svara, J. (ed.), 1994. *Facilitative Leadership in Local Government: Lessons from Successful Mayors and Chairpersons*, San Francisco, CA, Jossey-Bass.

Swianiewicz, P., 2005. 'Cities in Transition', in M. Haus, H. Heinelt and M. Stewart (eds), *Urban Governance and Democracy: Leadership and Community Involvement*, London, Routledge, pp. 102–128.

Tait, J., 1936. *The Medieval English Borough: Studies on Its Origins and Constitutional History*, Manchester University Press.

Taylor, M., 2000. 'Communities in the Lead: Organisational Capacity and Social Capital', *Urban Studies*, Vol. 37, Nos 5–6, pp. 1019–1035.

Tomaney, J., 2001. 'The New Governance of London: A Case of Post-Democracy?', *City*, Vol. 5, No. 2, pp. 225–248.

Travers, T., 2004. *The Politics of London: Governing an Ungovernable City*, Basingstoke, Palgrave Macmillan.

Van der Kolk, H., C. Rallings and M. Thrasher, 2004. 'Electing Mayors: A Comparison of Different Electoral Procedures', *Local Government Studies*, Vol. 30, No. 4, pp. 598–608.

Vandelli, L. 1997. *Sindaci e mito, sisifo, Tantalo e Damocle nell amministrazione local*, Bolgna, Il Mulino.

Wainwright, H., 1987. *Labour: A Tale of Two Parties*, London, Hogarth Press.

Wehling, H.G. 1999. 'Besonderheiten der auf Gemeindeebene', in H.H. Arnim (ed.), *Demokratie von neuen Herausforderungen*, Berlin, Druker and Humblot, pp. 91–102.

Wheeland, C., 1994. 'A Profile of a Facilitative Mayor: Mayor Betty Jo Rhea of Rock Hill, South Carolina', in J. Svara (ed.), *Facilitative Leadership in Local Government*, San Francisco, CA, Jossey-Bass, pp. 136–159.

Wollmann, H., 2004. 'Urban Leadership in German Local Politics: The Rise, Role and Performance of the Directly Elected (Chief Executive) Mayor', *International Journal of Urban and Regional Research*, Vol. 28, No. 1, pp. 150–165.

Wolman, H. and M. Goldsmith, 1992. *Urban Politics and Policy: A Comparative Approach*, Oxford, Basil Blackwell.

Working Party on the Internal Management of Local Authorities in England, 1993. *Community Leadership and Representation: Unlocking the Potential*, London, HMSO.

Yanez, C.J., 2004. 'Participatory Democracy and Political Opportunism: Municipal Experience in Italy and Spain (1960–93)', *International Journal of Urban and Regional Research*, Vol. 29, No. 4, pp. 819–838.

Young, K., 1975. *Local Politics and the Rise of Party: The London Municipal Society and the Conservative Intervention in Local Elections, 1894–1963*, Leicester University Press.

Young, K., 1989. 'Bright Hopes and Dark Fears: The Origins and Expectations of the County Councils', in K. Young (ed.), *New Directions for County Government*, London, Association of County Councils, pp. 4–21.

Young, K. and P. Garside, 1982. *Metropolitan London: Politics and Urban Change 1837–1981*, London, Edward Arnold.

Young, K. and N. Rao, 1994. *Coming to Terms with Change: The Local Government Councillor in 1993*, York, Joseph Rowntree Foundation.

Young, K. and N. Rao, 1995. 'Faith in Local Democracy', in J. Curtice, R. Jowell, L. Brook and A. Park (eds), *British Social Attitudes: The Twelfth Report*, Aldershot, Dartmouth, pp. 91–117.

Young, K. and N. Rao, 1997. *Local Government Since 1945*, Oxford, Basil Blackwell.

Index

Lightning Source UK Ltd.
Milton Keynes UK
UKHW02f1613260318
320063UK00004B/476/P